survival @ e-sp

transformation guide for pro   ss

survival @ e-speed

transformation guide for profitable Internet and mobile business

Peter Morath
American Management Systems

THE McGRAW-HILL COMPANIES

London • Burr Ridge IL • New York • St Louis • San Francisco • Auckland • Bogotá
Caracas • Lisbon • Madrid • Mexico • Milan • Montreal • New Delhi • Panama
Paris • San Juan • São Paulo • Singapore • Sydney • Tokyo • Toronto

Published by
McGraw-Hill Publishing Company
SHOPPENHANGERS ROAD, MAIDENHEAD, BERKSHIRE, SL6 2QL, ENGLAND
Telephone +44 (0)1628 502500
Fax: +44 (0)1628 770224 Web site: http://www.mcgraw-hill.co.uk

British Library Cataloguing in Publication Data
A catalogue record for this book is available from the British Library

ISBN 007 709838 2

Library of Congress Cataloguing-in-Publication Data
The LOC data for this book has been applied for and may be obtained from the
Library of Congress, Washington, D.C.

Further information on this and other McGraw-Hill titles is to be found at
http://www.mcgraw-hill.co.uk
Author's Website: http://www.mcgraw-hill.co.uk/books/morath

Publisher: Elizabeth Robinson
Produced by: Steven Gardiner Ltd, Cambridge
Cover by: Yvonne Booth
Typeset by: Mouse Nous, Cross in Hand
Printed in the United Kingdom by Bell and Bain Ltd, Glasgow

5   4   3   2   1   BB   5   4   3   2   1

For those seeing change as a new opportunity to excel

Of the four seasons none lasts forever; of the days, some are longer and others shorter, and of the moon, it sometimes waxes and sometimes wanes. He who can modify his tactics in accordance with the situation and thereby succeeds in winning may be said to be divine.

Sun Tzu, ancient Chinese strategist living around 500 BC

Contents

Figures

Tables

Foreword

You have heard the saying 'the Internet changes everything'. The truth is, in the past few years, the Internet really has changed everything in the consumer world. In the world of enterprise applications, however, the significant changes are only just beginning. And the companies that have the most to gain are not the 'dot.coms', but the companies with real revenue and real customers and earnings. They are the enterprises that will most profit from improving their business processes with Internet technologies.

I encourage you to read this book and to use the analysis provided to initiate the transformation of your enterprise. The data draws upon the experience of banks, telecom providers and other e-business pioneers, and applies across other industries. Banks offer a great field for analysis, because they are pioneers among the big enterprises, having started virtual customer interactions such as home and phone banking more than two decades ago.

Survival @ e-speed tracks how business dynamics have changed over time and presents best practices for customer treatment that have emerged. This book will help your organisation to quickly implement Internet technology as a competitive advantage.

The history of the Internet as a service delivery mechanism in the financial services sector began in the mid-1990s, when the first 'Internet-only' institutions were introduced. These institutions promised a new and more focused client experience without the overhead cost associated with the traditional 'bricks and mortar' institution. The predictions of the time were that the online-only, pure-Internet institutions would grow at an accelerated rate at the expense of the traditional 'bricks and mortar' institutions. Indeed, a report from the OECD published in 1998 stated that the cost of an online transaction was 89 per cent lower than that of a branch transaction and 78 per cent lower than that of a telephone-based transaction.

Today (November, 2000), management within many Internet-only institutions is discovering that the Web is not the panacea for financial services, but is merely another service delivery channel that is being used by segments of the total market for financial services. In the United States, Internet-only institutions have captured only 1–2 per cent of the regular online customer base, estimated at 19 million. In Europe, despite predictions from Datamonitor (*The Future of e-Banking in Europe: 1999–2004*) of growth rates of 37 per cent (CAGR), online banking has faltered when it comes to Internet-only institutions.

Pure-Internet banking was marketed as a next-generation convenience providing unlimited access to banking products and facilities. However, service to date has proved unreliable, with servers crashing and unreliable connections. In Europe there have been a number of well-publicised cases where client account details held by Internet-only banks were found to be publicly accessible. In addition, Internet-only banks have been slow to offer a full range of products and services to their clients.

Consequently, clients continue to choose the telephone for their banking business rather than access their account details via the Internet. And their comfort level for purchasing certain products, such as long-term savings plans, has not yet extended beyond the bank's branch – where details can be discussed in person – to the Web.

The slow growth of the online financial services market has led to slow revenue growth within the online financial services sector. While the marginal costs may be low for online institutions, many have high start-up costs. The Halifax plc, a bank based in the United Kingdom, for example, reported start-up costs of £145 million for its Internet-only subsidiary.

Rapid customer growth was also predicted for pure-Internet institutions. However, these new institutions tend to begin with no clients at all and have to spend significant amounts of seed capital on recruitment. To retain such clients, these institutions have to offer unprofitable returns that exceed the sector average. Inevitably, the competitive advantage offered by such high returns is quickly dissipated as other institutions modify their business models and offer similar rates of return.

Given the poor investment returns of Internet-only institutions, many have curtailed their activities and brought the returns offered into line with the sector. In the case of online subsidiaries, many have collapsed into their 'bricks and mortar' parent subsidiaries, offering products and services through a mix of channels. A number of the older Internet-only institutions, once committed to all-electronic, online service delivery, are now building branch-based infrastructures with a view to offering products and services via mixed delivery channels.

In the end, there is a growing realisation that the Internet is simply another delivery channel to be built into a financial institution's value chain. The evolution of a traditional 'bricks and mortar' financial institution to one with an online subsidiary, or a 'clicks and mortar' service, represents both an enormous opportunity and challenge to both staff and management.

I invite you to benefit from the experiences provided in this book and to select the approaches that might help you transform your business operations to become better, faster and more profitable.

Craig Conway,
President and Chief Executive Officer
PeopleSoft, Inc.

Introduction

@@@ Create customer delight by changing your enterprise to be empathic with your customers. @@@ Establish a strong organisation by empowering your employees to work up to their potential. @@@ Boost your performance by leveraging your traditional experience with online tools. @@@

Traditional companies are challenged by the new offerings that many little dot-coms create regularly. Quick deployment of new product packages and services is necessary to cope with the new offerings popping up daily on the Internet. Front-offices and back-offices need to work closer together and the staff of the enterprises need to acquire the tools necessary for quick decisions, as well as share a common view on their objectives and the customer perspective. The result has to be that new ideas can be implemented in days instead of weeks and that issues like customer complaints can be resolved in minutes instead of days. This book provides a practical guide for managing the organisational transitions imposed by the rapid changes in the competitive environment.

Companies that are capable of quickly implementing the ongoing innovations and have a clear strategy demonstrate a stock price evolution outperforming those who continue doing business as usual. Such strategies have to be clear and have to empower the business units to serve the customer flexibly while improving the shareholder returns too. Customer touch points have to be established and the services need to be flexibly reconfigurable as the market demand changes. The execution of transactions in the online portal, the call centre, the branch and in the back-office, must rely on an information pool and customer treatment policies triggering unambiguous and personalised interactions for the self-service customer, the call-centre staff and the staff in the branches and in the field.

This book with its many examples, practitioner's advice and practical worksheets will be useful for preparing your ongoing changes, if you are:

❏ the CEO, COO, or CIO of a 'brick and mortar' enterprise with the desire to change it to a 'click and mortar' company;

❏ a project manager in a big company in charge of going online;

❏ a senior manager or strategic planner who wants to speed up business processes and base decisions on the values generated for and by the customer;

❏ an information technology manager whose target is to make your team and environment ready for the changes in your enterprise.

Many articles on specific aspects of electronic business have been written for business and private readers on the one hand, and much research has been done on how to approach change in general on the other hand. But there is a new dimension to 'change' in the Web age: the *speed* of changes is permanently increasing; new *complexity* factors are added such as mobile commerce on top of e-business; and organisations must be ready to deal with several *parallel* waves of big changes including outsourcing and mergers. This book provides the full picture and gives advice on what to do for transforming an existing enterprise into a flexible online business: what opportunities to pursue, what partnerships to engage in, what tools to use and what to focus on at various points in your transformation. Written for executives and managers and for anybody curious about the customer treatment to be expected in the near future, it provides a guide on how to use new approaches and tools that will prove most beneficial.

The book provides strategic considerations and explains best-practice implementation approaches for organisational transitions involved in surviving e-business challenges. It addresses the objectives and concerns of all established companies and it provides examples and case studies from leading companies, in particular from the finance industry,* which has the longest experience in doing business online with home-banking, starting in the late seventies and progressing through various change cycles.

My goal for this book is to equip you with the necessary methodology for Web-enabling your activities. Using my 'e-business factory' concept, you will be able to generate continuously new innovative offerings which your online customers will like to buy. Following this pro-active and customer-focused concept, you can outperform both your traditional competitors who continue to work in the old way and the dot-coms that lack your experience.

If you are a private reader or a student, you will also benefit from this book. You will probably be most interested in a look behind the scenes at how electronic business is approached by the providers – and what improved interaction you can expect from them and their products and service providers. Key aspects are the emergence of 'communities' of which the consumers will find themselves becoming members, the transparency of prices with the opportunity to find the best offering quickly and easily, and the accessibility of services from a variety of providers through one portal.

The structure of the book

The book is structured in three parts. First, we look at an 'ideal' click and mortar enterprise from the customer perspective, viewing it from the outside, and so identify objectives for successful online companies. Second, we examine the inside of your company and discuss the components and disciplines that ensure sustained success during the changing cycles of e-business. This overall strategy is based on successful approaches implemented by e-business pioneers. These e-approaches lead to high performing, responsive, pro-active and profitable enterprises. Third, the implementation of necessary changes and the execution of a project transforming your organisation to an e-enterprise is described. These implementation discussions include worksheets to use in setting up and validating your own project approach.

* The finance industry is much advanced in terms of online innovation because capital can be easily transported around the globe, the products can be easily described and compared and for many banking interactions global standards for electronic exchange have been defined and implemented.

Part 1 explains *why* the growing customer demands as nurtured by the increasing number of convenient online services require better, faster and cheaper interactions with your business partners and with individual customers. This part addresses:

❏ the challenges fully developed companies are confronted with, due to the accelerating speed of changes and the increasing number of global competitors;

❏ improving interactions with your customers;

❏ providing a flexible product and service mix;

❏ matching customer needs with the services you offer;

❏ staying on top of change.

Part 2 first defines the basis of your current e-business readiness and responsiveness to change, and it recommends focal areas for different levels of development. Then it describes a strategy for intensifying and improving online customer interactions. It explains the core components of the future business, i.e. *what* should be in place in your envisioned click and mortar enterprise. We discuss what leading edge approaches you should adopt for refocusing your enterprise. Your teams and your customer treatment should focus on those areas where you can generate the highest value based on your competencies and the skills of your staff. It builds on best-practice examples in the context of the following approaches:

❏ the marketing approach: set-up of customer-focused portals with a special attention to mobile and UMTS offerings;

❏ the service approach in front and back-office: best leverage of people in end-to-end process integration with empowered staff supported by a modernised IT;

❏ the management approach to communicating central guidelines and policies in a way enabling and empowering local execution: personalised customer treatment supported by automatic analysis and decision-making.

Based on the approaches described in Part 2, Part 3 then describes *how* you can make your way towards your goal. The scope of various phases of your change initiative is outlined, timing considerations are discussed and the 'e-business factory' concept is described, with its strategy think tank, business re-engineering, system development and its appropriate tool-box, as well as a portrait of vendors.

The different facets of your e-nitiative are linked to a holistic perspective by underlining the end-to-end relationship of online Internet portals for PCs and mobile devices with call-centre interactions, all with personalised one-to-one marketing responsiveness and performance contribution appropriate to each customer. This is embedded in an overall leadership framework using measurable targets based on the balanced scorecard approach.

Readers with little time available will get the most important recommendations by reading the first chapter of each part of the book, the introductions to each chapter and the summary at the end of each chapter. Those who want to use the book as a programme manual should focus on the case studies and the worksheets provided throughout the book. Those worksheets can also be downloaded from my website: *www.success-at-e-business.com*.

Acknowledgements

I am grateful that so quickly after my last book Donovan Wright, Financial Services Director EMEA from PeopleSoft, encouraged me to go through a similar venture again, and that he provided me, despite his extremely busy schedule, with a broad set of case studies and best practice materials that facilitated my research.

Thanks to Elizabeth Robinson, my publisher, for her flexibility during the preparation of the book and for sponsoring the new idea from the beginning! And big thanks to Catherine Griffiths from the William Penney Laboratory at Imperial College in London, who advised me on my writing style to make my recommendations to the readers stand out clearly.

Many leaders in the banking and telecom industry who contributed to the book have to remain unnamed. It was a pleasure to reflect with you on ideas and to consolidate your recommendations from the perspective of your enterprises. I hope you have also drawn similar benefits from our discussions.

And I have appreciated the excellent 'catering service' provided by my wife and my daughter when I was swamped with research materials and draft print-outs, my mind concentrated on torturing my laptop, and forgetting to nurture my body. Thanks, Sigrid and Larissa, for all the coffee you brought silently and all the nice meals you slipped on to my to-do pile.

Site map

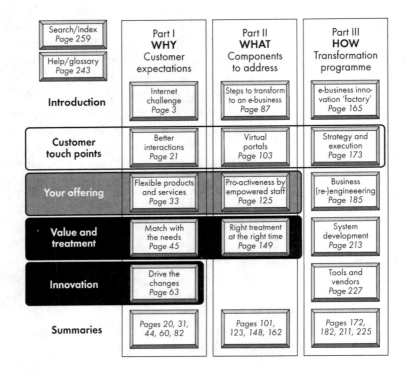

This practical book shows the leaders of established enterprises how they can transform their organisation to become excellent in e-business interactions. The site map above helps you to navigate through the key recommendations of the book:

❏ establish strong customer touch points incorporating portals on the Web and in your call centres;

❏ provide flexible products and services by highly motivated staff;

❏ optimise customer treatment by focusing on where the customer gets most value and where you gain the highest profitability;

❏ build a task force transforming your enterprise for ongoing changes. This task force should follow the concept of a factory producing continuously e-business innovations.

Many practical examples from the e-business pioneers – banks, telecom providers, dot-coms and entertainment – are used to high-light the key recommendations. Worksheets support your hands-on implementation.

Part 1

Improve the customer e-experience

1

The Internet challenge for established companies

@@@ Combine your operational experience from existing processes with emerging online business models to drive customer interactions to more profitable business transactions. @@@ Transform now from a slow 'brick and mortar' attitude to a flexible 'click and mortar' company. @@@

1.1 It is time to act

e-business has created lots of turmoil – on stock markets with stock prices of 'dot-coms' sky-rocketing for a long time and now getting back to a more reasonable price evolution, and in the merger and acquisition market, where newcomers have enough capital to take over traditional companies for unthought-of prices, like AOL acquiring Time Warner or Vodafone merging with Mannesmann. Now the first patterns in the Internet age are evolving, that distinguish successful companies from those falling back, being acquired or just disappearing.

❏ The first common pattern is the *flexibility* to respond to changes and to actually manage those changes. New competitive situations have to be assessed and new products or price plans launched almost every day. If you miss out on this velocity of change, you may be confronted with a similar situation as Time Warner or Mannesmann. Striving for such flexibility has to be reflected in your strategy, in your marketing and product offerings, and in your customer interactions.

❏ As a second common pattern, the surviving companies are not doing (or at least promising) everything for everybody. Instead, they have a *clear focus* and express this in their strategy, their policies and their customer treatment. Combined with the need for speed and flexibility, this requires a good central fine-tuning of the rules of the game and the tools to deploy and implement the new rules immediately in the field.

❏ The third common pattern is that *value chains* are revisited and redesigned frequently. This revisiting may identify outsourcing aspects that cannot be provided in-house at competitive prices, while new combinations of experience become a core competency and new alliances are built. For the end customer, the overall product or service looks seamlessly integrated, but many partners have to work together to actually market and produce the service. The classic 'front-office' and 'back-office' need to focus more on their own respective competency, but at the same time work closer together (in particular more quickly) than before. Actually, the main attention is on the front-office: marketing and research lead to more knowledge of how to keep customers' eyes on your website and what proposition to highlight in order to make the customer buy.

❏ Next, *co-operation* between everyone involved is very explicit: the management of the enterprise co-operates with staff via policies, treatment strategies, performance objectives, by monitoring achievements and by providing incentives for success. Front-office, back-office, product managers work closely together to create new products and services for the online customer. Everyone in the enterprise shares a single view of the customer to keep messages to each individual customer consistent, no matter whether he receives a marketing mailing, is online on the Web, talks to a call-centre agent, speaks to a representative in the branch, or gets visited by field service staff. The co-operation and communication of the enterprise with the external partners is performed with formalised renegotiations of the mutual value contribution and online exchanges of information, such as electronic offers, online service requests or invoices presented and paid electronically.

❏ Finally, *new tools*, processes, and information technology (IT) systems are used as created by the pioneers of e-business. The internal tools include balanced scorecards to define the business focus and to monitor achievements; customer-value models to understand customer preferences and profitability drivers; and easy-to-use tools such as product configurators and pricing schemes for creating new products and services. The tools for external communication include electronic marketplaces, online auctions and supply chain management via the Web.

For your business survival you have to define which of the new e-business potentials to exploit first. Is it supply chain management or business-to-business sales? Then look at the globally available electronic marketplaces for online bidding, auctions, logistics and payments for the various industries. Or do you sell to consumer markets? Then look at the examples of trendsetters for online and mobile commerce, such as the Scandinavian countries, global business travellers – and of course your children! Business-to-consumer interactions have started to sky-rocket as now customers do not need to have a Web-enabled PC at home or use their employer's, as additional Internet access from mobile phones and TV sets is broadly available.

Companies that have been in business for quite a while, either as an e-business start-up or as a traditional brick and mortar enterprise, have to revisit their business approaches in the light of the attention shift to the business-to-consumer market. While 'traditional' competition continues being fierce, additional challenges come from e-business start-ups as well as companies expanding out of their traditional business area into other market areas or geographic regions. In the finance industry, for example, traditional banks are challenged by newcomers such as online discount brokers (for example, Charles Schwab, *www.schwab.com*), by first-e (*www.first-e.com*), by insurance companies offering saving plans – and even by car manufacturers that offer interest-bearing investments or by supermarkets providing cash advances. The successful companies focus on their core competencies, outsource all 'overhead' activities and thus create a quicker organisation and save costs, and of course offer better prices to their customers. In addition, their marketing spending is more than the industry average – so they attack their competitors on all fronts, in terms of process efficiencies, price advantages and a strong perceived presence.

It will not suffice, though, just to copy a successful business model – at least not in the country where it was invented. The first innovators have the biggest advantage to gain the market share necessary to be profitable, and to further improve on process efficiencies. So add your specific experience and flavour to the business models to distinguish yourself from them – and be ready for an online marketing war. If you are importing business models from another country, do not forget to consider the local preferences: first look at differences in geography and language, opening times of shops, logistics to get your goods to the customers and how people like to be approached.

With all the examples at your fingertips, it is a great time for you to analyse the constituents of your core competencies, revisit your value proposition, look for new partners, rank your business areas according to their contribution to your bottom line, streamline your internal processes and redesign your organisation to formulate your e-business proposition.

Players such as Amazon, AOL, Vodafone and Yahoo occupy the key roles and the pole positions in the global Internet race. But you have the operational experience of your traditional business. If you use the time now to increase your responsiveness to catch up with the pace of e-business speed, you can still get a good position in the market and use the best practices of both the traditional business world and the e-business pioneer experiences. While the players in the new markets begin to be confronted with cash problems,* you benefit from the fact that the initial hype concerning 'dot-com' start-up has gone. Venture capitalists and stock markets look more closely now at the business plans of the small companies, and highly motivated but inexperienced entrepreneurs have started to learn the lesson that profitability is the key to survival. Many of those companies provide interesting stories you can learn from – some of them might be a candidate for you to partner with (or even to acquire) in order to get a head start with e-business, or some of their staff may be interested in trading in the chaos and empty promises of dot-com for the steady success of a solid enterprise. And the online market is still huge: depending on the country your customers are living in, the percentage of customers already locked in to a particular service provider is in the worst case between 40 per cent and 50 per cent of the population (in the Nordic

---

* According to a survey conducted by PricewaterhouseCoopers from July 2000, 20 out of 56 assessed companies newly floated on the stock exchange are running the risk of using up their capital in the next half year: 2 out of 7 Internet service providers, 1 out of 8 multimedia producers, 9 out of 20 software companies and 8 out of 17 e-commerce vendors.

hemisphere – USA, Scandinavia, Iceland, Canada). So the other half of the population waits for you to attract them with a new, enticing product or service. In other areas of the globe such as Australia or the various European countries, 70 per cent to 80 per cent of the population are still waiting for the Internet revolution to bring benefits to them.

While large enterprises are used to a steady fine-tuning of the results in terms of small increments, increased competitive pressures make it necessary to regularly take big steps, following – or even better anticipating – market dynamics.

1.2 Business models: sound online value propositions

Cornerstones of e-business

There are four cornerstones for services offered on the Internet:

❏ Communication – this is the focus of telecom providers offering services which range from cable network, through end terminals (fixed-wire telephones, mobile phones, PCs), to value-added services such as e-mail, chatting and news or any of the three other aspects listed below.

❏ Information – this is a broad field where many companies from different industries are fighting for market share. Services include intermediary services such as stock brokerage, travel arrangements, online shops and electronic marketplaces. Others offer 'pure' information, for example, newspapers or magazines, research in databases containing archived articles, research in business databases or the provision of training courses.

❏ Entertainment – most private Internet use is for entertainment. It includes listening to music, chatting with friends or strangers, playing games (alone or with remote partners), and watching videos. Surfing the Web has become a hobby in itself, just as 'zapping' through the TV channels is a hobby for people not patient enough to wait for the outcome of a film. And all websites compete for visitors' attention. The most successful are those that most quickly attract the visitor's interest, keep him or her interested in using the service for a long time and stimulate his or her active participation.

❏ Payment – most transactions on the Web require eventually some payment, either as a per-transaction charge ('micro-payment'), or as a recurring charge like membership fees or subscriptions. This should be the field where banks dominate, but actually many other providers have acquired a part of the market share, such as telecom operators, content providers or payment consolidators.

Your Internet formula

Use the basic 'information' and 'entertainment' aspects listed above according to your business model and contents to create your own Internet formula:*

❏ **Market segment command:** define a segment and establish a powerful service in that area, such as the Bank of Montreal (*www.bmo.com*) has done for the college market.
Objectives: get the biggest market share in a segment, establish temporary monopolies.
Success factors: know the market segment, use efficient processes to handle services, get on the same wavelength as your customers, be aware of where the customers are price-sensitive and where not.
Profitability criteria: premium prices for products or services where you are superior to the competition; economies of scale for mass products

❏ **Information content control:** content is the prime selling point that this business model exploits. Examples are: the *Financial Times* (*www.ft.com*), providing full research capabilities for listed companies including multi-year charts and background archives – only a broker function is currently missing; Reuters business research (*www.reuters.com*) or entertainment such as Disney (*www.disney.com*).
Objectives: create an electronic product (information, music, videos, games) that can easily be distributed electronically, establish temporary monopolies.
Success factors: production capabilities or access to content, market interest in content, clarity concerning where the customers are price-sensitive and where not.

* From: AMS University, e-business portal *http://learn.amsinc.com/amsu* with annotations from the author.

Profitability criteria: premium prices for services and goods where only you can meet demand, cost of content production.

❑ **Category dominance:** create a special identity built around a broad range of associated services. Examples are: Amazon (*www.amazon.co.uk* or *www.amazon.com*) with sales of books, CDs, software, auctions, and entertainment; Webvan (*www.webvan.com*) with a new logistical approach for delivering all kinds of grocery (including fresh products like fruits, frozen goods like ice-cream, or fresh lobster) across the USA within 24 hours with a delivery precision of 30 minutes; m-tv (*www.mtv.com*) with its global broadcast TV entertainment dominance and related online lifestyle shopping.
Objectives: invent and exploit a new business model, get big fast.
Success factors: uniqueness of idea, first-mover advantage, readiness in the market to accept product or service, patience on the part of venture capitalists in funding operations throughout loss-bearing growth phase.
Profitability criteria: customer size and transaction volume forecast in the time-frame estimated when drawing up the business plan, preventing competitors eating into the same market.

❑ **Efficiency curves:** utilise electronic means to streamline, automate, or improve functions and processes – usually leveraging economies of scale like Cisco (*www.cisco.com*) with their complete back end process and systems integration.
Objectives: throw competitors out of the market through price competition, cut back operational overheads, focus on value generation where your core competencies are.
Success factors: permanent fine-tuning of operations, outsourcing of overheads to reliable partners, internal knowledge management to expand core competencies, maintaining high customer satisfaction.
Profitability criteria: maintaining guaranteed service levels to customers and from suppliers, managing the risks of outsourced supplies, for example, price changes, supplier defaults, transportation difficulties.

❑ **Event control:** establish a unique experience based on all activities associated with a specific event, such as travelling – like the organiser of traveller communities Cabana (*www.cabana.com*).

Objectives: establish customer loyalty by providing an environment and a community they belong to, get big fast.

Success factors: generating network effects where the customer group grows exponentially by referrals from one customer to the next, outsourcing the generation of contents to customers and partners, one-to-one targeting of prospective customers possible for advertising and sales.

Profitability criteria: enough commissions for banner advertising, together with profit from sales.

❏ **Value chain integration:** link partners in an electronic supply chain or sales force chain to create services or products new to an industry, e.g. TradeLC.com with its 24-hour international trade finance service provided by three banks working together and operating electronically in different time zones of the globe.

Objectives: make the sum of the parts more powerful than the sum of the individual powers, combine individual experience and customer relationships to provide a unique service.

Success factors: make the different components and approaches involved compatible, get the best out of each partner without compromising his or her other sales activities.

Profitability criteria: premium prices for services or products where your group offers something unique, economies of scale for mass products.

Select one of those strategic business models and become excellent in it. Existing enterprises can usually build on their strengths and have an advantage in pursuing market segment command, information content control, or efficiency curves. They require less radical changes than the other models, so they can be implemented as an initial initiative.

Electronic bill presentment and consolidation

Payment transactions depend on agreements between the service provider and the customer. Traditionally, the payment channel preferred by the customer is used, for example, credit card, bank transfer or cheque payment. Therefore, economies of scale have been restricted as each customer usually has only few transactions and small amounts to pay. When you manage to follow the preference of the provider instead, such economies of scale can be achieved more easily, and the transaction costs can be cut back.

In the US, we see an interesting example of providers funnelling transactions to a billing and payment consolidator. The bills are compiled from various providers (for example, mail-order companies, telecom providers, utilities) and presented to the customer via the Internet; the payment consolidator is in charge of getting the money from the customer and to the provider. It is basically the same function as in traditional banking, but instead of waiting until the customer takes action by filling out a transfer slip or a cheque, the payment consolidator takes the initiative. In contrast to a factoring company, the payment consolidators do not buy the assets and step into risk management, they just settle the payment. The general approach is shown in Figure 1.

Depending on the degree to which providers want to outsource their billing and payment operations, thin or thick consolidation is applied. The thin consolidator model (top part of Figure 1) just obtains the totals of the providers' invoices, consolidates them into one statement for the consumer, presents it and settles the payments. No invoice or payment details will be available in the electronic presentation – and no handling of complaints is possible except for a rejection of a total invoice.

In contrast, the thick consolidator model (lower part of Figure 1) shows all items of the providers' invoices. Thus the providers do not need their own invoicing system; this is all handled by the thick consolidator. Even the generation of accounting entries can be outsourced to the consolidator. The consolidation is obviously more complex and requires building up specific know-how. John Sandifer, AMS' Vice President for Financial Services Europe, recommends building up 'a middleware infrastructure for preparing a homogenous presentation of invoice items from heterogeneous billing sources for complex requirements, but as a start the adoption of the thin consolidator model is definitely easier'. The benefit of the thick consolidator model is that customers get a full picture of their invoices and dispute resolution procedures can be automated on specific invoice items. Actually, the dispute function can even be aligned with the customer's behaviour: for customers with a good risk profile, for example, you can allow that small amounts (up to five Euros for example) can occasionally (such as once per quarter) be credited without expensive manual dispute handling.

In both consolidator models, marketing messages can be included with the bill – either from the providers of the bills (and the actual goods and services) or from third parties. Currently, the companies

Thin consolidator model

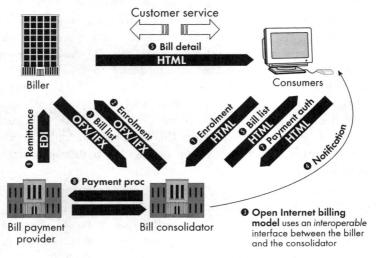

Thick consolidator model

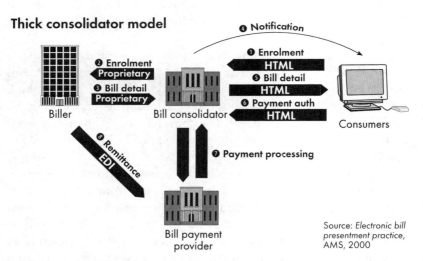

Source: *Electronic bill presentment practice,* AMS, 2000

Figure 1   Electronic bill presentment: thin versus thick consolidator

with strong relationships with customers are the initial players in the payment consolidator market:

❑ Credit card companies extend their traditional settlement of credit card transactions, by also processing transactions from other channels. The issue for many of those companies, however, has been that the commission on electronic bill presentment and payment is significantly less than traditional credit card acquiring fees. So there is still some reluctance to cannibalise their profitable credit card business revenues by a low-cost payment consolidation.

❑ Banks extend their basic account management by offering liquidity management based on all invoices compiled for consolidated payments. Even additional loan demand can be triggered by offering the customers an optimisation of the payment plan that includes consideration of what the costs of third-party credits are (for example, for the credit card company) or which early-payment discounts can be achieved. The issue for most of the banks has been that they do not have all the customers' invoices. So creative thinking is necessary. Others have been creative and have started to make payment consolidation an area contributing to their success – for example Bank of America (*www.bankofamerica.com*), by helping the customer to plan his budget and liquidity.

❑ Telecom providers leverage the fact that they have a relationship with the customer that triggers regular (usually monthly) payment interactions. And they have built up huge billing systems for tracking and charging each single call. With those systems it is easy to process one or two more transactions per customer and day – and the additional income on commissions for the payment handling is always welcome. Like the banks, the telecom providers need to get invoices from partners, and so far, primarily invoices from sales partners are included in the monthly bill, for example, from Mannesmann's mobile phone franchise shops (*www.d2privat.de*).

Presenting the bill electronically is a good feature for your website – see the Web demo from Avolent (*www.avolent.com*). Customers can visit your website to check invoices and release payments (fully or partially), they can issue disputes that you help them to sort out and all the time you have the opportunity to feed them with marketing messages. Start with your own invoices or statements and include the invoices from partners step by step.

1.3 The priorities

The good news is that you have not (yet!) missed the race. It is ongoing and many of your competitors face similar problems. A recent survey by Bain & Company (in January 2000) showed that the media and entertainment industry has gained the biggest lead with their Internet services while others lag behind. Out of almost 800 companies from 18 industries surveyed, media and entertainment scored 43 per cent more than the average; IT, telecom, financial services, the public sector, retail and logistics were all around the average; with construction, and the automotive and chemical industries falling back the most. However, in all industries, the interviewed leaders felt they were not doing enough to bring their latest services and products sufficiently quickly onto the market.

Two key points stand out from this survey: e-business is not a project you start now and finish at a predefined time; it is rather an ongoing journey – and you can learn from the interactive approaches of the leading media and entertainment industry. So, a 'big bang' approach is not good for that explorative exercise and it is more risky than a stepwise evolution. It takes a long time to prepare the big bang; during that time the market requirements can change, a competitor can come up with the same idea and your big investment can be in vain. Small steps will allow you to grab market positions early, learn from your marketing and operational experience and fine-tune your service. Your customers will appreciate being able to use your services quickly and in more convenient ways. They like to see ongoing improvements step by step instead of being forced to wait until everything's ready for a big bang. Therefore, get your priorities right!

An issue often seen in larger organisations is that there are a few excellent business areas with great market perception and lots of contribution generated. But the majority of business areas just show a mediocre performance. And the result of all those areas is often eaten up by one or two under-performing business units – see the chart in Figure 2 depicting the value generation throughout all customer segments. The most profitable customers are shown on the left-hand side of the chart. The first 10 per cent of customers create more than $1.5m profits, that is, more than 50 per cent of the overall profitability. These are the customers you should focus on to expand the business! The one-third of the customers depicted on the right hand side are, on the other hand, eating up more than a million dollars of the profitability.

But this situation gives you an opportunity for a quick win even before you start going online: if you terminate your engagement with the customers identified as 'losers', you will be more

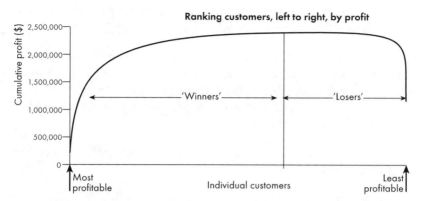

Figure 2   Value contribution by customer segments

profitable. You may do it in a friendly way: increase the prices for them, then they can decide if they want to leave (which would be profitable for you, because you stop your losses) or if they want to accept your higher prices (which would be eventually more profitable, because they now generate a contribution). And now for the left-hand side customers, the profitable ones – these are the customers to whom you should initially address your online service to expand your engagement with them.

Let us look at it more systematically. What you should do is an A/B/C analysis. That is, identify the best (A), the average (B) and the worst (C) segments. (A) would be those with a high profit contribution, (B) would generate little contribution and (C) are the loss generators. Perform this analysis by customer segments, by regions, by sales channels and by product segments. You are probably aware of those areas; if this is not the case, a quick look on your performance figures structured by the aforementioned dimensions should suffice. Then, as already indicated above, *focus on the best and on the worst segments* and identify the key actions in those areas by envisioning the alternatives:

❏ for A-segments: extending customer engagement, penetrating the region further, increasing sales channel use, enhancing the product or service on offer;

❏ for C-segments: terminating the customer engagement (or pricing up), pulling out of a region (or requesting additional fees), discontinuing the sales channel use (or changing the commissioning approach), cutting the product features back.

While a separate team can handle the C-segments, your Internet task force should create an attractive online service or product. Here is some advice: online business transactions have in principle two positive and two negative effects (for the service provider). Those effects are:

☺ easier accessibility for customers and thus less costly sales closure than in physical stores or branches;

☺ cheaper operation through a neat integration of the Web front end with the operations, the suppliers and the information technology back end

☹ focus of customers is on price comparisons due to full transparency on the Web;

☹ global competition.

If you look at it in more detail, you will see that the importance of those effects is different in each business area. With your top performer, your customers are probably less price-sensitive, because your market reputation is so high and you have managed to distinguish your product from competitors' commodities. The Web will allow you to add some quality to your top services and products, and to reduce fees carefully at the same time, for example, for customers using self-service. In this area, you should rely as much as possible on the recommendations of your staff – their past success proves that they know what they are doing! Also include the customers in the improvement processes: they will appreciate it if their wishes are reflected and will become even more loyal.

If you do not want to terminate the engagement with your worst performers (or increase prices), you should check to see if you can cut back your operational overheads sufficiently that you actually make the product or service profitable. This may be done by highly automating it, by outsourcing the areas you are struggling with because they are not within your core competencies or by getting better prices from your suppliers, for example, via electronic marketplaces. But do not underestimate the effort it takes to actually manage all those external dependencies – so maybe you still should get out of these segments; it is easier anyway.

For the top performers, while I recommend that you start making more effort to sell more and to engage with the customers online, you may be afraid of changing the relationship with the A-customers or changing the positive market perception of your A-products. But remember that if you do not improve the best of your services and products, your competitors may overtake you by offering a Web version and steal your customers! Strengthen your strengths!

Once you have analysed your best and your worst areas and change initiatives are underway, you can go through the mediocre areas as well. Probably you will find some similar patterns and can re-use the analysis and the change experience.

To allow rapid changes, you also should stay clear of perfectionist ideas. It is OK to have people on the teams who highlight what can be improved, but do not allow them to drive the decisions. Those decisions should be guided instead by Pareto's 80:20 rule – with 20 per cent of the effort you can reach 80 per cent of the results! With an analysis of the operational cost versus the value contribution as indicated in Figure 2, you can drive your efforts towards the most valuable customer segments. For analysing the cost and subsequently assigning the appropriate treatment to each customer you need to get an end-to-end perspective on all aspects of your customer acquisition, production and service interactions.

1.4 Preparing the infrastructure for flexible decisions

In contrast to the Internet start-up firms that have created their business from the bottom up and started with the implementation of technology tools, fully developed enterprises should plan their e-business activities and the reconfiguration of their overall business top down.

The initial analysis for setting the priorities as discussed above should be relatively easy. You either get the numbers from your accounting system or you can make some *ad hoc* evaluations.

For an ongoing monitoring of your performance, you should establish tools in addition to purely financial accounting, indicating trends, goal achievement and quality aspects. Such tools will allow you to see the impact of earlier decisions, learn from that experience and adjust your decisions regularly, for example, monthly instead of the current annual budgeting cycles.

Such monitoring should highlight:

❏ ranking of financial performance by customer segments, products, regions and sales channels;

❏ market penetration analysis with market shares, marketing response rates, product pipeline and innovation cycles;

❏ margin analysis and trend evaluation;

❏ trend analysis of costs such as investments, operations and staff, partnership fees and refinancing;

❏ service quality, such as response times in call centres, decision times for transaction approvals, completion times of orders;

❏ staff quality, development and competencies, measured, for example, by contribution or decision speed and quality.

Based on the financial and the non-financial data, monitoring and reporting on all levels of the enterprise and for all different business segments has to be consistently supported. This will allow a clear communication of objectives and success stories throughout the enterprise.

Some of these data should be available in your data warehouses and just need to be included in the reporting. Several of your data may show inconsistencies such as different cost-accounting philosophies in different regions or in different product responsibility areas. For these, a consistent presentation needs to be set up: identify the key information needs with the data entities and attributes, as well as the tables and fields of your various applications. Define the contents of those fields, validation rules and conventions, and establish data quality checks – and if necessary perform a data cleansing to get the data consistent. Other data, in particular those on the non-financial aspects, need to be reflected in your business processes; you have to start compiling and storing it.

Altogether, you should build up a new information warehouse allowing you a focused attitude to your customers – with real-time decision support for your online product and price offerings, your call-centre interactions and your marketing activities. Even off-the-shelf tools are available now to support such an enterprise perform-ance management (EPM) integrated with actionable customer rela-tionship management (CRM). Creating an information warehouse, doing the data-cleansing and setting up new management data are projects in themselves, but let us not get distracted by this from the specific goals for your e-business. In fact, frame those projects in the same brief development cycles as your e-business programme (see Part 3 for details of the programme).

In younger companies, even the financial data may not yet exist, but it is absolutely critical to compile and monitor them. Without proper planning and without measuring progress against plans, the financial behaviour of the company is not predictable – and the stock markets have started punishing the owners of companies without controlling tools by severe stock price reductions.

1.5 Your new exposure to the customers

In order to get a better bottom-line result with improved customer interactions, you need to refocus on several aspects of the customer experience. Those aspects are summarised in Figure 3.

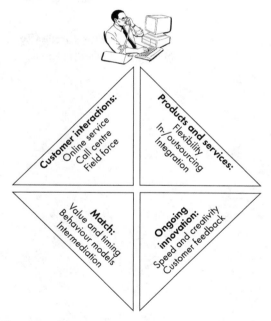

Figure 3   The customer e-experience

Each of these aspects will be discussed in the subsequent chapters:

❑ improving the customer interactions;

❑ offering a flexible product and service mix;

❏ matching your proposition with customer needs;

❏ making ongoing improvements to drive the changes.

1.6 Summary: issues requiring your decision

The foremost objective for you as leader of your enterprise is to define a crystal-clear e-business vision addressing:

❏ which customer segments to serve online;

❏ which Web services to make that leverage your traditional execution strengths and provide an added online value;

❏ which regions to approach – with which specific local refinements of the customer segments and services;

❏ which mix of traditional and 'virtual' sales and service channels to use;

❏ which operational aspects to fine-tune internally and what to outsource to optimise efficiency and effectiveness.

2

Better customer interactions

@@@ Give the online customers convenient access to your service touch points and provide immediate confirmation for the online transactions and a feedback on execution and delivery capabilities. @@@

Customers in the Internet age expect to obtain a consistent level and content of services no matter which channel they use: the Web, a call centre or the branch. They want to pay the world-wide lowest price for a Web transaction – and be treated like 'king customer' in the good old high street shop, where they were known with their preferences, their past orders and complaints and the agreed conditions.

In lieu of customer loyalty supported by personal relationships between the customer and his or her agent in the branch or at the counter, electronic means have to be used to achieve customer loyalty and to maximise the number of clients looking at your service. Additionally, 'brands are peculiarly vulnerable on the Internet. Take the case of a bank. In the world of bricks and mortar, a bank can assure its customers that their money is safe by housing it in impressive buildings. But how is the online bank to generate that sense of trust? Online, service and experience dominate, even over content and application.'* Let us have a look first at the customer touch points, that is, the instances (or portals) where your customers are actually interacting with your enterprise.

---

* Source: PeopleSoft Essentials Document, *Improving Shareholder Value in the eWorld*, 2000

2.1   Using the right touch points for virtual customer interactions

I use a broad definition of 'virtual interactions'; namely, they take place whenever traditional encounters by one of your sales staff with your customers in a branch are replaced by an interaction where they are outside your branches.

There are four ways for your customers to interact with you virtually:

1. Internet interactions: the already classic PC applications – such as home banking, brokerage services, online catalogues and orders, online auctions, entertainment. All these interactions use the sophisticated navigation and animation possibilities of the Web, combined in a portal inviting the customer to visit you and stay with you for a long time while he or she is entertained and shops. Alternatively, mobile phones can now be used – the upside is that the market penetration of mobile phones in Europe and Asia is much higher than PC penetration, so the Internet vision of ubiquity can more easily become reality. The downside is that applications and interactions need to be restricted in their scope as screens on mobile phones are so small (normally just four or five lines with approximately twenty characters each). Therefore, not much advertising is possible and surfing is not very convenient. We will discuss some implementation examples from Europe and Japan in Part 2 of the book. Personal digital assistants (PDAs) offer a better screen with better surfing capabilities, but the market penetration is still very small. Thirdly, TV-based Internet offers a good way for addressing the mass market. This will probably be successful for goods where animation is critical and PC availability cannot be expected, such as for selling fashion or for approaching more elderly customers. The least you should offer on the Web on top of your 'brochureware', that is, in addition to the catalogues of your products and services, is the possibility for the customer to get in contact with you via e-mail (and you also should establish processes to actually respond to the e-mails within a maximum of 24 hours). For your primary products, you should additionally make it possible to order them online.

2. Call centre: this provides a human voice and ear for customer enquiries and concerns while securing permanent availability to the customers. At the same time it maximises your flexibility for

change – you can scale up and down more easily than with a physical branch network and you can roll out new products or change the processes more easily. At each change, you can test it with a dedicated group of call-centre staff (the appropriate calls can be routed directly to them), and for the subsequent broad release you benefit from the fact that your staff are in the same place and thus can be trained more easily. With computer telephone integration (CTI) you can even handle standard cases such as providing the last account balance, fully automated. Provide your call-centre staff with the tools to inform customers about the availability of your products, to accept orders and deal with complaints.

3. Mailings: for messages you want to send to your customers, you have the choice between traditional paper mail, e-mail, and SMS (short message services sent to your customers' mobile phones). When you find the channel to most easily attract the customers' attention with the least cost, you can save a fortune on broadcast marketing. Currently the most interesting option is e-mail – customer attention is pretty high, because there are fewer distracters than in paper mail (often a waste of the postage fee and printing costs), the customers can pick the mail up when it is convenient and it can be sent at virtually no cost.

4. Your sales force field agents: for customer situations where you need to have a face-to-face contact, for example, for life insurance applications, your agents can be equipped with electronic order forms from an intranet. This reduces errors when filling in the forms and cuts back the effort of making multiple data entries. Thus, the order handling processes are accelerated, some overheads for manual correctness checking are reduced and customer satisfaction is increased.

Each of those touch points will play an important role in your transformation to a highly flexible enterprise. Approaching the customer with an individualised message is often referred to as 'one-to-one' marketing. It requires you to understand the customer preferences and buying profiles, and to 'remember' the last enquiries and purchases – like in the old high street shop with the friendly owner knowing each customer.

In general, the service offered to your customers must be consistent across all touch points or service and delivery channels –

no matter if he or she shows up in a branch or uses one of the
virtual touch points – and the messages must be very specific:

> With the Internet, consumer tolerance for broadcasted
> communications falls. The art changes from being one of
> predicting the product service that will appeal to the most
> people, to the art of understanding a complexity of needs
> and designing mass customisable solutions to meet them.*

Examples of smart usages of the new channels even from
production companies, that is, the earlier mentioned 'late starters'
in the online world, include *www.gmbuypower.com*, where General
Motors has set up a great consumer portal to enable customers to get
a feel for the GM way of life, the driving experience, the service
commitment – and the opportunity to order, obtain a loan and get
the car delivered right to their door. Large companies are also
leading the way in linking sales and purchase transactions with
their suppliers 'virtually'. Again, the automotive industry has set
up the electronic marketplace Covisint (*www.covisint.com*), where
Ford, GM, DaimlerChrysler, Renault/Nissan and Toyota share
communication channels for getting quotes from their suppliers,
placing orders and organising bulk orders for better prices.

For enriching your organisation with such 'virtual' channels,
different approaches exist that will be discussed next.

2.2   Creating e-business touch points

Customers have a specific perception of your enterprise brand. Most
of the banks, for example, have created an impression of solidity and
security. Surfing on the Web, on the other hand, is hip and fun. This
perception conflict is too big to solve in one step; instead you have to
move your brand step by step out of the 'brick and mortar' corner.
After a while you can create an image of an empathic and pro-active
helper serving customer needs according to his demands without
violating the strengths of your initial brand.

Those expectations created by your brand need to be supported
with the appropriate channel mix as discussed above. At the same
time, you want to achieve performance improvements and cost
savings by automating the back-office and the front-office. The key

---

* Source: *CRM as Strategy*, PeopleSoft Whitepaper, 2000.

is to be found where benefits for your customers exist: customers like to have things under control by, for example, being informed about the current state of their transactions such as orders, complaints or statements of accounts. You still have to make the service you offer different from that of your competitors and provide additional features in order to fight the possible perception of being a commodity broker, which might end up in margin-eating price reductions.

For defining the appropriate speed of change for your enterprise, you can learn from the following approaches.

❑ First, you can spin off a particular unit of your company in charge of e-business. This can either use your existing brand or a modernised sub-brand. For marketing purposes, you can disguise the initial test as a specific service or product offered to a small customer segment. This is the approach with the least friction in the market and for the organisation of your overall enterprise. But it requires careful management of the new unit: it is effectively a new company requiring capital, a proper legal umbrella, changes to existing employment contracts and pension plans. And you need to identify clearly the handover of interactions between your e-business company and the other units. The biggest benefit of spinning off is the clear and explicit value proposition – and the possibility to monitor the e-business performance separately.

❑ Second, you can go through an overall redesign of your activities. This will create some turmoil among your staff, but will leave the external boundaries of your enterprise unchanged. If you do it slowly, you can also gradually adjust the perception of your company in the marketplace.

❑ Or third, you can redefine your value proposition, seek new partners and alliances and thus create a completely new group of companies. This is the approach with the highest benefit potential due to the focus on respective core competencies, but at the same time the biggest risks due to complete disassembly and reassembly of several enterprises and thus a high upfront investment need.

We will discuss examples of all three approaches – actually, all are success stories, and you should adopt the approach that most suits your risk appetite and your time-to-market objectives.

Deutsche Bank 24 (*www.bank24.de*)*

Let us first take a look at Deutsche Bank. They spun-off their mass-market operations into Deutsche Bank 24, that is, a 24-hour call centre and Web-based efficiently organised low-cost unit. This sub-brand initially did not have any branches; it only used the call centre and Web for client interactions. Also, new customers were initially acquired by the new sub-brand. They attracted new types of customers: younger, higher educated individuals who wanted to have the burden of their financial transactions taken care of conveniently by a reliable partner. With those initial customers, Deutsche Bank 24 gained experience of how to operate an online bank, what back-office capacities to maintain at which times of the day, week and year, and how to fine-tune the processes.

In a second step, after a few million customers were satisfied with the service quality, Deutsche Bank transferred their existing mass-market customers (with less than 100.000 Euros in funds to manage) to Deutsche Bank 24 (DB 24). At that time, some of the physical branches were reallocated from Deutsche Bank to DB 24, while others were closed down and only a few kept by Deutsche Bank for relationship management with non-mass-market customers that was centralised in some key regions. Most of the transferred customers accepted the change, in particular because the new bank asked for smaller transaction costs and fewer recurring charges. And if customers complained, they were allowed to stay with 'mother' Deutsche.

The board of DB 24 has a strong marketing perspective; they experiment with different pricing schemes, for example, discounts for online orders, aggressive referral programmes for winning new customers and massive advertising.

Bank of Montreal (*www.bmo.com*)

The Bank of Montreal took a different approach. As an established financial service provider, they managed to change the perception their customers had of them from initially an arrogant and detached

---

* To allow you to compare the banks' situation with your enterprise, let me provide some figures: Deutsche Bank is the largest Germany-based bank. They have more than 800 billion Euros in assets; more than 90,000 staff serve 13 million customers from more than 2,000 branches in 60 countries. The Bank of Montreal has $238 billion in assets, and over 32,000 employees in Canada, the United States and around the world. TradeLC.com targets a market for trade processing services of nearly $10 billion.

institution to a friendly and empathic adviser, close to their customers, by:

❑ aligning the business processes to focus on the customer;

❑ enabling the employees and the systems to come up with pro-active proposals;

❑ empowering them to quickly approve client transactions such as loan or mortgage applications.

The client now obtains the same treatment no matter if he or she uses Web online interactions, calls the call centre or shows up in one of the remaining branches. This is achieved because the processes and systems are seamlessly integrated and customer profiles and histories together with the appropriate treatment policy are available for each interaction channel. The Bank of Montreal has several behaviour models to predict client interactions, for example the customer life-cycle model, as well as customer value and risk models. As a result of those models, each customer or prospective customer is assigned to one or several profiles. At the time of treatment decisions (for a loan approval, for example), the profiles and the currently available treatments are mapped automatically to optimise overall performance, to spend time and effort on those cases where high returns can be expected, and to apply only a little effort when only a little contribution is probable. In most cases, even an automatic decision is possible.

And the top managers of the Bank of Montreal set good examples of becoming customer-friendly by publicising their curriculum vitae, and providing value by publishing their speeches and presentations via the Web – not only to stock analysts or conference participants, but to every customer.

The key issues the Bank of Montreal had to resolve were how to change their legacy, that is, how to streamline their processes, reorient their middle management and staff (including reassigning and relocating people), and how to extend and embed their existing information technology into the new approach.

TradeLC.com

TradeLC.com (*www.tradelc.com*) is the joint venture of three banks: ANZ (Australia and New Zealand Bank), Barclays Bank and the Bank of Montreal. They have created an e-business unit to handle all international trade finance and letter of credit transactions. This business was traditionally difficult, because specialists needed to check the freight documents before payments could be released. So exporters often had to wait a long time for their money. The new idea from TradeLC.com is to pool specialists from the participating banks, allow customers to submit key documents electronically and provide 24-hour specialist availability.

Their service is geared towards corporate customers, that is, to importers and exporters in the various countries. With their centres of activity around the globe, online interfaces to their customers and internal electronic co-operation between the centres, Web-based interactions for opening letters of credit, checking documents, and releasing payments, they beat the traditional 'nine-to-five' attitude by far. How did they organise their initiative? They jointly went through several months of strategic redefinition of their value proposition, a close examination of their business process quality levels and their execution strengths and started to position themselves as a global provider of trade finance services. Then they implemented a new organisation with two key components: local sales and marketing forces to engage with their customers and central facilities for processing transactions – that is, local front-offices and a globally centralised back-office. The front-offices are distributed around the world in the locations where customer segments were identified as having the highest population. And the back-office operations were implemented where the best service levels for a defined cost could be achieved. This approach resembles and finally implements IBM's 1980s slogan: think global – act local.

The biggest issue for TradeLC.com is to cope with the 'little' differences the standard banking products handling requires in the different countries, plus the multilingual issue. A massive effort to explain the 'standard' product needs to be launched.

Advantages and disadvantages

Let us compare the approaches of the three banks. The most important factor in common is the combination of an easy transition for the customers, a careful evolution of the brand, a clear vision created by company leaders and stable top management support. The selected approach and the execution details differ significantly, though. While the Bank of Montreal effected the transition with the normal day-to-day operations continuing, Deutsche Bank created a new area of operation where they started from scratch, fine-tuned the approach and finally transferred the customer base to the new organisation. And TradeLC.com starts with an empty slate for implementing processes and IT (without constraining their views of existing enterprises, current product definitions and procedures) before transferring their customers and operations altogether to the new organisation. Therefore, management attention and areas for ongoing monitoring were different: the Bank of Montreal had to look at the number of new interaction channels activated, the service levels in each of them and the consistency of the service across the channels. Deutsche Bank had to focus on acquiring new customers for the young self-service brand while scaling up their organisation and information technology simultaneously. And TradeLC.com must ensure the implementation is ready in time – and keep the customers motivated to go through the transition with them, for example, by offering better professional services.

All of these approaches reduce the costs per transaction due to the economies of scale but each requires significant upfront investments, in particular for information technology and call-centre infrastructure. The 'ongoing changes' approach from the Bank of Montreal and the 'new area first' approach from Deutsche Bank both needed a relatively small initial investment with a flexible implementation starting in a relatively small environment. Subsequently, this environment has been scaled up according to the current size of the business. TradeLC.com, on the other hand, uses a 'brute force' approach by completely reshuffling front-offices and back-offices around the globe. The results still need to be seen.

The Bank of Montreal needed more than a decade to offer initial services to the customer, with many little changes to manage, while DB 24 started small but then made a 'big bang' change – altogether less than five years were sufficient to expose the majority of their customers to rebranding and reservicing. During that time, DB 24 faced the key problem of not earning money, because they were in permanent growth and investment mode. So subsidising from Deutsche Bank was necessary, while the parent company had still to carry the cost of the legacy environment. TradeLC.com plans to implement all its changes in two years, so it will be the fastest approach – and the one with the highest upfront investment. The key difference between these approaches is that the amount of subsidies is very explicit for the managers of Deutsche Bank and of TradeLC.com, while at the Bank of Montreal cost accounting has had to struggle with cost allocations between new and old ways of doing business.

It is interesting to see the evolving approach to change at the Bank of Montreal. First, they were one of the pioneers to gain online experience by implementing the necessary changes customer segment by customer segment – and now, with their experience from this slow and piecemeal project, they have adopted the big-bang approach in the TradeLC.com venture. A new team of players in the joint venture, a new way of approaching the market and a new technology! Actually, another player in the team had also had important experience. Barclays was already using electronic co-operation between specialists in different fields: for a decade they had distributed key business processes in trade finance over various geographic units. Between those units they forwarded images of specific documents to the appropriate specialist. Creating TradeLC.com from scratch without the earlier experience would probably have meant risking money and reputation, but now the stakeholders are a strong team of Web-experienced marketeers, remote co-operation specialists and technologists. What you can learn from this is that there is a high strategic value to 'getting your hands dirty' with initially small Web projects so as to gain experience and develop models of how your customers react and interact, and then later increase the size and impact of your Web presence to market dominance in the targeted areas. The little difference that makes the difference is – no surprise – experience.

Let me emphasise once more the most important similarity between the three approaches: in all cases the top management was and is fully committed to the new approach, put all its energies into it and invested creativity and energy in motivating staff and customers to accept the new way of business. Some of the leading companies even have chief imagination officers (CImO) or chief electronic commerce officers (CeCO) to underline the importance of innovation and e-business and to demonstrate interest at board level.

A common theme of all approaches is the utmost flexibility, leading to a shorter time to market. This flexibility is usually achieved by a stable information technology and operations backbone combined with a 'best of breed' approach for components, where outsourcing partners, insourced service units and software packages can be 'pulled out' and 'plugged in' according to the most recent business strategy. But this is not enough! Additionally, close monitoring tools for overall performance (financial figures, customer growth, staff attrition and innovation speed) have to be implemented and used throughout all the organisational units.

2.3 Summary: objectives requiring your attention

Do you see a lot of problems for transforming your enterprise to focus on customer interests and interactions? You are right, but those companies that did not want to go through such massive changes and offered just an add-on channel for offering or distributing their products have been less successful. Some of the providers have even discontinued their Web presence. So, do it right – or wait until you get bought (or disappear). Key points to consider are:

❑ support 24-hours a day, 7 days a week customer interactions;

❑ allow the customer to choose between traditional and virtual channels, in particular call centres and online services;

❑ integrate these channels to maintain high quality services with a consistent profile;

❑ share cost savings with customers to foster your competitive advantage;

❑ gain Web interaction experience through some smaller projects and then get online for your whole customer base fast!

3

Flexible product and service creation

@@@ Allow your customers the choice between different product and service configurations by integrating all value-generating units of your organisation flexibly so as to scale up or down, and to allow for adapting co-operation between internal units and external partners. @@@ Keep your time-to-market faster than your competitors. @@@

The speed of change on the Web is faster than any traditional company can absorb internally. Imagine the huge number of global competitors on the one hand and the time it takes to define traditional organisational competencies, processes and to implement supporting software solutions on the other hand. So the customer touch points discussed in the last chapter need to be established as a buffer, where new packages or prices can be presented to your customers without actually changing the contents. But repackaging the same contents will not be enough; you still need to refocus your processes to maintain customer loyalty (and revenues).

To comply with the speed of change Internet customers demand, you need additionally to structure your organisation more flexibly than in the past. The key point is to build units capable of working independently, each providing specific parts of your overall value chain. These independent units can be more easily reconfigured, in particular scaled up or scaled down. Some activities can be outsourced if better performance can be found on the market, or you can support other companies by offering them a particular service. The process of making your enterprise more flexible should be based on an analysis of trends, plus your forecast of what changes you expect in customer demand, in the competitive evolution, and in your product offerings. In this chapter, we will examine the most important trends for the various units in an enterprise, discuss the impact of insourcing versus outsourcing and assess some specific implications and megatrends for the finance industry.

3.1 Trends for providing high value services

'Customers want service − not just stuff.'* The Web increases competitive pressures by allowing customers to compare providers' capabilities and prices with a few mouse clicks − the market thus becomes very transparent. This transparency, the speed of innovations and the eroding margins force each unit of an enterprise to permanently rethink their value proposition and to adjust their focus and services again and again. Before we consider the strengths and weaknesses of insourcing and outsourcing, let me share with you the particular trends for each value-generating unit, in Table 1.

As an additional recommendation for customer interactions discussed in the last chapter, you should make sure you inform your customer about key developments coming from each of the units mentioned above, such as a new patent for your company, exhibitions and conferences, special offers, new products or service features and achievements of your field force.

3.2 Insourcing versus outsourcing

The trends described in Table 1 indicate how traditional boundaries between the different industries and providers are disappearing. In fact, you should prepare your company for that change, too, by making units independent from each other and by being explicit about their contribution of services. This independence provides your company with a large range of flexible opportunities depending on performance and business evolution.

---

* Frederick Newell in his book *loyalty.com*.

Table 1   Trends and characteristics of value-generating units

Unit	Trend	Considerations & Characteristics
Research & Development	The refinement of existing products is achieved in just a few centres on the globe. New product ideas are generated by small companies, e.g. dot coms.	Is it more effective to do it alone? The automobile industry shifts to massive mergers like Daimler and Chrysler exploiting the synergies of combining the global car design and development activities. The finance industry has a few places (e.g. London and New York) that currently drive the innovation. Most companies plan to cut back on R&D
Marketing (traditional)	The Internet is the primary marketing 'machine' for the current decade. Investments into it and its penetration will continue to grow.	Who will be the winners of the battle for customer attention? The disappearance of the first dot coms underlines the fact that a prerequisite for success is a good brand-image combined with a large number of customer contacts. So the long-term winners will be well-known companies (no matter from which traditional business area), like big telecom and network operators, top banks, radio and TV stations with many listeners or viewers and emerging top Internet players (like amazon or eBay). They may sell a broad range of third-party products and prosper from the commissions they get. With the increasing refinement of customer segments, too, the number of marketing channel operators will grow, too.
One-to-one marketing and sales closure	The concepts are clear, but implementation of highly automated solutions are still rare.	These are pretty new disciplines in the Web world. Traditionally, the sales person or sales agent was the one to translate a company's product into the exact needs of the customer. Today, your systems need to 'read between the lines' to find out more quickly what a Web visitor wants and to offer it pro-actively. At the same time, they need to provide the necessary risk coverage such as identifying and authenticating the customer, ensuring payment, checking warranty obligations and providing for the execution or delivery capabilities. Companies that strive to be a significant bit better than the competition get stunning improvements in their sales figures – like the head start Amazon made with its book-selling.
Production	The traditional focus on production of the actual goods shifts to the services around the product – but the production of marketing materials will grow.	Some highly specialised companies will emerge to produce actual goods with very specific features for the target market segments. Possibly, other companies will package products and provide marketing materials with the specific information for target segments
Servicing	Providing customised services in the regions to complement the basics produced in a few global centres will see considerable growth.	Products that require delivery, configuration, assembly or repair at the client location, will create new service requirements. Imagine the sophisticated logistics for just-in-time delivery of the grocery goods necessary for cooking a meal for friends based on a recipe downloaded from the Web.
Payment	Credit card companies still play the biggest role for Web-based sales but telco operators eat into that market.	Who should own the payment streams for Web-based sales? The finance industry is confronted with the issue of shrinking influence, but partnership agreements might help out. Telco providers and the operators of online shops start to build up their own risk management systems in order to get their share of the current credit card transaction fees.

Each of the units has to come up with a very clear perspective on the value they generate. What is the core competency, who are the customers (consumers, other companies, internal units), what is the specific value as part of an overall offering to the market, has the evolution of value generation been growing or shrinking in the past and what is the expectation for the future? With this 'purpose of life' in mind, each unit should establish explicit contracts with their customers concerning the product or service to be provided with specific service level agreements.

Once the strategies of the units and their approaches are redefined, you can compare their performance with the performance of similar operations offered by third parties. Some services may not be needed in the online world any more, while for others in high demand you may currently not have sufficient resources. With the discussed explicit contracts and service levels in place, you have triggers to indicate the need to scale operations up or down. In the cases where your own units are not capable of dealing with the large number of transactions, you can outsource in order to deal with the overload. Units with a good performance but excess capacity can offer their services on the intercompany market.

Moreover, you can reassemble your overall value proposition. For the new online value proposition, you can adopt either of two basic strategies:

❏ you can increase the breadth of your offering to exploit economies of scale and scope;

❏ or you shrink it to be the primary player in specific market niches.

In the first case, you should look at adjacent business fields where you can build up additional services when your earlier markets become more and more quickly saturated. The additional services may be created in-house or they can be packaged with third-party components – maybe the 'package' is even formed by a merger. Mergers, though, may create a big headache for you; according to long-term studies only fifty per cent are successful. And even worse for your clear perception of your brand,

> ... merged firms often feel very different, and to people – staff, shareholders and analysts alike – feelings matter. Important issues include how to retain and motivate the best people within the enterprise, to bring disparate

cultures together, as well as how to sell the merger to its public, both customers and markets.

Source: *Improving Shareholder Value*, PeopleSoft essentials document, 2000

In the second case, you spin off or outsource those areas of operations where you do not have a specific value generation and no economies of scale. Classic examples are the cleaning services which in the old days (who remembers them still?) were done by the enterprise's cleaning ladies – and now are outsourced to highly professional cleaning agencies.

The main point you need to assess is where your most competitive strengths are, i.e. to identify your core competencies. The list of value chain elements discussed at the beginning of this section indicates key trends (listed below according to expected change in importance).

↗One-to-one marketing and sales closure

↗Regional and local servicing

↗Traditional marketing

→Payment

↘Research and Development

↘Production of goods and back-office service execution

Where are your core competencies? Ask yourself what distinguishes you from your competitors, where customers get value from and what you can leverage for generating new business ideas. Are there assets you own such as patents, brands, standards or procedures that can be used in additional areas? The area of your core competency should then be built up quickly to a supreme position. Invest in it significantly to extend your strategic assets (such as brands, patents, rights, networks) and to realign your processes on the new target markets: use to advantage your creativity, energy, money, excellent staff and your personal attention. If this core competency is in one of the areas of growing importance leverage it by inviting partners to join a broad-based network – such as TradeLC.com did. If you are lacking core competencies in the areas where strong future demand is expected, seek a partner quickly before one chases you. Thus you can continue to exploit your existing competencies (such as research or production) and complement it with your partner's marketing strengths.

What about under-performing areas? You have to optimise them, too. If you can afford it, you can take your time by applying some gentle modifications, streamlining processes, standardising activities and cutting the costs of operations. Your financial situation, the competitors and the shareholders may force you, though, to perform optimisation more quickly. In order not to distract too much of your managerial attention from pushing your core competencies to even higher excellence, delegate the problem and its solution. If your middle management is good enough to handle it, define the objectives in terms of service levels and costs, allocate a reasonable deadline and see if they can fix it. If it works out OK, you can decide if you want to keep the unit in-house or to spin it off into a separate unit. Spin-offs motivate your staff and should lead to even bigger improvements in operations, but the downside is that you are then dependent on an external entity you can control only pretty remotely. For this case, you would need also a 'Plan B' in case that external entity does not perform to your requirements.

If, on the other hand, the results of the initial optimisation programme are not consistent with the objectives or if you are under more severe pressures, you can decide to take a more drastic step. For example, hand over that business unit of yours to another company that specialises in such operations and buy the services back from them (like 'sell and lease back') or from other sources. Making an analysis of what is available on the market will also give a good benchmark for service levels and the reasonable costs for such services.

The process of making units and co-operation between units more flexible, and establishing formal agreements with a large number of internal and external partners, is often labelled as disintermediation and reintermediation. This new construction of the value chain is necessary to allow the customer a range of choices.

To identify the areas to outsource, you should go through a value chain analysis – let us see what *www.tradelc.com* come up with:

They distinguish between four areas:

❑ the front-office to stay unchanged by TradeLC offers;

❑ the middle-office, the conceptual cut of the traditional back-office that defines those processes to be kept by TradeLC's customers;

Figure 4   TradeLC's value proposition

❏ the outsourced part of the back-office TradeLC can use economies of scale for document processing;

❏ and the basic bank products that are kept in the bank (in the traditional back-office).

This approach leaves the front-office functions of the banks (and also of each of the TradeLC founders) untouched: the relationship with end customers stays with the original bank. Strategic areas such as product management, risk management and pricing also stay with the bank. Those areas are handled by TradeLC, where the focus is on efficient processing of the documents 24 hours per day: the examination of documents presented; the handling of payments with all the variations (for example, partial, deferred, in various currencies and countries); messaging (that is, electronic communication with SWIFT and with the exporters or importers); and the handling of all operational issues. So the customers of TradeLC can expect less costly processing of trade finance products than if they build up (or keep) their in-house solution – and TradeLC is smart enough not to challenge the relationship with the banks' customers.

3.3   Allow the customer a range of choices

For me as a customer it is easy to shop around until I find exactly what I want. When I am looking for banking services, I can open a current account at first-e (*www.first-e.com*), yielding 6 per cent interest, open a credit card account that earns bonus airmiles upon each transaction, find a discount mortgage and select from many insurance providers. For you as provider it is hard to supply exactly the pre-configured product or service I need. So instead of anticipating my entire configuration desires, why not offer me the possibility to pick and choose, as I like? If you have some entertainment on your website the picking and choosing will prevent me from shopping around too much – in particular as searching the lowest price provider is still time-consuming on the Web.

The basic 'products' of the providers are increasingly similar, but the branding, terminology and packaging for the various customers can be quite diverse. You need to offer a broad set of components (from within your organisation or through a partnership with another provider) and allow a flexible configuration. Anticipate situations where I as a customer want to gamble a bit on the stock exchange, but make sure that I always get back at least 80 per cent of my investment.* Or where I want to save some money during my working years in order to retire at the age of fifty, sail a boat and provide a good education for my children. If you let me play on your website with different amounts to save every month, different combinations of investment, allow me to configure the right mix of risk and return, allow me additionally to have a game portfolio for fun, and if you are able to support my dreams, e.g. by showing me the sailing boat I can own later, or give me a feeling of the university flair I intend to provide for my children, I will more likely sign up for your savings plan (or whatever the package name is).

Sounds great, but will such an approach work for you? Nobody can tell you up front. The only way is to try it out systematically, test if it works, that is, count how many eyes have been viewing

---

* Banks offer investment portfolios where a good part of the funds are deposited in secured assets, such as government bonds, and only the remainder is invested in stocks. Combined with a minimum duration of the investment of various years, the banks' expectation is that they will not run a risk with that guarantee, and many customers have accepted such a service due to perceived security.

your website and how customers have ordered, use another approach in parallel, compare the results and then use the better of both. Once the better approach is implemented, try out yet another approach in order to continuously improve.

The design of your Web portal should allow enough choices of configuration, each at a reasonable cost, to keep customers' and prospective customers' attention on your website – and persuade the customer to eventually buy from you. Many traditional enterprises do not have their core strengths in marketing. So you should partner with companies that already have relationships with your customers. These relationships may be traditional, or even better, through exploiting new channels such as telecom operators, radio or TV stations – or in partnership with your customers' employers.

American Express provides an interesting example with their 'corporate card' service of how to use employers as a marketing multiplier. They have special offers for enterprises which commit themselves to a bulk purchase. Everybody wins: Amex makes an important closure with just one contract negotiation; the employees pay lower fees and the companies get an analysis of expense profiles, for their travelling costs, for example, allowing them to conduct discount negotiations with their travel providers. Oh – and the online part to it: Amex offers employees a Web application to claim their travel cost reimbursement from their employer based on credit card statements. Customer loyalty is achieved by the many mutual relationships and benefits that exist around the core service of payment processing – and by moving their corporate customers (the employers) into the role of sales staff to their employees.

3.4   Link the Web sales with your back-office organisation

There is more than just the basic core product, that is, your marketed product. How is it embedded in support services? Is it easy for me as the customer to understand the 'small print' of your tariffs, insurance regulations, payment terms, warranty regulations? Can I easily obtain your products and services or are cumbersome application procedures necessary? How quickly can you confirm the acceptance of my order – and how quickly can I get the ordered goods? What if I want to change some of our agreements later, for example, use another cost model, change the pay-out times of my pension fund, or what if I sell the house I got the mortgage for? How do you protect me against risks during our relationship? How difficult is it to resolve complaints, terminate agreements, or raise claims?

The better you understand the situations your clients are in, the more empathy you generate; and the better the contents and design of your website, the higher the chances of creating additional business via the Web.

It is also advisable to allow your customers to 'configure' the intensity of human interaction – and implicitly the price of your services. Do they want to be treated personally by your agents in the field? For such customers, you had better only offer products and tariffs that support the cost of your field force! Do customers want to use your call centre heavily? Then apply a medium charge. Or are they pushing for a highly effective and automated operation at little cost and with high yields? Then you had better offer a straightforward website without many gimmicks and distractions around the core business functionality and you had better be very concise in dealing with such customers personally, for example, through efficient discussions with specially trained call-centre staff.

Again, Deutsche Bank/DB 24 is an example of how to implement such an implicit segmentation of customer-approach. If I want to be taken care of by my individual account representative and am ready to pay higher prices, then I stick to the traditional institution. If on the other hand, I want to have close personal control of my portfolio and I seek highly performing money and stock services with real-time trading round the globe, and do not mind an unknown number of staff and systems dealing with my requests, I use the DB 24 self-service.

So the 'ingredients' and the quality of your core product plus the services around it are key. For improving services, you should systematically identify events throughout the customer relationship cycle when there are interactions between him or her and your organisation, for example, general requests for information, comparisons with your competitors' offering such as pricing/risks/benefits, order or application compilation and submission, configuration of components, changes and extensions, complaints, reductions and terminations of existing agreements.

For each of these events, you should find and implement appropriate responses, for example, through call-centre scripts or online dialogues, that optimise the returns for your customer and you. Look at examples, from leading providers in various industries. Catalogue selection, order entry and order handling is well implemented in the book market (for example, by its pioneer Amazon, *www.amazon.com*) and by telecom operators or Internet service providers (ISPs such as AOL, *www.aol.com*). A great product configurator can be found with Cisco (*www.cisco.com*) where more than 10,000 different components can be configured by customers — and the production facilities then tailor the system according to the customer request.

3.5 Customer value versus treatment costs

When you record and monitor the interactions mentioned above, you will find out on which occasions and through which events an individual customer has the tendency to buy a particular product or to request a specific service. It does not reflect, though, what the value of this is for you, because we have not looked at the costs yet. Therefore, for each of the anticipated transactions and customer contact, you should also have an expected cost assigned.

In the long run, you should aim to optimise your results by putting most effort into the areas with the largest expected returns. Several things need to be in place for such an outcome. You need to understand the cost situation of your enterprise in detail, that is, the cost of a 'unit' of the things you are selling. Then you need to add to this basic cost the cost of related services such as marketing, sales, dealing with orders and transactions, cost of supplies, complaint handling.

In more advanced models you will include the value potential, too. How much cross-selling is to be aimed at customers in a specific segment for additional products and how does the overall expected value of the customer look then? When is it right not to throw additional marketing money at a client who will not decide to buy your product or service anyway?

Then, by looking at the result of a particular customer relationship and the necessary costs incurred, you (or your automatic decisioning system) can rank various treatment options to the associated value. Imagine sales and processing costs of 300 Euros for a transaction with a value of just 200 Euros — it would have been better not to start the transaction at all! You still need to monitor how often such opportunities occur. Once you manage to cut your costs to half, that is, to just 150 Euros, it will be a profitable business.

To decide on the appropriate approach to particular customers for example, whether to offer them a discount when they visit you on your website, or when they call the call centre, you have to store the customer profile and have the appropriate action triggered by your systems.

3.6   Summary: actions to take

Key aspects for shortening your time to market and for being flexible in reacting to changing customer demands are:

❏ focus your enterprise on your core competencies and complement these with products and services from partner companies where you cannot provide for excellence yourself;

❏ provide strong online marketing – either by yourself or with support from a partner – and package what you offer via the Web with many convenient options;

❏ integrate your Web front end customer interactions with the back-office organisation;

❏ organise your units to quickly scale up or down and to extend or adjust the particular service they contribute to your overall service or product;

❏ spin off units that are not capable of handling the necessary speed of change.

4

Match customer needs

@@@ Provide the right value proposition for the right customer at the right time to make a profit while online markets and prices have become fully transparent and traditional industry borders start to erode. @@@

Catalysts for buying decisions (and eventually loyalty) are primarily the value customers receive or perceive for their money, plus the timing of your proposition.

4.1   Value for the customer and loyalty

Customer motives and needs

'Our biggest problems don't result from a lack of knowledge but from a lack of guidance and orientation. We are confused, not ignorant', says Norbert Bolz, Professor of Communication Science at the University of Essen. With the growing number of similar products and services, customers are becoming more and more lost in the Internet world. To cope with such a challenge, let us discuss some marketing basics first. Buying decisions are always triggered by a bundle of motives. The basic motives are physical needs, such as food and sleep. Then people think ahead and look for an orderly life consisting of work, a roof over their heads and clothes on their backs. Once these needs are at least minimally met, people of all generations want to socialise, be respected by other citizens (in particular their peer group or community) – even make them jealous or gain power and influence over them. At the same time they care for those close to them, and try to create an environment where they can all comfortably live. Additionally, as more and more leisure time is available, people look for entertainment of all kinds: TV, music, reading, games, sport, travel and now also surfing the Web 'just for fun' and chatting with people in other places.

The better you can identify the needs profile of your customer target group and the better you support their overall communication and socialisation needs, the better you can mix and balance the components in the package of services or goods you offer them. Look at the campaigns for mobile phones: it is fashionable now to have one, they are available in crazy colours, the tariff structures make it possible to have a hot button to get connected with your lover (for the young ones) – or with friends or family for the more mature customers. The mobile phone is not only the technical means for generic communication, but it serves the purpose of staying in touch with the most important other people in your life no matter where you are and where the other people are. This increases the perceived value of mobile phones very much – and who cares if, for that purpose, that it may cost three times more than talking over an old-style fixed telephone!

So you should dress up your goods and services and your marketing, in line with your customers' needs and the benefits they perceive. In the finance industry, such packaging has been done to some extent by life insurance companies, but no real boost for business has been triggered by traditional sales campaigning. In contrast, companies such as Equity & Law (now AXA Sun Life; a subsidiary of the AXA group – *www.sunlife.co.uk*) that extended their basic product with the opportunity to improve capital returns by investments on the stock exchange have been very successful: they appeal to the greed of many of us human beings: you can start with little money, and there is a fun factor attached to it. Here, the perceived value is high. Also successful is the campaign of the Bank of Montreal offering 'BrainMoney' for their students and creating a student community which a huge percentage of Canadian students favour and have subscribed to.

Communities and network effects

As long as you are not able to get your product out of the commodity corner, the criteria the customer uses will be just price. Imagine, for example, the needs of a young family who wants to provide their child with a good education. Depending on the timing of the decision this could be 'implemented' by a stock saving plan if the child is still very young, a bond saving plan, or a loan if the child is already about to start his or her education. But that will not be enough to persuade the customer to decide on your product and to create customer loyalty. You had better combine this product with value-added services in line with the underlying needs of the customer, for example, with a university course (or various courses for each field of education), with accommodation assistance for the young person who is studying away from home – and of course with a one-stop-shopping package for the student: student account, student car insurance, student travel. Think about the rich data set you obtain when the customer shares his or her desires with you – and how you can use this knowledge to enhance what you offer! Update your concept of customer loyalty:

> 'To the degree that customer loyalty of the past was partly a product of habit, ignorance of alternatives, perceived high switching costs, loyalty will still be under greater pressure. ... A heightened value will be placed on quality customer service and understanding, with a real premium on adaptability, responsiveness, clarity and dependability. ... The links of voice-mail, e-mail and the Internet support a stronger and stronger sense of [community] and personal connection in our increasingly distributed global activities.'*

Put emotional value at the forefront instead of monetary bean-counting! Years ago I learned in my Marketing 101 class that 'people don't buy drills, they buy holes'. Today I would say people do not buy holes, they want to buy dreams they can hang on the nail in the hole someone drilled for them.

An important value for customers is also the feeling of being a member of a large community. The human need is to communicate and to be among people of similar interests. So if you manage to create sufficient trust among your joint user base so that they want to share their views (like Amazon readers with their book reviews, or eBay's scoring of the quality of private sellers), you create an emotional home for your customers. Additionally, the efficiency of your services increases with the growing number of community members. The classic example is telefax: with a growing number of fax users, the overall service developed its value and usability. More

---

* Source: *Clicks and Mortar* by David S. Pottruck (President of Charles Schwab) and Terry Pearce

recent examples are SMS messages via mobile phone and e-mail access, and also, as mentioned previously, Amazon and eBay customer groups reviews with their growing number of reviews. This positive circle of self-induced growth is called network effects – the better you play them, the quicker you can outperform your competitors. Currently the leading business concept purely built on network effects are directory and contact services, for example, the global directory service PlanetAll (*www.planetall.com*), which allows its currently more than two million subscribers to stay up to date with their friends by providing their most recent addresses – no matter where they move on the globe; or flirting and dating services such as *www.matchmaker.com*. Through such services, you can be informed when a friend is moving from or to places that interest you and you can organise to meet him or her again.

Pricing approach

Use a pricing approach for your products that downplays the monetary side. Your customers may be sensitive to recurring monthly charges (as currently in the telecom environment), so offer a price plan with low monthly charges, but usage fees which are a bit higher. Customers may dislike being charged for each and every transaction (as happened in banking a few years ago), so charge them an annual lump sum. They may not like to pay you money at all – so get your money from third parties (as we currently see from the free ISPs living from banner ads and telephone charges).

The details of your financial plans may be pretty difficult to understand for the normal customer, anyway – in particular if you include down-payments and deferred refunds as in the banking and insurance business and now also starting in telecoms where you can subscribe (with a regular lump sum) to discount price plans. How many customers are capable of doing a cash flow analysis, or even a discounted cash flow analysis, or even consider risk premiums for the various transactions? Even well-educated people often do not use their knowledge of mathematics to check if 0.95 Euro today is more or less than what 1 Euro will be in two years – not to mention looking ahead ten or twenty years.

Empathy with the customer

Your product managers and staff (and maybe even your brand) should be different for each of the customer segments you are serving. Imagine, for example, the different attitudes of young families compared with young entrepreneurs or with elderly couples. They use different language codes, have different lifestyles and wear different clothing, so different examples have to be given and different objectives have to be used. The young entrepreneurs need to get professional advice for their industry, may quickly need a few millions for their next investment – or are cash-rich but are looking for a very profitable (say more than 20 percent annual yield) excursion on the stock market. The elderly couple may want to securely maximise the return of their funds in order to maintain a good standard of living, enjoy many more holidays and be able to afford all medical costs that may occur.

In view of this, you should organise your staff with a focus on customer groups and extend your marketing and sales accordingly, instead of organising your people around your products. Additionally you need to teach and enable your staff to translate the core services and goods of your company and your partners into those meaningful packages for your customers.

This focus on specific customer segments can be more easily accomplished when your customer-contact facilities are based on call centres – or even spun-off into a separate business unit or legal entity. There you also can learn from the experience of your staff and develop their capabilities: provide opportunities for call-centre staff to talk about the dynamics of their sales talks for specific customer segments, appoint people to disseminate that experience, grow with their knowledge and see them grow, too!

Trends and changes to come

The trend is to provide the customer with lots of information and have your actual product or service as just one of many items on your website – a 'by the way: you can buy great stuff here, if you like'. One of the companies awarded with the Internet marketing award Tenagra, the Virtual Vineyard (*www.virtualvin.com*) offers, for example, tales of past viticulturists in France, anecdotes and information of interest to those in the industry as well as people who just enjoy wine, provides cooking tips and recommendations for wines for different occasions, and you can order the wine, too.

In the middle of the turmoil created by market changes are the financial service providers. The monopoly of banks for customer payments will soon be over. Such services are now being taken over by telecom providers, collecting payments from customers via the telephone bill and reimbursing content providers (see the example of Paybox in Chapter 12.3) and also by companies specialising in credit-worthiness decision-making and payment (see the example of Competix, also in Chapter 12.3). So the banks are even more than other industries forced to review their value proposition and core competencies. During more than the first half of the last century, they were focused on providing liquidity for manufacturing plus obtaining some fee income from managing payment streams (bills of exchange, foreign exchange, foreign trade, documentary business and later credit cards). In the last third of the century, the focus shifted to the investment market with the 'private', that is, wealthy, customer, or to interbank deals. Now the stock exchange boom is slowing down or even retreating, and a normal pace of stock price development can be observed again. At the same time the costs of this business are increasing due to excessive salaries for top stockbrokers and analysts plus expenses for global treasury and credit derivative risk management systems. With the profitability in the treasure sector beginning to deteriorate, the next pillar of profitability has to be built up.

The next generation of banking will focus on specific customer segments – actually many new brands will be generated to engage with such segments (see example in Chapter 7.2). Many specific services for different customer contexts will emerge, in particular for the various huge mass-market segments. No longer will discussions with customers be based on the fact that your competitor offers a five-Euro smaller monthly cost for a loan or a one basis point higher yield for an investment. Instead, you should win the customer by being able to recommend the best universities for his or her child's education, when talking about a saving plan for the child's studies, or by demonstrating the best analysis tools for monitoring the customer's stock investment.

The increasing transparency of the online market, together with the erosion of borders between traditional industries, will force service providers to combine services with those of their partners and to organise around customer interests. Consider yourself the intermediary between the customers needs and what is available on the market (including, of course, your own products) and express the strengths of your package as advantages for the customer. So one of the key responsibilities of your staff is to think ahead and define new types of services, products and packages.

Once this understanding about different packaging, customer approaches and success rates has evolved in the case of initial customer segments and products, you can implement similar packages and similar types of dialogues on your website for the segments and products you decide to deal with next. The difference between the website approach and your physical branches and call centre is that you need to think ahead more: certain customer needs have to be anticipated and pre-packaged. On the other hand, with the configuration possibilities for your packages we discussed in the last chapter, you should use the 'feedback' from your customers obtained from measuring what configuration parameters they primarily use, so that you can systematically adjust the product or service you are offering.

4.2 Timing

The customer groups mentioned above are usually stable for several years – but the details of their interest may shift and there are additional events and business opportunities to be considered for each of the groups.

For the customers with a focus on their private life, events throughout the year can be used for additional sales of your products or those of your partners. You can help your customers to organise birthdays – their own and those in their social environment. Your customers' birthdays can be used to issue congratulations from you to the customer combined with the offer of a special yield birthday investment. The birthdays of the customers' friends can be stored, to trigger birthday greetings (combined with a referral proposal), to select and purchase gifts for the friend, allowing you to link with gift shops, handle payments, or even finance a large gift. Even parties can be organised (again possibly embedded in a referral programme) – why not consider a birthday party 'sponsored by' you! Holidays trigger travelling ideas and you can offer route planning, plane, train and hotel reservations, sightseeing trips and entertainment (all with a commission for you); you can take care of providing the necessary foreign money, deliver payments and organise house-sitting at home. Seasonal events trigger a similar set of services: in winter, organising Christmas gifts, providing for oil to heat the house, selling winter tyres for the car and supplying skiing gear; in spring, gardening materials and house repair; in summer holidays, sports or outdoor parties; in autumn, the new school year and family events. I have mentioned a broad set of examples and you should decide which of them to pick for specific customer segments – this is part of your redesign of the value proposition. If your core competencies can be expanded, for example, so that you become a bank with attached travel agency, the choice will obviously be different than if you decide to become a telecom operator with attached entertainment activities, or an electronics provider with an attached event organisation.

For customers with a primarily professional interest, events throughout the year also trigger sales opportunities. During budgeting times there is often the need for agreeing on additional loans, and at the end of the fiscal year tax advice will be appreciated – including some ideas to 'park' available funds in a tax-free way, and when big payments are received the customer may want to make a short term/high yield investment.

If your staff dedicated to each customer target group are more creative and pro-active than those of your competitor, you can gain more market share. Learn from the mail-order companies. They issue separate catalogues for clothing (per market segments: teenagers, families, young professionals, mature people; and distinguished by gender), gardening, do-it-yourself, children, games.

Make sure, though, not to allow confusion – there must be a clear lead from the top, outlining the direction your enterprise should take with some defined focal areas. Are you in the business of serving the customer throughout the seasons? Then offer seasonal brochureware and organise seasonal events – and make sure that you can predict from the customer's behaviour when he or she is about to leave for the annual holiday and what products he or she will buy from you then! If you have never tried such a seasonal approach, test it in a small segment so as to gain experience, and then extend it to all appropriate segments. The key for success is systematic testing – do not change all parameters at once!

4.3 Consumer behaviour models

The testing mentioned in the last section has to be based on an understanding of the customers' expectations and what they want to tell you, for example:

1. 'I expect you to have mastered the *basics* of what you are in business to do. If you haven't, I will switch to a different source. Even if you have that alone is not enough to keep me loyal.'

2. 'I expect you to go beyond the basics and provide me with that which I *value*. If you do, you will have a *loyal* customer. If not, my business is up for grabs.'

3. 'Some things you do *irritate* me, but they are not important enough to drive me away. Besides, your competitors do the same things.'

4. 'Some things you do, I *don't care* anything about.' *

If you do not fulfil the first customer expectation, you can best see this from complaints, so watch closely what the customers are actively telling you there: categorise the contents of complaints, count how many you get from each category and check trends. For the second item, you can use classic market research, that is, ask your customers why they use your products or services and you can analyse events and situations when customers buy and use what you are selling: use the models described below for defining such triggering events. For the third and fourth items, you need to become aware of the assumptions you have been operating under and formulate explicit policies: when do you offer which product actively, when do you highlight which prices, what is on the top of your homepage, which banners are on there, how frequently are they shown, what exact words do you use for payment reminders, how friendly are your staff? Each of those policy details has to be changed for a test group of customers and the impact should be checked. If no particular impact can be seen, go back to the old approach and change the next thing you do. In this way you can permanently adjust your understanding of the customer behaviour and interactions.

Now for the analytical models for customer behaviour. These models anticipate certain customer situations (for example, buying decision, termination decision). You identify what factors or triggers are indicators for a certain customer behaviour (for example, a buying decision). With these factors or triggers you can undertake a systematic testing and adjusting: change the factor in a test group, compare customer responsiveness with the rest of your customers, and then set the more favourable factor or trigger for all customers. Repeat the testing and adjusting with the next factor or trigger.

---

* From: *loyalty.com* by Frederick Newell

Marketing models

Figure 5 indicates the two major marketing models you can use for the consumer market, namely the buying preference model and the customer life stage model.

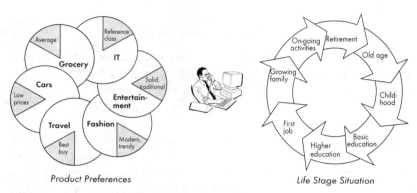

Product Preferences   Life Stage Situation

Figure 5   Models for consumer marketing

Product preferences: for different needs, your customer may show different buying preferences. He or she may wear the latest trendy and expensive fashion, but rationalise on expenses for his or her car and travel. Or a computer addict may have the latest electronics at home, but be a sloppy buyer in all other areas.

Life stages: at different life stages, your customers have obviously different needs and thus different buying behaviours. The most interesting points for sales decisions are whenever customers get into their next life stage situation. At this point in time, they are actively looking for the best provider to support their new needs – and often they stay loyal to this provider throughout that new life stage. Apart from buying preferences, the payment risk is also different at the different stages.

There are two ways to identify these preferences. One is just to talk to your customers; in a small market you can do that yourself, in larger markets you will need to engage a market research company. The second approach is to monitor the behaviour of your customers with more or less sophisticated statistical tools starting with a sales count in a small environment and ending with complex data-mining activities crunching millions of data records to find out the patterns of customer behaviour in very large markets.

Monitoring customer responses

In Figure 6 you see a model which suggests how you can refine measurements and assign customers to specific profiles based on their past buying (or referral) behaviour.

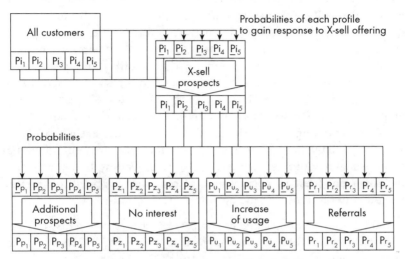

Figure 6   Measurement of behaviour probabilities

With the example of measurement mentioned previously, the probabilities for cross-selling success can be monitored. For each customer segment and campaign a probability in percentage terms can be stored and monitored, if customers purchase an additional product, if they show no interest, if they increase their use of the contracted product or service or if they make referrals. In mass-marketing, it has proven successful to run similar, but slightly different campaigns as a test in parallel, to compare outcomes and then to use the better one for a full coverage of your targeted segments. This comparison should not be only a one-off activity, but you should perform this on an ongoing basis. So you will always have a standard marketing campaign running, using the current 'champion' strategy and a new 'challenger' to the existing strategy which may outperform the former champion. Thus you permanently adjust your marketing activities. These models should not only reflect the customer, but also his or her environment. Many buying decisions are made jointly by several members of a family, for example most purchases can be vetoed by either husband or wife.

The customer behaviour model has proved important in a few large enterprises, for example at the Bank of Montreal discussed earlier, but the broad application is still missing. The main reason is that the underlying data have not been available for a long time. Even data warehouse projects have not always delivered the expected results, because too little attention has been paid to data quality. With the Web, you have an additional lever, namely to show your customers the key data you have stored about them. This entails two benefits: first to ensure that profiles and preferences accurately reflect the customers' actual desires, and second to encourage customers to interact with you, and so that you can emphasise to customers that you are interested in their feedback.

When you implement the models, do not leave them to your statistical analysts, but add the everyday measurement of actual customer behaviour as outlined in Figure 6, leading to a continuous improvement (that is, correctness) of recorded probabilities for the various interactions. Let me outline a brief action-plan:

1. model your customer behaviour by reflecting key events in his or her life-cycle, throughout the year, in your production life-cycle, in response to marketing campaigns;

2. measure (count) his or her buying or termination behaviour;

3. ask your statistical analysts to build different customer groups (segments); for each group check the different behaviour patterns (profiles);

4. define customer approaches (for example, a cross-selling campaign, an early-adopter sales event, a discount campaign) for the specific segments and run the campaigns;

5. measure the customer responsiveness – and adjust your model, that is, start again at step 1. After an appropriate time, extend the operation to a broader group of customers and internal users. Initially, it is just an exercise for statisticians; in the end every agent in your call centres has to be familiar with customer profiles and their implication for customer dialogues.

This approach allows you to understand more and more clearly what your customers do and when, what the chances are for a positive buying reaction and when customers are most inclined to give you their attention. The customer segments will get smaller and smaller and your approach, that is, your marketing campaigns or responses in the call centre, will become more and more refined. Thus, you are on the right track to developing one-to-one marketing capabilities.

4.4 Dis-intermediation and re-intermediation: megatrends in the finance industry

In the last chapter, we briefly touched on the re-assembly of value chains. Let us take a closer look at what this dis-intermediation and re-intermediation can look like. The finance industry provides a good example of how enterprises strive to match customer needs while erosion of company boundaries has been going on for some time.

Financial services are growing. For example, payments are expected to grow by 6 per cent annually in Europe and America, and even more in Asia/Pacific, and cross-border payments are expected to grow between 8 per cent and 15 per cent annually in the years until 2007.* But will this growth feed the banks? Customers can get now insurance services, for example, pension plans, from their bank while traditional insurances offer interest on saving accounts and allow customers to optimise the returns on their life insurance by configuring their individual stock investment plans. Banking and insurance converge and become bancassurance, banking and capital markets converge to trading and brokerage and insurance and capital markets converge into commercial insurance – see Figure 7.

Such convergence also includes players from other industries, such as car manufacturers. DaimlerChrysler, for example, has issued bonds on the Web. The business idea was to save on the bank's margin on a loan DaimlerChrysler needed and split it between themselves and the private money investors. As a financing instrument it was successful and attracted enough investors, but it is doubtful if this approach will be repeated regularly because it requires a lot of overhead and is not DaimlerChrysler's core competency.

An approach even more dangerous for the finance industry's market position, can be seen in the UK – this was even initially supported by the banks to cut transaction costs: retail stores and supermarkets were entitled to provide cash advances. So they were quickly grabbing the customer relationship and could start cross-

* Source: AMS survey: *The BankFactory.com*, March 2000.

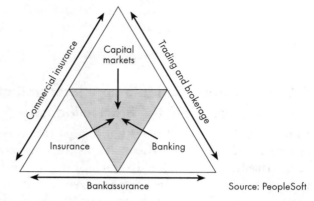

Source: PeopleSoft

Figure 7   Global competitive megatrends

selling; the banks got rid of some costs but also lost revenues! This example of a short-sighted cost-saving initiative shows the dangers of focusing too much on the cost perspective.

Instead of (or at least additionally to) focusing on the cost savings, the Internet should rather be used to exploit new markets and to launch additional marketing campaigns. This is particularly important, because the market for banking activities is still growing dramatically (see Figure 8) – if you do not at least support this growth, your market share and your importance will steadily diminish!

Therefore, use the technologies at hand to maintain or extend your market share.

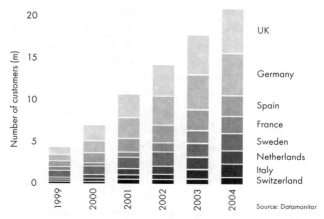

Source: Datamonitor

Figure 8   Expected growth in Internet banking customers, 1999–2004

'The technology of delivering services from a central point has developed rapidly. This technology has also been widely accepted by the customer base as a better and more convenient means of interacting with the bank, rather than using branches. The key advances in order of development have been:

❏ automatic teller machines (ATMs);

❏ telephone banking;

❏ centralisation of bank back-office functions;

❏ electronic banking services;

❏ in-store supermarket banking kiosks and branches;

❏ kiosk based multimedia terminals at off-branch sites;

❏ integrated telephone/electronic banking – mobile phone/personal digital assistant (PDA) services;

for 24-hour support, no more queues, self-service and no need to travel to a traditional high street bank. These new channels have gained widespread acceptance as customer lifestyles have changed and the technology has evolved... The traditional bank–branch–client relationship is being eroded by the banks' drive to generate cost savings by closing branches and using technology as the means of service delivery.'*

Still, the big banks in Europe in particular feel protected because they have built up a market oligarchy: a few players 'own' the vast majority of the banking customers, for example, 'in the UK the top seven banks have 84 per cent of the account share. In France the market is similarly concentrated with 96 per cent of the assets being owned by the top seven banks. The most highly concentrated market in Europe is in the Netherlands where the top three banks account for about 90 per cent of the banking business ... Germany is characterised by having three large institutions, each with a global presence, and large number of regional banks, which are either wholly or partly owned by the big three institutions.'*

* Source: PeopleSoft Essentials Document: *Managing Change in the eWorld*

But this feeling of protection may be wishful thinking, because not only are the margins eroding, but intruders into the financial market take potential important customers: in Scandinavia and Japan, telecom providers have started to offer mobile phone payment services on a large scale – you can book a ticket (cinema, theatre, music, train) via your mobile phone on your way to the train station or airport. The 'ticket' is just the electronic certification number on the mobile phone that can be checked off by the ticket inspector: instead of presenting a piece of paper to the ticket inspector, the visitor shows his mobile phone displaying the certificate. The telecom operator processes the money transaction and of course keeps the payment commission. So, the mobile phone is like a credit card. You are invited to find a name for this industry – is it TeleCredit or PayComm?

When will the banks begin to come up with similarly new services which eat into previously unrelated markets? The current prime pillar for profitability, namely investment management and trading, is already starting to erode, so the next pillar needs to be built soon. At least the banks should provide excellent online services for their core business – see some leading examples in Chapter 7.

4.5   Summary: quick win candidates

Make your service customer-compatible, so that customers like the results they can achieve with your products and services. Allow customers to configure products and services according to their needs. Build up personalised marketing activities based on sophisticated measurement and analysis of customer behaviour and operational execution. Here are some ways to get started:

❏ identify the customers that contribute the most to your bottom-line products and services and check what distinguishes them from the other customers;

❏ assess the indications that a prospective customer is ready to buy, or that an existing customer is ready to buy again – in particular in the case of customer segments contributing a high value;

❏ identify the products and services that contribute the most to your bottom line and check which customers order them and when (for example, at what time in the customer life-cycle, time in the day/week/month/ year do customers perform transactions);

❏ identify events that can be used for personalised marketing activities and monitor the customer responsiveness to each personalised marketing activity;

❏ trigger additional sales by a personalised service or product at the time you expect the customer to be ready to buy;

❏ check how customers configure your offerings (product features, payment terms, risk and return preferences, service demand, for example) – get rid of the frills nobody demands and offer additional details in frequently used options;

❏ start building up your statistical models based on measuring customer responsiveness to your initial personalised marketing campaigns and adjust your marketing approaches accordingly.

5

Ongoing innovations: drive the changes

@@@ Extend your steering gear to pilot your company not only based on financial navigation, but also to drive the speed of change, innovations and quality of service. @@@

5.1   Acceleration of innovation cycles

In all industries, innovation cycles are accelerating. Start-ups do not need a decade any more before going public but just a year; development of new cars is down from four years to a little over one year; and companies are planning in years or quarter-years now instead of the earlier three- to five-year plans. Innovation cycles in e-business and the underlying software development projects are down from one to two years to half a year or a quarter of a year. Independent from industry, success in the online market place is driven by speed and size: the faster you are, the better you can adjust to market requirements, and the bigger you are, the more interactions can be funnelled through your revenue-generating portals. This can be condensed into the often-heard e-business recommendation: get big fast! While this recommendation was initially meant for start-ups, it is also valid for the e-business activities of established enterprises – here 'big' is the given, but 'fast' is the issue. Many established companies that had their Web presence just as a back-burner activity and have not conducted a regular update of the website's contents, have been disappointed by the small number of visitors. They are deciding now to either close their website down – or to invest again and do it right this time, that is, look for wide access and keep their website contents interesting and frequently updated.

So, the size of your customer base should be OK for the moment, but as you grow, lack of flexibility can make you more vulnerable to the challenges you are exposed to from Internet start-ups. Website contents, product descriptions, fun and entertainment components need to be adjusted and extended day by day. So you are in the middle of a big conflict. On one hand, the time frame for change has shrunk to zero, but on the other hand a lot of experience and research has proved that you cannot change a whole enterprise very quickly. Daryl R. Conner, a well-known change guru, writing in *Managing at the Speed of Change*, summarises the difficulties of change:

> 'People can face an unlimited amount of uncertainty and newness but when they exceed their absorption threshold, they begin to display signs of dysfunction: fatigue, emotional burnout, inefficiency, sickness, drug abuse.'

It takes a long time for you to change the direction of a large enterprise. Conner also indicates, though, a way out: from time to time when there is a crisis (either a threat or a big opportunity) people are willing to invest mental and physical energy in getting through the crisis – like Internet pioneers creating new business ideas and working seventy- to eighty-hour weeks. You have to generate a really positive spirit, eagerness for new frontiers, and flexibility of pioneer hours along the dot-com paradigm 'work hard, work long, get rich' while carefully making sure that you do not risk the dysfunctions mentioned earlier. Moreover, you should always seek the next quick win, that is, some significant improvement you can achieve with relatively little effort.

For creating a pioneer spirit, you need to relax administrative and political control and empower and enable your employees to do certain tasks as a measure of their own growing responsibility. Are your employees driven by hierarchical and title targets, do they stop their discussions when they fear their opinion is contrary to their boss's opinion, or are they motivated to achieve customer benefits? Decrease the number of detailed rules while enforcing key policies – and align your financial and non-financial incentives with the achievements of your company and of the individuals.

There is an interesting test area for such changes: think of the days, weeks and months when you prepare your annual report – a similar presentation to the public needs to be updated daily on the Web, plus the contents need to be even more concrete and tangible, because they will be the base for customer buying decisions. So it may be a Quick Win to update your 'annual report' with, say, monthly amendments on the Web. Is your company ready to delegate this delicate topic to a group of young writers and Web designers who are closely linked with your product managers and corporate marketing – and who are entitled to adjust the public image of your company every day?

If your enterprise passes this test, then you can create small new operational units that radically differ from the legacy of the traditional enterprise – think of DB 24, who were allowed to follow a trial and error approach very different from good old Deutsche Bank.

5.2 Creation of new business ideas

You will not have the luxury of experimenting with the full range of trial and error possibilities; it would be just too risky – that is rather the area of the whole group of start-ups taken together. Possibly even one of the many new business ideas will be strong enough to actually challenge your position. But you can and must watch them closely and identify where the start-ups have created a business idea that can become potentially dangerous for you, or that you could adopt and benefit from. And you can also look out for trends that can be beneficial to your business proposition:

❏ What is it that newcomers to the Web are offering?

❏ How can you adapt some of the components of their ideas to your proposition?

❏ Check foreign industries and foreign cultures for online approaches you can exploit – for example, ethnic minorities offering products on the Web and dealing with logistical issues (*www.folkart.com*), or entertainment providers generating a high degree of customer loyalty.

❏ Analyse newspapers from other regions of the world to see if some of the issues or solutions described trigger an extension of your products and services.

And you do have a great wealth of experience and strength that none of the start-ups or competitors can copy. These strengths can be a certain knowledge of the industries that you can leverage for an adjacent area (such as banking and insurance, or fixed-wire communication and mobile communication, or TV video production and Internet infotainment) or the knowledge of the needs of a well-defined customer group. This was the approach of DB 24, namely adjusting banking and brokerage services for the mass market in such a way that they could offer better services for lower prices.

With the fresh look at the core competencies of your units and at your enterprise's assets that we have taken in the last chapters, you can now also leverage the skills in areas not directly related to your customer groups or industry. Look at the telecom market in Europe, where earlier monopolists or state-owned companies spun off fixed-wire or mobile operators like Infostrada (which emerged from the Italian railway and the German Mannesmann steel and pipeline company, now owned by the mobile carrier Vodafone); Cegetel (owned by Vivendi, British Telecom and Vodafone/Mannesmann, Southwestern Bell SBC) in France; or Arcor in Germany (again railway and Mannesmann).

Why are former railway and utility companies mentioned so often? Well, they had the important asset of 'right of way' for railway tracks, pipelines or power lines – and invented 're-use' in laying kilometres of cable for telecommunication connections. They have another advantage in common and a core competency many start-ups are lacking: their well-proven methodologies. They know how to successfully run multi-million Euro infrastructure projects such as building a countrywide radio or telephone switch network or implementing complex customer care and billing systems. In addition, their fierce procurement groups squeeze out any advantage they can get from their suppliers and infrastructure vendors. Another advantage lies in the continuing social circles and communities where former civil servants impart their experience to emerging best-practice groups. They have now also acquired the competency of operating large call centres and are starting to use these for additional business ideas such as buying transactions for partner companies as a payment consolidator that results in commissions income and payment fees.

In addition to such assets and methodologies, you have the experience of all your staff – often they have not realised that you are interested in exploiting that wealth of knowledge. Work systematically to understand the 'mechanics' of your business and to adjust the key points. We will discuss ways of accessing this pool of experience in Chapters 8 and 11. For successful innovative projects you need to step outside day-to-day operations and make yourself aware of the end-to-end processes. What are the events which cause processes to start, what are the decisions that need to be made *en route*, who has the competency to make those decisions, how are the results communicated back to the customer and how do you measure the results of the processes?

Many companies are still focused on the departmental perspective instead of understanding the 'big picture'. Once you are able to describe events and decision steps, you can start counting how often such events happen, what data are used in order to make decisions, what the quality of the decisions is – and you can create models to support your decisions. Take credit scoring as a classical example, where statistical models are a great tool to even automatically supported loan decisions. But before that was possible, the whole credit application process had to be understood, the relevant data for deciding on an application had to be analysed and statisticians had to come up with scorecards.

Similar systematic work is necessary for the current areas in focus, namely for marketing and sales activities in order to zoom in on the most promising customers, and for customer service and call-centre activities in order to invest staff time efficiently in maximising the outcome in customer satisfaction, referrals and cross-selling.

So far, we have discussed improvements to your existing products and services. For bigger leaps in the generation of new business ideas, a good exercise is to change your perspective and to create new business ideas by checking what is missing in your industry and what has been disregarded so far – like 'poor' customers for banking, 'lazy' people for shopping, a home delivery service for new cars, or the most 'crazy' complaint one of your customers was raising. With this approach, you avoid a head-on confrontation with a large number of traditional competitors, and you circumvent their market penetration by offering a completely new service or product. Set aside a time and a place for creative sessions, such as a weekend tour which is both fun and physically challenging (river rafting, climbing or hiking) and by doing some mentally challenging brainstorming. GE (the former 'General Electric', and today one of the most innovative companies in the world) call their creativity meetings 'Dreaming Sessions'; anybody is allowed to come up with proposals that can be tested for validity – no matter how crazy they sound. Play with the future and with its possibilities. Ask the 'why not' questions to squeeze out really creative ideas:

❑ Why not deliver whatever you provide in 5 per cent of the time and for 10 per cent of the cost – such as a loan approval within one minute, or furniture delivered the same day, or a car delivered within 24 hours, or a house built within a week?

❑ Why does every schoolboy or girl not use your services when he or she plays with (or trades) Pokémon cards? Why do your employees not play with children's games and check out if there are overlaps with your value proposition?

❑ Why does every teenager not use your service when he or she uses the latest hip mobile phone/buys concert tickets/looks for trendy fashion? Why do you not invite the teens to play with your products or services?

❑ Why not promote your products via SMS and e-mail?

❑ Why is your product or service not as entertaining and funny as the Simpsons/Dilbert/m-tv/Star Wars/football? Depending on the target group!

❑ Why does every student not see the benefits of your products and services when he or she needs to accumulate knowledge for the next examination or when looking for a job?

❑ Why does every parent not reduce the daily hassle by using your products or services?

❑ Why is your icon not on every PC?

❑ Why do senior citizens not enjoy your products or services?

❑ Why did you not double your revenues in the last period?

The answers are not intended to provide an excuse, but to trigger action to increase your market share and to get into everybody's mind! Document the ideas, test them in small, controllable market segments to see if they work; if yes, roll them out to the whole market, if not, look for a better idea.

5.3   Unique source for improvement suggestions

The most reliable source regarding the needs and ideas of your customers are: your customers. There are two particular groups of customer interactions that offer you a broad range of insights: call-centre enquiries and customer complaints. From these you can often derive ideas for your next product generation or an improved service offering.

Microsoft is a company that has built up its customer service in an excellent way for providing structured feedback combined with free-form comments. Which additional functions would the customer like as part of the software applications? How could usability be improved? What additional leverage is possible by using functions across various components (such as pictures in text documents, or text formatting in presentations)?

Mail order companies systematically assess their client feedback. Customers are asked to indicate the reasons for returning goods. Sweepstakes are used to compile the wishes of customers in various segments. Some selected customers get early copies of catalogues, so that they can submit early orders plus indicate additional product likes and dislikes. And complaints are used to identify customer concerns and to increase customer retention.

How can you translate the approaches from these enterprises to your environment? Build on the examples and extend them by understanding and empathising with customer needs! Leading providers in most of the industries have started experiments with hotline services. They offer 'tape recorded' answers to frequently asked questions (and count how often they are used); they store and maintain product descriptions and supporting explanations in their document management system and make them accessible via the Web in a help-text format. Again, they assess where the greatest customer confusion is, that is, where the largest number of questions is raised. They have their call-centre staff store key words of the customer interactions and scan the text of customer complaints for frequently occurring issues.

This systematic, and automatically supported listening to your customers, provides you with market research that is much cheaper and much more exact than that provided by staff in the field or interview agencies running around and looking for answers to hypothetical questions. And there is one more benefit: the ideas your customers raise in interacting with you are proprietary to your company – none of your competitors can anticipate or imagine that wealth of detailed insights.

5.4 Getting started

Gary Hamel, professor at the London Business School, highlights in his great book *Leading the Revolution* four different types of innovation:

Table 2   Innovation characteristics

Change severity	Application to	Examples
Incremental change	Single component	Traditional optimisation projects, e.g. ERP, Supplier negotiations,
Incremental change	Whole organisation: Business Process Improvement	TQM, ISO 9000, supply chain integration/just in time
Radical change	Non-linear innovation of one or few components	Mobile telecom operators
Radical change	Whole business: Business Concept Innovation	Amazon, Charles Schwab, Yahoo

When companies have gained experience of how to go through incremental changes, radical changes still need to be learned. The orientation needs to change from procedural improvements to creating new business ideas, from cutting costs to identifying and exploiting potential, and from a relaxed 'nine-to-five' attitude to a demanding environment where entrepreneurial-minded people like to share their contribution no matter at what time of the day or week. The key points are a powerful leadership communicating its vision and the value of the changes to motivate staff and customers; a proper management of the transitional activities and forward-looking handling of peoples' concerns (for example, of customers when two companies merge: how will the services be provided in the future); and a clear focus on targets and their achievement.

Guidance and leadership

As leader on any level of an existing large enterprise who is taking steps towards a pro-active online proposition, you will achieve personal and professional success by the right mix of

❏ *Strategy and vision:* give your team a clear picture of what the future looks like and how customers will be served. And clearly indicate what you do not want to do and do not want them to do, in order to avoid distraction.

❏ *Energy:* the will to succeed is the most important success factor. If you can create this will in your team, you have taken the most important step towards getting rid of the attitude of an old and dusty enterprise and towards motivating your troops for the e-business adventure.

❏ *Flexibility:* be ready to disregard existing procedures, rules or even policies that block your success – actually that is something you need to sort out with your superiors and peers in order to arrive at the right set of new directives.

❏ *Experience:* select those aspects of the tradition of your enterprise that other companies cannot copy. One such aspect can be corporate approaches (as in the examples of telecom and banking mentioned earlier); it can also be knowledge embedded in behavioural data of your customers – mail order providers, credit card companies and other mass marketers have plenty of such data, and it can be hidden in your procedures (as in credit approval procedures). Distil the core competencies and make them available for the new venture!

❏ *Solidity:* a good employee base, trust, good customer relationships, sound book-keeping and profitability are the traditional virtues of a business person – and they need to be embedded in the overall strategy and vision.

I have not addressed 'change' or 'transition' explicitly yet. Actually, that was on purpose. As long as you feel aware of changes and of each step you make you have not reached a state of ongoing improvement and transition yet. Such permanent improvement with its ongoing changes should rather be the persistent objective of your undertaking – not only a hassle you need to go through before you can relax again and build up any new routine and legacy. Once you have reached a stage of 'transition maturity', you, your team and the whole enterprise will have internalised change as an ongoing task in order to improve your products or services and your processes. Refer to Part 3 of the book for how to get prepared for such ongoing changes.

A similar consideration applies to life-long learning. Forget that big concept – 'life' is too abstract. Ask your staff and yourself instead what you have learned today and what you intend to learn tomorrow!

Do organisational responsibilities, like the many steps needed for approving a loan or the many people to ask before laying a cable to connect a customer, stop your staff from being more pro-active? Erase any one of the steps if it does not provide significant and measurable value!

Is the next milestone your overall goal? OK, that is your next target, but it is just the basic one. What is the expected quantum leap once you have reached the milestone? How do you create subsequent breakthrough ideas, to become even better? And why do you need to wait to implement the next breakthrough idea until after the next milestone? You might as well start implementation immediately.

Change management

If you approach the issues described in the section above from your new assertive perspective, people may get frightened. Your staff might be more concerned about their career future in the changing environment than about your new strategic objectives. And customers might be confused about the changes in their interaction with you.

You need to offer your staff as a 'life belt' and as a learning aid lots of communication:

❑ Immediate care on personal issues – without hierarchical constraints.

❑ Discussion forums within peer groups and within expert groups on work-related and private topics.

❑ Success stories concerning the new approach from all levels of the enterprise.

❑ Risk-aware (not risk-averse!) progress reporting with early identification of potential risks and mitigation strategies – do not sweep problems under the carpet! Let your team know what you believe could go wrong, ask them for their damage-limitation ideas and let them identify additional risks. That wins you a lot of goodwill towards the approach, increases the probability of success and reduces the 'need' for chit-chat behind your back if they think you are not responding to the challenges.

❏ Quick and clear information given to customers on what improvements they can expect – remember, only employees who are confident that improvements are on their way will be able to maintain the trust of the customers.

Intensive communication of this sort provides an ideal area for the internal use of a web, that is, an intranet, or similar tool for distributed work-group environments (such as Lotus Notes). Additionally, of course, formalised electronic communications need to be supported by person-to-person and informal communication. Social events within your team and possibly with customers, regular conferences on specific topics and accessibility of everybody by everybody in the team by e-mail and voice-mail is a must. This intranet is another area where you can test your approaches, try out various designs and navigation aspects and acquire experience running the systems and keeping the contents current.

A similar approach is advisable for intense communication with your customers and explaining in depth why you are changing your ways of operating and how will they benefit from it. Here is a little war story quoted from PeopleSoft's White paper on CRM: 'As one bank in New York City found out, the recently launched new ATMs actually needed staff talking to customers in ATM queues on the streets for a time. But whilst this might seem to be an extreme measure, it proved to be an extremely beneficial PR exercise too.'

An example

Let us look at an example of how systematic work has lead to significant bottom-line improvements. This is an example from a small business field, but the good thing about it is that we have been able to trace in detail the results of the initiative.* It concerns collecting the money for the products or services from the customers. Traditional approaches in the companies where I worked included low-cost activities such as sending out reminder letters or

---

* Many factors contribute to success. When you have identified one factor, you need to systematically apply different treatments for this factor in one customer segment and compare the result of that treatment with the performance of the other comparable segments. The better treatment has then to be applied to all segments. Thus, you systematically improve the overall performance. As at the same time usually the competitive situation and the customer interactions change, too, it is often difficult to exactly measure how big the financial impact of all the fine-tuning steps has been.

brute force activities such as intensive calls from a collection centre or handling by a collections agency. The first approach has the disadvantage that the customer can ignore the letters, so in many cases even the low-cost effort is a waste. The second approach has the disadvantage of very high costs relative to the collection amount.

Then we segmented customers using the data available in the different situations, for example through service used or product purchased; through payment pattern (such as the time it usually takes until they pay their bill); through socio-demographic situation (age, gender, place of domicile) and through other available credit worthiness data. We further split each of the segments into two groups and tested the results of different strategies. Such strategies had many ingredients: reminder letters versus outbound collection calls by the call centre; frequency and timing of action taken, for example, one week after due date, one month after due date; timing of disabling the service or using available collaterals; insourced steps versus action taken by a collections agency. All those parameters needed to be checked for relevance and improved step by step. Of course there were common patterns, such as the earlier you start collections, the better are your results. The key point for our discussion, however, is to see if the performance improvement is steady over years (see Figure 9).

Over a period of four monitored years, processes improved most when the initial analysis was completed and a new balance between call-centre activities and written activities was defined (and when simultaneously a software tool modelling the collections workflow, automatically triggering the appropriate collections action and monitoring its results was implemented). That is year 3 in the chart. Regular reviews of the strategies still show improving results in subsequent periods, but only in small increments.

You should apply a similar approach to the key business areas you want to change – look at the processes and workflows, identify the contributing factors and continue adjusting them.

5.5   Innovation benchmarks

Let us learn from the leading industries how to maintain an openness towards creativity and change combined with an eagerness to learn. Consultancy and marketing companies, for example, are excellent at motivating and enabling their employees to stay on top of innovations. In those companies, employees feel like

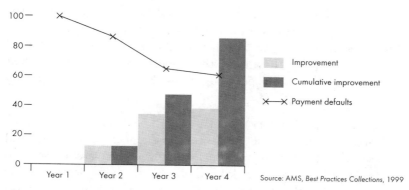

Figure 9 Bottom-line improvements by systematic adjustment

entrepreneurs, because they have to define a value proposition tailored to each customer situation. Their career progress is triggered by their merit and the measurable contribution they have generated – both in terms of money and reusable assets and experience. The key components of the consultancy approach are:

❏ One project manager is put in charge of dealing with the client. This person is accountable for the client relationship and the project success. He defines the skills needed for the project and pulls together the resources, that is, staff and materials, for the project.

❏ Everyone is committed to success for both the client and the enterprise. The definition of what 'success' means is one of the key initial project objectives – and it may require integrating the services of external partners or subcontractors.

❏ The team environment is created as needed. Often there are cross-departmental and cross-regional expert pools, but no permanent physical place for them, that is, no predefined desk areas or hardware and software environments. Instead, the teams are built according to certain recommended structures, and they create their environment from either some predefined, off-the-shelf configuration that the company provides or they go out and build up their profit centre like a real new company – starting with renting rooms at the project or client site.

❏ The team members draw upon the experience of their colleagues through in-depth examination of the cases of other clients which can be found in the internal communication system (such as the intranet), plus the human network supported by the fact that the team members rotate regularly between different types of projects, that is, they have the opportunity to increase their experience and their personal network through a continually changing work setting.

❑ Each staff member has to make himself or herself useful at the level of the internal labour market. Those who are most in demand (and earn the highest salaries and incentives) are those who manage to have the best skills applicable to the widest customer situations. This implies the perfection of market principles within the companies.

The combination of these key components leads to an ongoing fine-tuning of the overall proposition through the combined experience of a team of excellent employees. This will achieve an important balance of top-down leadership with delivery capabilities growing and improving bottom-up.

5.6   Maintaining oversight

Some of the new approaches I recommend and the accelerated pace of business change may make you afraid of losing control. As Donovan Wright from PeopleSoft puts it:

> 'Bosses realise the limitations of a "command and control" approach and have rather to encourage the knowledge worker with a devolved sense of responsibility and ability to make decisions.'

This limitation of control can be difficult for you to accept, if you grew up in a brick and mortar company where staff and management experienced success as the result of carefully engineered products, well-defined procedures and clear hierarchical rules. You are actually right as long as the term 'control' means for you that you can command your staff, get predictable results for an approved cost, with a defined quality at an agreed date. Altogether, this is an internally based view of 'control'.

Now, what is different from that meaning of 'control' versus the control an e-business stakeholder, say a venture capitalist, applies? Their view is driven by external factors, some of which are even 'soft' factors. Such soft factors are items not as easily countable as financial figures or production input and output (for example, number of staff, tons of steel produced). Some key soft factors are brand recognition and preference, staff experience, culture, process effectiveness, client satisfaction and loyalty and flexibility.

Most of those soft factors are directly related to your corporate culture. Most companies believe they have a corporate culture, but as long as it is undocumented and unspoken, people can only support it in a haphazard way. During the initial definition of specific measurable soft factors, you have the opportunity to discuss (or review) your corporate culture and values explicitly – it helps your staff to see they are contributing to something larger, and it helps you to give a more positive image to your brand, that is, to have your customers really like you. Invite your stakeholders and employees to dream in order to find how their dreams can match their daily work and link with customers' dreams in order to create affection and loyalty.

While you should be able to eventually document your corporate values and culture on one page (or on a large poster displayed in key places) and while these values and culture should last for a long time, your operational targets and their achievement require a full-blown specification and comprehensive reporting. Such reports should be available online and be monitored regularly, together with the review of your financial results. Let me go back to the word 'comprehensive'. I strongly recommend you develop key indicators for various underlying details in order to allow you a quick navigation through reports – and to be able to easily communicate achievement in your organisation. It is much easier to find out 'Overall, our customer satisfaction is on target, but our customers in the Southern Region made 15 per cent more complaints than anticipated' and to trigger the appropriate action than shuffling hundreds of pages of reports around.

Such reviews and monitoring are already performed by your stock analysts during their reviews, and you should base your regular management decisions on those factors. We will discuss the implementation of this approach in further detail later on; it is often referred to as the balanced scorecard approach, because it balances financial and non-financial figures and builds a score that can be easily used for communicating both the plan and success measurements. Let me mention some illustrative examples for the underlying measurements complementing your financial reporting:

❑ brand recognition and preference: Web hit statistics; click stream analysis/usage of links to your site and from your site; market research; buying behaviour; market share (by product, region, customer segment);

❑ client satisfaction and loyalty: duration of website visit, customer retention and propensity to buy expressed as date of most recent purchase; frequency of purchases;

❑ staff experience: number of online forums with facilitators from your company; number of registered patents; number of publications and press coverage; number of students and interns trained by your staff;

❑ process effectiveness: service levels (average, maximum and minimum), for example, time needed for decisions such as a loan approval, waiting time in your call centres, response time for complaints; product and service price and quality, for example, fee structure compared with competitors, payment schemes, number of different supportable regulations such as local tax rules; bundling and unbundling options – both with own products and services and third-party components (examples for the finance industry: loan for purchasing stocks, life insurance for mortgage); number of product variations the customer can configure in self-service;

❑ flexibility: product configuration on the Web; regular refinement of products and services, for example, average age of products, number of products in the pipeline.

You may already measure some of those items, but if the measurements are diverse and not integrated into overall models (like the ones defined in Section 4.3), you will not know what to do with the reports. Therefore, these observations together with the financial data have to be condensed and analysed to obtain actionable information. An example of such meaningful online information is provided in Figure 10 – please look at the areas where the deviations from the expected results are shown. This triggers action, both when time expectations are not met (as in the forecast accuracy report) or when values are not according to plans (as in the sales deals analysis).

In order to make the information functional, you should find out where actual situations deviate from your plan, for example in terms of number of complaints, achievement of response times,

Figure 10   Sample measurement

number of escalated client issues, backlog or orders. Additionally, you will be able to answer broader questions such as suggested in Tables 3–7. (See my website for softcopy of each of these tables.)

In the following worksheets, I recommend some areas to measure – please adjust them to your requirements. But whatever you adjust, maintain the focus on the customer.

Table 3   Marketing effectiveness measurements

Questions to trigger subsequent actions	Measurements
Which lead profiles have responded to which campaigns?	Examples: High usage customers, prospects from certain regions/certain income categories etc.
Is the campaign on a path to success?	Cross-check against expectations, e.g. response rate by certain dates
Is the campaign being managed successfully within its budget?	Compare the forecasted costs of the campaign with the accrued costs (if necessary pro-rated)
How's the correlation between buying patterns in the past and the responses to the current campaign?	Assess buying patterns like: When did the customer buy from you last time, how often does he buy, what's the average value of his purchases?
Basic measurements	Profit and loss per customer (over given time periods) Value of purchases (with averages) Response rate to campaign (by customer segments)
Compound measurements	Product mix purchased (product portfolio) Repeated purchases of same product (affinity) Revenue analysis (by customer segments, product segments, discounts granted) Updated forecast of campaign success and ROI

Table 4   Sales effectiveness measurements

Questions to trigger subsequent actions	Measurements
What are the most effective sales approaches?	Examples: online sales, call-centre sales, branch sales – check whatever is individually generated by the particular channel against the channel specific costs
What are the main drivers for revenues per sales representative?	Check for patterns such as regions, time of closure, customer profiles, size of transaction
Where are unexploited market areas where additional sales resources can be allocated?	Check for gaps such as regions or segments with less than average market penetration
Where do sales representatives encounter difficulty in the sales process?	Interview the sales representatives, monitor the closure of competitors
Are representatives accurate in forecasting?	Benchmark forecast accuracy against each other
Is our sales process on track to achieve the forecasted revenue goals?	Re-forecasted figures

Table 5   Support effectiveness measurements

Questions to trigger subsequent actions	Measurements
Which product quality issues are most prevalent?	Number of questions or complaints by categories
Are the support representatives effectively handling customer issues?	Length of time from raising a question or complaint to closing it
What is the cost to support our customers and products?	Effort for fixing problems (per product, service activity, customer segment, region)
How has call-centre performance changed from last year to this year?	Number of calls handled per hour, number of complaints closed per agent
How effective are support staff at creating cross-selling opportunities?	Number of orders closed on the phone, revenue generated over the phone

Table 6   Field service effectiveness measurements

Questions to trigger subsequent actions	Measurements
Are site visits being used effectively to solve customer issues?	Duration of site visits (per category, product, service unit, with benchmarks against each other)
Are repair parts located in the right place at the right time?	Time needed to transport repair parts to repair site
What are the costs associated with warranty contract or SLA repairs?	Efforts per category
Measurements	Number of problems (per product, category) Mean time between failure Case attributes (duration, efforts, costs) Call escalation Inventory analysis

Table 7   Customer satisfaction and profitability measurements

Questions to trigger subsequent actions	Measurements
What are the features most valuable for the customers – what makes them buy and what makes them terminate the relationship?	Ask your customers, e.g. by formalised welcome interviews and termination interviews allowing free form answers
Where do you get the most referrals from?	Track referring customer
How profitable is it to sell each product and what are the prime factors driving the costs and the margins?	Cost and revenues broken down by cost centres, business processes, locations
Which products, customers or channels are most profitable and what characteristics stand out?	Ranking of products, customers, channels, assessment by regions, sales representatives (including interviews)
Which discounts trigger additional sales?	Track customer behaviour
How is the evolution of your margin? How is the trend of profitability over time?	Comparison of figures over a longer period of time (usually in a data warehouse)
How effective are customer interactions?	Duration of interaction handling, percentage of unsuccessful interaction, percentage of achieved successful completion of interactions

Strategy effectiveness – that is the umbrella for all the measurements above. What is the optimal mix of products and customers to achieve maximal profitability? Perform the A/B/C analysis as discussed in Section 1.3. Check which variations in the major goods or services in your industry have been successful in positioning what you offer distinctly from what your competitors offer.* In fact, checking this will enable you to see how you are distinct from your competitors. If you do not measure this, you will not achieve distinction. Another key area to monitor is which challenger strategy outperformed the current treatment strategy –

---

* An example of an undistinguished and bad strategy is, how most big banks in Germany were focused during the last decade on winning more of the beloved 'upper class, high net worth, low risk' customers with an annual income of greater than 50,000 Euros, liquid assets of greater than 100,000 Euro and a small mortgage. These dream customers were supposedly ignorant enough of the better deals available on the market to let their banks continue generating a solid contribution from them. As all banks pursued this segment like lemmings, the margins began to erode there, too – as they had already eroded with their average customers with less than 20,000 Euro annual income and little or no assets. Other enterprises have been more successful in gaining market share and contribution that came up with a distinctive strategy, for example, focusing on proper risk management for 'mass market' customers like KKB/Citibank or focusing on solid advice for performance-seeking private investors such as advance.bank.

and by how much? Change the parameters systematically and find out what impact it makes, as in the example in Section 5.4.

You can develop your own reporting tool, but it is easier to implement one of the off-the-shelf solutions that are available for ongoing monitoring.

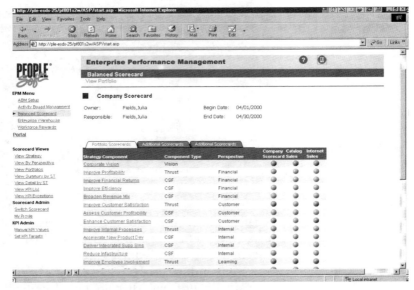

Figure 11   Sample Balanced Scorecard monitor

With such off-the-shelf solutions you can get a cascade of reports providing details of transactions (similar to most of the financial reports you have in place, but extended by non-financial data), summarised to a medium level of aggregation as the example in Figure 10, and even condensed to the balanced scorecard values for top management reporting – see screen shot in Figure 11. This example shows how achievement of plans can be reflected in a way easy to understand and easy to communicate with its symbols in the right-hand columns, and the option to focus on details by clicking on the components listed in the left and middle columns.

5.7 Summary

Innovation has to be driven based on measurements which express unambiguously your current baseline and your targeted future vision. The measurable items and the progress compared with the plan need to be clearly reported and communicated. Include measurable targets for:

❏ speed, in particular speed of innovation, readiness to change, time to market, speed to execute orders, speed to handle complaints;

❏ quality, in particular customer interactions, satisfaction and value

❏ organisational knowledge, market reputation and effectiveness of operations, for example, percentage of closed deals, service level achievement;

❏ financial performance.

Make your goal and its measurement understood across all business units, departments and regions – just as your cost reports, profit and loss calculations or performance statistics are currently understood by all your managers.

To achieve your goal, define the key processes, identify the decision points, work on models that help improve decisions, and systematically measure and monitor your goal-achievement in an unambiguous way. Then strive for a permanent improvement on the scale of success you have defined for your enterprise with a step-by-step fine-tuning of customer relations.

Part 2

Strategy for achieving e-speed
and optimising shareholder value

6

Major steps to transform to an e-business

@@@ Pursue the big changes step by step while deepening your experience. @@@ First, create a front-office to interact online and via call centres with the customers, then integrate the back-office processes for quicker and consistent services, and finally transform your enterprise in alliance with your partners into a powerful and self-adjusting service provider. @@@ Target your cycles of design, development, operations, innovations in very short time frames – a three-month duration is a good goal. @@@

What is your e-challenge today? Do you see some initial challenges from cyberspace – like the investment brokers who experienced their first signs of change in the mid 1990s with boutiques like Aufhauser & Co using the Web for first online transactions? Or does the online competition roll over you like the online broker with significant TV ads and permanent presence in sports such as baseball, football and tennis sponsoring? Or is it already as bad as for Merrill Lynch, the earlier market leader, who realised after Christmas 1998 that their market capitalisation was outperformed 'suddenly' by Charles Schwab? If so, now is your last opportunity to get organised and strike back, offer customers your products at prices similar to those of your online competitors – and extend them by your experience and the service capability of your large enterprise!

When you are about to decide to make your enterprise fit for e-business, you need to be clear about targeted customer segments, products and services, sales channel specifics and regional settings.

An example of these dimensions is depicted in Figure 12. For your first initiative, you should select one of the many segments, gain experience, and then expand to additional areas.

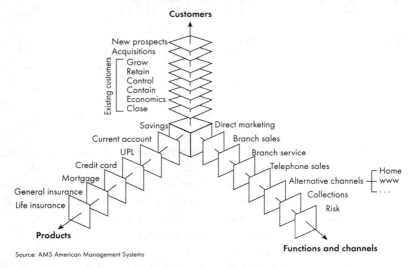

Source: AMS American Management Systems

Figure 12   Dimension for scoping an e-business initiative

As discussed before, start with the segment (customers, products, channels) with the highest contribution and the one with the lowest contribution. With the best segment, develop the methods as described in Part 1 of the book, and implement the components we discuss in the subsequent chapters. For the worst segment, check how you can use the components for reducing service costs or winding activities down. Then exploit that experience for the next best and worst segments.

All phases of your e-business initiative have to be embedded in a long-term approach, where various levels of e-business maturity should be pursued step by step.

6.1   Long-term target and approach

Based on the dimensions of your e-business project you should plan your overall initiative: how many sales representatives and customer service personnel will deal with the targeted segments and products? How much of your business will be affected? How long did it take your competitors to carry through such projects and how much time was necessary for earlier similar activities in your enterprise?

So does it look like a multi-year activity? Yes, you are correct. Does it resemble earlier huge projects? No – that view has to be avoided as it would lead you to making a major mistake, namely to approach it like all your other big projects. If this were so, you would not be able to change your enterprise towards customer-centred approaches, leaner processes and openness for flexible changes.

In contrast to traditional project approaches, you have to look for very short implementation cycles. Each cycle should start with a clear definition of the goal of that phase and it should include the actual development of processes, Web front-office and back-office integration based upon reviews of past lessons learned and past successes. Here is the first time that software development creeps in – and you have guessed it right, it is on purpose. But do not let the project be driven by technology! Your business priorities and organisational changes have to be first. Then, with very strict phasing, software and hardware selection, off-the-shelf implementation and rapidly prototyped extensions can take place. You should not wait to declare a phase completed until all acceptance procedures have been meticulously run through with 100 per cent perfect results, but much earlier, namely as soon as it is evident that the result of the phase is better than the last increment. Hopefully, this can be achieved after short periods of time, for example three months. The remaining adjustments and extensions can be included in the next phase, provided they are still considered important.

Telecom providers are in the lead with such short implementation cycles. They create new products with a weekly or bi-weekly frequency. Peter Manning, the Chief Operating Officer, now appointed Chief Executive Officer and President, of COLT-Telecom expressed the objective of a wide-spanning re-engineering e-business initiative in this way:

'We need to continually improve the customer online experience. In order to do so, we have to release a new version of our online offering every 90 days. I want to be able to build up progressively on the experience of each step – and to even throw away the results of a phase if that is necessary to meet the changing demands of our customers.'

This structured test and improvement approach allows a very flexible fine-tuning of the long-term development plans. It is much easier and much less expensive to correct mistakes every three months than to suffer through several years a long process of system design, development and roll-out projects.

6.2 Levels of e-business maturity

We have discussed the overall target of making an enterprise excellent in ongoing improvements. Experience shows that getting there would be too big a leap for any company. Therefore, practitioners have identified four appropriate levels of e-business maturity. These are the first indications for breaking your initiative down into major phases. The components of the phases are as follows.

At level one, only static information is provided via the Web. This is like the glossy brochures you send to your customers and prospective customers. No specific interaction with your customers and prospective customers is possible. Only a little investment and time is necessary to have such an initial Web presence – the costs can also be compared with printed brochures. All big enterprises have usually gone past that stage.

At level two, some interaction is possible: customers get some personalised information, the goods and services you offer (or at least some of them) can be ordered directly via the Web and you should be able to give an immediate confirmation of the order back to your customers. This requires integrating your back-office. In fact, your infrastructure should include real-time inventory keeping, interfaces with your suppliers in order to inform your customers about expected time for delivery, and you should have a support centre or call centre in place in order to quickly answer customers' e-mails. In fact, the majority of e-businesses are at that stage.

The next level, now level three, offers additional personalisation. This is the level most companies try to achieve. In particular, it requires you to implement a customer value model in order to follow the one-to-one marketing approach. This means that your website should be supported by decisioning systems:

❏ to guide the customer through what you offer;

❏ to highlight such goods and services you assume your customer has a high propensity to buy;

❏ to offer the appropriate price, packaging, delivery service and payment approach you want to use for the particular customer.

The final level, at the current time level four, will allow extensive self-service. Your customers will be able to configure your services and goods interactively on the screen, they can 'negotiate' service levels and prices and they will get pro-active and responsive support. And your enterprise is to set up in such a way that is consistently fine-tuning itself to come up with even newer and better products and services. You need to innovate products and services more quickly than your competitors in order to keep the customer loyal.

This goal goes beyond the implementation of even the most advanced current e-businesses. Some companies are striving for this level, but it has not yet been implemented in all its aspects. One of the few companies that have most of the characteristics of this level is Cisco with 70 per cent of the revenues generated via the Web and the whole service culture aligned with opportunities for interactive customer support.

To make this maturity model more tangible, let me share a survey from the German Computer Zeitung (22/2000) with you. Most

Figure 13   Four levels of e-business maturity

companies do have a website ('level one' according to the model described above): percentages range between 96 or 98 per cent of IT providers, banks, insurances companies and production industries, to 83 and 94 per cent of retailers and network providers, respectively. Only half of them, though, offer some electronic interaction ('level two' according to the model): relative leaders are network providers and retailers with 61 and 58 per cent, while less than 50 per cent of the other industries provide e-commerce transactions.

So much for generic discussions. Let us look closer at the finance industry now.

Online banking maturity

Research done by the author into the Web offerings of the top five banks in the European (EU) countries and a variety of project experience shows an almost complete coverage of online 'brochure ware'. So, the banking industry is at least on level one. There are interesting differences, between banks, though, if you compare how many of the products are on the Web – and how long responses to e-mail enquiries take. You find the full range from five minutes to fifteen days!

The majority of the banks have progressed to level two: what most of the big banks offer is account-keeping with online statements and money transfers as well as the buying and selling of stocks. As with the difference of the degree of responsiveness to e-mail enquiries, there is also a huge difference in the degree of integration with back-office processes and systems. While some banks stick to the basic Web functions and implement the service by manual handling, for example by another data entry in the existing legacy back-office systems, others allow for 24-hour trading accessing directly a variety of stock exchanges, derivatives and futures exchanges, or funds, in most of the currencies and around the globe. The more progressive banks also provide smart extensions to the basic 'current account' such as credit cards or insurances or automatic saving functions combined with loans and mortgages.

In the case of some segments, clearly targeted marketing campaigns and a tight back-office integration with self-service have also been achieved – such as ordering new cheque books or blocking specific cheques, entering and updating standing orders, or even changing one's own credit limit. This cannot usually be observed across the full spectrum of offerings, customer groups and regions – and it actually would not make sense. In such segments as these, level three has been reached. Online opening of an account of a new customer or online approval of a new loan application, though, is still very rare.

Some banks or units even partner with vendors of specific goods – you can order your car via the Web and pay with an online approved loan (refer to *www.gmbuypower.com* or *www.smart.com*). But even here, no thorough implementation of the customer value perspective can usually be found, for example no systematic modelling of what discounts can be afforded for which individual customer is usually implemented. Thus, no really personalised offerings can be made, and also the ongoing web-based innovation is still pending. In general, the newly founded banks are a bit more advanced – it is notable that they are experimenting to implement some of these targets. But you still have the time to catch up, if you start soon!

Online insurance maturity

In the insurance business, Europe has seen even fewer online customer interactions than in banking. Some smaller players offer their e-services for customers who like to experiment with new tools such as *www.insurancecity.de*, or serve in niche markets, such as discount car insurance. For their internal handling, though, insurance companies equip their agents with electronic application forms on their laptops or by process facilitation when collecting and submitting insurance claims.

The mass-market breakthrough is still to be expected, because the industry has not yet defined the easy-to-handle forms that are as neat as a bank transfer slip. Here, you can exploit the first mover advantages or enjoy the luxury of watching the development a bit further until you need to decide what emerging business model to adopt. Interesting examples you can learn from are US companies such as *www.InsWeb.com* or *www.QuoteSmith.com*, providing quotes for all types of insurance – the intriguing business concept for a broad acceptance in the diverse European markets is still up to you to create.

6.3   Focal areas per maturity level

In general, 'the focus must shift from attending to the functions a firm aims to perform, to the strategic objectives it wishes to achieve' (*Creating Shareholder Value*, PeopleSoft Whitepaper, 2000). For translating that into an action plan, we will use the e-business maturity model as discussed above and explain the specific focus per maturity level. To get from one maturity level to the next one, you should anticipate various design and development steps. In the following discussion, we will call those steps a cycle to underline its iterative and repetitive nature. In each cycle, you gain more experience with online customer interactions and improve strategic objectives more and more.

Level one objectives

For level one, online 'brochures', that is descriptions of your services and products, have to be available for all products within the scope of the e-business initiative. Moreover, they have to be translated into all target languages and the regional specialities have to be reflected. I assume that you have already achieved that stage when you read this book.

Level two objectives

At level two, where many big corporations still are, a consistent and complete handling (starting with key products and customer segments) of order/transaction entry has to be achieved. At this stage, some manual interfaces to the back-office processing can still be tolerated – those manual interfaces require less development effort, but the handling costs are pretty high, in particular as you need to ensure the response times expected in the online marketplace. The benchmarks are set by companies who have integrated their back-office systems, so usually customers get confirmation within seconds to a maximum of a few minutes. So your back-office will be challenged to ensure such service levels with manual processes.

The key benefits at this level are that your customers can get in contact with you using modern online capabilities and that your call centres and back-office operations gain experience through a closer customer encounter. An important point here is that the data definitions (such as status information on a customer order) need to change their semantics from an internal, procedure-oriented and even sometimes encoded nature to a meaningful text that allows the customer to act upon this information. Some customers may even want to build their own automated processes on top of the interactions with you! This new experience for your organisation can be gained no matter to what extent the automation and integration of the back-office processes is possible in the respective cycle. But keep in mind that you need to carefully examine the transaction progress and status data. Also at this level, you can start to build up your metrics and models for service levels. How many staff are necessary in the call centre, at which times of the day or week? How does it influence the service levels (for example, response times in the call centre, end-to-end processing times for a transaction, duration of handling complaints) and your costs if you work with some over-capacities or staff shortages? These figures should be used then to size and configure your organisation in the subsequent project phases.

To also gain experience with technical integration, data from your back-office systems should be provided at the Web front-office. For example, account statements should be offered as soon as better security features are in place than for the pure entry of transactions. With such a stepwise project execution, you can check if your integration approach and the tools used are solid – and how Web visitors have an impact on your existing IT architecture.

Level three objectives

For level three you need to complete the modelling of business transactions identifying events, responsible parties (or 'actors') and end-to-end information flow. This phase offers you all kind of challenges:

❏ changing organisational responsibilities (in particular in the call centres and other customer-centred entities);

❏ re-engineering your processes;

❏ implementing analytical and decision support models to support one-to-one marketing and customer relationship management (CRM); and

❏ setting up a new IT infrastructure. This usually includes the definition of a data warehouse (DWH), implementation of your tools for performance metrics based on on-line analytical processing (OLAP) and tools for a simplified integration of the back-office systems such as EAI.

The focus at this level is on treating your customers more efficiently. Recent surveys show that companies expect huge improvements in revenue through dedicated one-to-one marketing and focused cross-selling. A study from the Chartered Institute of Banking (CIB) from 1999 indicates, for example, that new customer acquisition has a weight of 38 per cent, increased customer retention 52 per cent and increased cross-selling 72 per cent. Analysis shows that long-term customer relationships have a higher profitability by a factor three to five than new customers. If you perform your cross-selling activities with one-to-one marketing activities, you do not even incur big costs for your campaigns – but you need to have significant up-front investments for the infrastructure described above and you need to fine-tune your approaches permanently.

So it is good that you have already gained some experience with the speed of changes during the phases before – and you should know at this stage how to balance customer dynamics and increased business with necessary investments. I am sure that you have a pretty solid impression what the first points of the list above mean for you, but I bet that you are terrified about the item regarding IT. It smells like a fortune of money to spend. Unfortunately, you are right.* There are some ways, though, to spend it more efficiently.

The key for good IT investments is a clear integration architecture combined with a solid roadmap for regular release iterations of all related systems. You probably already sense the difference – you must not allow separate fiefdoms within your IT group! Everybody must co-operate, across functional borderlines, across country borders, across systems borders (for example, mainframe and client server) and across tool responsibilities. The key success factors mentioned further this cross-border attitude by the intrinsic need to design the solution components with the overall business and IT perspectives in mind. The transformation of the IT approach from a legacy attitude to a pro-active business support is a big change project in itself. Such projects are outlined in Chapters 10 to 13 with the necessary strategic roadmap, with their respective disciplines, with a quick-look assessment to be performed for defining the new service levels, and with the respective system development tasks.

---

* A Datamonitor survey from Spring 1999 shows that for CRM systems alone, European banks spent 950 million Euros in 1998, an increase of 41 per cent over 1997, with similar growth expected.

Enterprise application integration (EAI) architecture

EAI refers to an approach that started more than a decade ago, which is based on the experience that in large enterprises no neatly integrated IT environment usually exists. Even before the days of frequent mergers, various business units had purchased software and hardware that was best for their local objectives. The investments were approved based on their individual business cases – and no real need for integration was seen. After this had continued for a while, the top managers realised that they did not have a complete and consistent picture of the company's performance any more – and people doing the day-to-day business experienced the lack of a complete view of the customer. Often customer data were kept in several separate systems, which meant that the processing of a change of address for a customer was a mess – and risk management or value considerations were pretty difficult if not impossible, too. In some cases, governments even had to step in to prevent bankruptcies due to lack of risk management (remember the capital adequacy directive for banks).

Therefore, systems were integrated and central data repositories or data warehouses (DWH) were built up. Data integration was often a point-to-point connection where data were exported and imported in a fashion just sufficient for the two related systems. And the number of interfaces grew exponentially, because over time almost every system had to be interfaced with every other. More clever approaches created some layers in between the systems that had to exchange data. Two prominent examples are, first the 'bus' concept where a data publishing system sends out its data and others can 'subscribe' to it, and second, the 'message broker' concept: a system which provides methods for the entities it contains, and handles the situation when other systems need to pull up or change data of the provider system. The handling of such requests is done by the message broker. While initially, the approaches implemented different mechanisms, namely the bus concept a 'push' mechanism, and the broker concept a 'pull' mechanism, today both approaches have been extended and refined to support either philosophy. With either approach, the overall development effort is reduced, because the number of interfaces do not grow exponentially any more, but each system has only to have an adapter or connector to the central middleware. That means, only n middleware adapters (or connectors) need to be developed instead of $(n-1)^2$ direct interfaces for n systems to be connected with each other.

So much for the connection and transport of data between different systems. In most cases, the data are different, though, from one system to another. So, in order to store data in the central data warehouse, the data requires a transformation from one format to another. This job is often not done properly, because the development staff still have traditional interface descriptions in mind and perform direct mapping (that is, translation) from one system to another. Instead, a common format should be defined – like the format of the data warehouse – and the methods that can be applied to certain entities, like a customer, have to be standardised too. Imagine the example of a customer changing his address: some systems may provide directly the function 'change address from (old address) to (new address)', other may distinguish between mailing addresses, site addresses and so on. So the central method and data repository needs to find the appropriate functions in each system for such a perceivably trivial event. In modern EAI solutions, this is handled by a 'business rules' component. But this component needs to be configured, too, that is, the events must be documented, the related functions in the various systems must be identified and linked to events and the data mapping has to be done thoroughly. That is also quite a bit of work, but the good news is again that you need to do that 'only' once per system to be integrated. And you will be able to explain much more clearly to your business people what is possible in your IT environment and what your systems cannot handle.

Up to now, we have discussed the activities necessary for interfacing which require development investments. What are the benefits of those investments? Actually quite a few: fewer data handling problems, fewer data quality issues and an increased ability to perform risk and value management. Altogether: a better view of data with the possibility to slice and dice your data and to get an analytical view.

An example of such an analytical view on a detailed level is shown in Figure 14. The particular contribution is shown by customer segment, by channel (branch, call centre, ATM, Internet) and by lines of business (mortgage, car loans, savings accounts, current accounts), each with the financial value on top of each cube, a score for the achievement of service levels at the front of each cube and an indicator for customer satisfaction on the right of each cube.

And there are more benefits to come! Have a look at Figure 15, where the strategic layers of EAI use are shown. Once you have

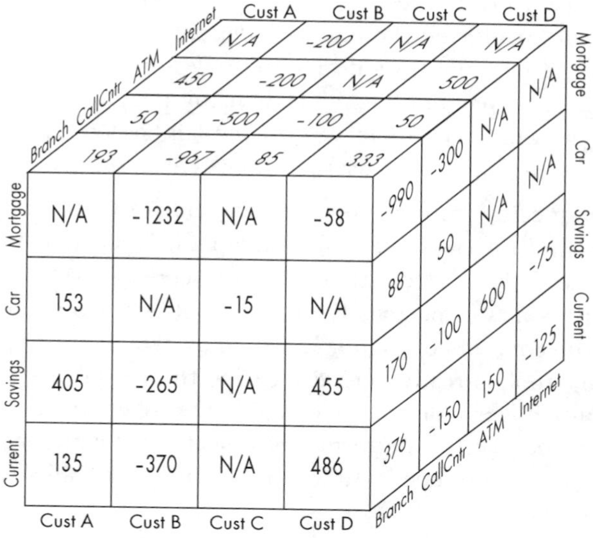

Figure 14 Analytical slicing and dicing

implemented the higher layers you can achieve a huge leap in monitoring your throughput. The process definitions you have prepared for the changes in your business are the base for measuring the *process flow*, that is the duration a certain transaction needs to be processed by a particular system. Operations tools highlight bottlenecks – and you can quickly see if particular units in your organisation or specific systems work at their capacity borders. This knowledge allows you to fine-tune your operations; namely organisational units, software and hardware!

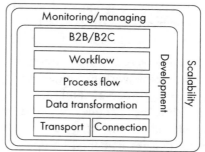

Source: AMS American Management Systems, EAI Solution Centre

Figure 15 Layers of strategic EAI use

On the next layer, then, complete customer interactions can be monitored in specific end-to-end *workflows*. How good is your online availability? How long does it take to process a bank transfer, to increase a limit, to pay out a loan? How many people are engaged and how long do they need to answer a complaint? How often has your field force to return from a customer home without having met them?

Finally, specific online interfaces can be provided for business customers and for consumers, for example off-the-shelf Web front-ends. Around these layers that form the core of EAI, middleware software packages come usually bundled with development tools for defining the contents of each layer (such as data mapping) and with monitoring tools already referred to for the actual display of the throughput at each of the layers. For the selection of a specific package, of course the performance objectives have to be met and the implementation needs to be accordingly scalable with your business growth.

I have seen so many companies struggle because they lack the capabilities of proper integration that I recommend you should follow the discussed leading-edge approaches! The flexibility you gain is worth the undertaking. We will come back to that in Part 3 of the book, where I will highlight some EAI vendors with their strengths and weaknesses.

Level four objectives

Level four is for the most companies still an outlook on the future. With all things in place discussed so far, that is, with a concise reporting and pro-active steering of the enterprise, you can go for an adaptable, learning organisation. The metrics will then be reflected in feedback loops, policies based on those metrics will be defined and their success rate can be compared with improved policies and rules. So your implemented business strategies will be permanently challenged by extended and refined strategies.

People will be empowered to work freely and to the best of their capabilities in the framework provided by these policies. Good people will have a lot of liberty – and 'good' will not be defined by some wilful act, but by parameters publicly communicated. So everybody can strive for the next level of personal growth and excellence. And cross-departmental co-operation will be the norm instead of the exception. With this approach everybody wins: you get the full performance out of your staff, your people will like to live up to their potential and your customers will appreciate a better service.

Functionally and technically, your systems will be refined and extended: the data warehouses, together with the customer relationship management (CRM) systems will trigger personalised marketing activities and Web contents and the customers will be able to choose their product and service configurations from a wide set of options – and influence the prices in a transparent way by cutting or adding features. Again, everybody wins: you get a better closure rate on your products and services, save the money wasted on unnecessary effort, wasted stamps and paper, your staff can focus on more demanding and satisfying tasks, and customers will not get junk mail they are not interested in, but instead receive valuable information when it helps them.

6.4 Summary: what requires your specific attention

As the overall programme is huge, you have to permanently set a specific focus balancing the 'magic triangle' of time—cost—quality. In the Internet age, attention has shifted very much to time, so you need to define project packages small enough to fit into the defined slot of time (three-month cycles for example). Those project packages still have to provide significant and measurable steps forward in online service quality. Do not allow your staff to do too much at once, but focus on a particular area (such as customer segment, product, or service function) in each step while maintaining and extending a forward-looking roadmap where all good ideas and suggestions are reflected.

The co-operation across your organisation, in particular between marketing, customer-oriented groups, back-office and information technology needs to get more intense. Joint teams need to progress on business and IT re-designs.

Structure activities in cycles reflecting design, development, operations, and define the service levels to be achieved at the end of each cycle. Wait with the implementation of some ideas until your overall organisation has reached the necessary level of maturity and customer focus with the respective level of integration between front-office and back-office operations. Adopt a sequence of focal areas:

❑ online availability of brochureware (usually widely implemented);

❏ online transaction entry with various electronic and manual interfaces to the back-office systems and transaction handling;

❏ streamlined responsibility for customer relationships and performance based on end-to-end integration of the Web front-end with the back-office systems;

❏ value-driven processes supported by personalised messages and recommendations to the customers and usage of individual cross-selling campaigns.

6.5 The disciplines of your initiative

We went through the improved customer experience in Part 1 and you probably sense now the size of your overall e-nitiative. While we were looking at the customer experience in Part 1 from an outside-in perspective, now we focus upon the components you have to set up to provide for such experience. We discuss those components now with an inside-out perspective. Here is the structure of the following chapters.

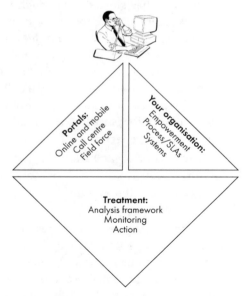

Figure 16   Disciplines of your e-nitiative

7

Portal set-up for maximising customer orders

@@@ The portal is your door to your customers – and their door to you. @@@ Welcome each customer with the news, services and products he or she is interested to see. @@@ Guide customers through your portal to an entertaining business closure. @@@ Make ordering as enjoyable, easy and convenient as possible. @@@

Virtual portals today have the same purpose in cyberworld as had earlier the physical doors at your giant buildings, the great windows presenting your goods and the large number of staff running around and demonstrating the size and importance of a traditional enterprise. This purpose was and is to impress the customer, create trust and motivate him or her to buy one of the presented offers, or talk to a clerk for a more customised offer.

Compared with such an impressive physical presence, cyberworld portals have some constraints, but they also offer tremendous new opportunities. The main constraint are the tiny windows to look into cyberworld. While cyberworld is large, your customer's window to it is just some eleven to seventeen inches in diameter from his or her standard PC display. There is an acoustic portal, too, namely the channel to your call-centre staff, but what is that compared with a face-to-face dialogue?

You can make up for those constraints by using other elements of technology, namely a better (though formalised) understanding of your customers. This understanding is expressed in customer profiles allowing targeted marketing such as one-to-one approaches.

Customer profiles are a combination of the information the customer volunteers to share with you, such as preferred products, preferred services, price and risk sensitivities, with the information you obtain from analysing customer interactions. This includes purchasing patterns, payment patterns and service request patterns from past interactions. Additionally, you need to interpret the current Web visit: which top notch products was the visitor looking at – or how many of your discount offers did he or she check in the last few minutes? Is he or she coming from a competitor, a link partner or a search engine reference? As you want to maximise the probability of a closure, the portal should be set up in such a way as to anticipate customer demand. Depending on the individual customer profile, this means to

❏ highlight specific news and messages that you believe are interesting for a particular customer;

❏ use a prominent place on the Portal for the particular product this customer should be most willing to buy;

❏ show such banner ads for your own products or links to partners where you have seen a propensity to buy.

We will discuss now the various considerations necessary for making up good portals on the various channels, that is for PC based Internet, for the call centre, the field staff and mobile portals.

7.1 Marketing

The classic rules of marketing still apply in the Internet age – only the number of companies competing for your customers' attention has increased. If you want to rely on your existing brand, you have the advantage of being well known. This comes at the price of possibly being perceived as a bit old-fashioned. The 'modern' e-brands have fresh names such as Amazon, DoCoMo, eBay, Vizzavi, Yahoo and Yollo. Building up such new brands requires the usual investment in a combination of classic advertising and PR campaigns plus a strong online presence.

Companies from different industries may join forces to produce good complementary market coverage and to defend themselves against the big portal providers such as AOL or Yahoo. The objective is to come up with their own portal, providing wide spanning and interesting content. For example, the market leader of the Spanish telecom providers is now offering an entertainment portal together with the Dutch TV producer Endemol, and the Dutch 'incumbent' KPN and the large bank ABN Amro are approaching the Benelux and German insurance and mortgage market in a joint venture called 'Money Planet'. And CanalWeb leverages the experience from more than 100 different customer segments identified by their subscription to the specific broadcast channel (yes, they have 120 different customer segments!) to target-market the merchandise products. These companies have enough immediate access to a large number of customers to allow them to win a market share for their own or their partners' products, services and contents from the large 'pure' telecom Portal providers.

To produce a good image and to ensure acceptance in the market, your marketing specialists have to come up with a clear picture of the targeted customers for the various products and services – and they need to create the right flashlight messages and a nicely packaged and entertaining website environment. What is the gender and age of your target segment? How are they educated and where do they live? What are their current online habits? The appropriate language code, pictures and entertaining elements have to be created for the core of your target areas.

At the same time a balance is necessary with the image your customers currently have of your enterprise. The trust you have created with your traditional business has to be transformed into a similar trust in your online channel. If your customers perceive you as a market leader (as IBM was perceived even at times when they were not at the peak of their performance), you need to support that authority by your Web presence. In this case, you have to emphasise your industry leadership by highlighting recent product developments, the knowledge you have acquired (by showing the patents you own for example), the prizes you have won and the benefits your enterprise will create. The online business you perform has to be supported by similar guarantees to those of your traditional business – maybe you should even extend the guarantees in order to reduce the entry hurdles for your online customers and to maximise the hurdles for your competitors.

An interesting example here is the design compromise Deutsche Bank came up with for their online service. Influenced by virtual figures from TV stations, they created the avatar Cor@ (see Figure 17). She is appealing to the young – but in contrast with the sexy cybergirls from TV stations, she still implies the serious Deutsche

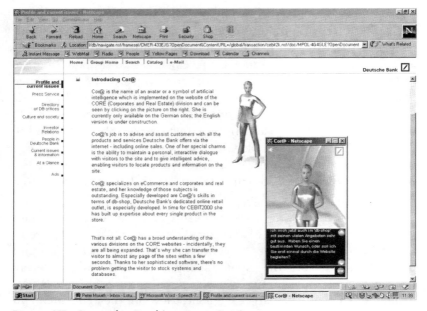

Figure 17   Deutsche Bank's avatar Cor@

Bank attitude. And of course, she does provide help to the visitor who has questions when navigating through Deutsche Bank's website. In the meantime, some companies have even started to offer different avatars to the different target groups; select the preferred gender, give it the appropriate age and appeal – and let your customers play with the length of the skirt or the size of the tie.

Depending on the maturity level of your online presence, you have to put more and more emphasis on customer interactions. At the first level, you just should provide a good site map and direct accessibility to the various 'brochures' you have available online. On the next levels, when customers can submit orders, trigger transactions, or make enquiries, broad sets of interaction options are to be made available for the different users:

❑ quick data entry into an online form for 'expert users';

❑ configuring services following an online questionnaire for more inexperienced users;

❑ browsing through a catalogue and filling a shopping cart;

❑ or even closure decisions during a game.

For each of those interaction types, the relevant marketing messages have to be put across. Deutsche Bank does not have only the portal with Cor@ for their private investment customers, they also have the 'low end' Bank 24 brand for the mass market – and now they have launched one more portal for their business customers, *www.db-business-direct.de*. With those sub-brands they already have three market segments that can be approached separately. And further refinements will come. The target is one-to-one marketing, that is, no waste of stamps on mailings, no waste of customer attention, just being right on target.

Establish a high-performing Web publishing team with traditional marketing knowledge, online design background and good system usability experience. This team should design interactions based on flow-charts that show step by step how often the customers must click with their mice and when they get confirmations or questions back. When pulling or pushing information, it has to be decided to what extent only pure navigation support is to be given or when certain marketing aspects should be included, as for cross-selling opportunities. This is a multi-dimensional challenge – and perfect answers do not exist yet, but the earlier you start to practise and measure responsiveness from the market, the faster your online penetration will grow.

You also have to adjust your Web presence to the specific channel – PC-based Internet attracts the more 'mature' customers, say primarily twenty to thirty years of age, while the mobile phone focus has now shifted from professional users to a big cluster in the young and hip segments, say ten to twenty years old. And the market penetration in this latter group is growing most quickly.

Once you have achieved a good penetration of your target population, you should try to get your visitors actively engaged on your website. The best concept is communities. These communities reflect (and create) the trust of all the visitors or customers together. Amazon started such a community with reader reviews of books and music, eBay extended it to a kind of risk and service ranking for all sellers of goods (including private persons) who participated in their auctions, and now communities have become an aim in themselves. Chat rooms where people communicate in groups or in couples, or date or flirt, are more private services – and forums are used to channel thoughts, questions, experience and recommendations in any private and business field. Such forums and communities can be of any size. For example there is a small active community of readers of my last book consisting of a few hundred people (approximately 5 per cent of the readers) who exchange their experience of e-business launches around the globe. And there are big clubs such as Walt Disney's Club Blast where people can access games and entertainment – and exchange their private concerns and questions; this club is one of the largest 'machines' for market research and campaign execution. By the way, Russ Gillam, the manager at Disney for online-business, works with more than twenty Web designers on the permanent fine-tuning of the website in order to convert as many Web visitors as possible to subscribers. They regularly test the extent to which small changes in Web navigation and marketing messages influence the percentage of successfully acquired subscribers. And a little note here regarding product management and speed: Disney's CEO Michael Eisner has demanded that his enterprise has to create a new product every five minutes (!), for example a film, a CD, a book, or some merchandise.

One last thing on marketing and on attracting customer attention: the visitors can zap away much more quickly than if they were in your physical outlet! For a more personal touch, videos of your board members, or pre-recorded messages from customer care staff, should be available. And you compete against a lot of entertainment on the Web. The best thing you can do is to add entertainment to your website, too – at least for those customers who are attracted by it. Also, a careful dose of games can help. Solid products such as those in banking can be enriched by stock games using a trial portfolio, even with competitions between your various customers, or by an online version of classic Monopoly. Content has to be added to traditionally content-free services such as telecom services – they can be made more personal by chatting, dating and relating to friends and 'buddies online'. And why not have a news ticker streaming across your website with some special information for your different customer segments, for example

❏ the latest news on the local party scene for your student customers;

❏ money and stock news for young professionals without kids;

❏ tips for kids, house and garden for young families;

❏ health recommendations for those at retirement age.

7.2   Contents and design

It was not too easy to come up with a good website design, when only PC-based Internet existed. And now it is even more difficult, as you also have to consider several variations on how your customer can be in touch with you on the Web.

I want to highlight two types of business interactions that should be at the core of your interaction design.

❏ New customer handling: depending on security and privacy requirements, a combination of paper contracts, validation of customer identity and evaluation of customer credit history, and check of delivery capabilities will apply. Then a customer record can be created in the system and access to the different relevant channels can be activated.

❏ Transactions handling: the basic approach is to use the existing forms and to just put them on the Web. This does not, however, reflect the best design approach. A better interaction design goes through a stepwise data entry. Many customer master data should be stored in a profile (such as the address and regular payment information), so only the specifics for the transaction have to be entered. Depending on the transaction, the customer has to get a confirmation back about the status of its processing. Look at the Amazon approach, how customers are kept in the loop regarding the delivery status of an ordered book or music CD. Similar approaches can be envisioned in other industries – imagine the service of a stockbroker, where the customer has placed an order within a limit and the stock price is getting close to the limit, but does not reach it. Why not inform the customer about this fact, that the stock price is just a few cents away from the limit and suggest that the customer adjusts the limit? That would provide the customer with an added value at little cost for you!

Let us have a closer look at how interactions should be implemented for different formats:

❏ PC-based Internet: different bandwidths are possible. The customer might use a normal modem at a relatively low speed where colourful and detailed pictures may already create a problem: he or she may be an ISDN user with a medium speed data transmission; or he or she may be one of the DSL users that have a very high bandwidth and are even able to watch video streams with a decent quality.

❏ SMS (short message service), where transactions can be executed by swapping pre-defined message formats.

❏ WAP (wireless access protocol), that is, mobile phone websites – where unfortunately the phones from different vendors do have different screen formats.

❏ UMTS (universal mobile telecommunication system), the new mobile telecommunication standard about to replace the current GSM network during the next few years with bandwidths even larger than the current fixed wire ISDN implementations.

❏ Mobile PDAs (personal digital assistants), large mobile phones with a screen and small keyboard – you could also call them small laptops with an integrated phone.

On an SMS or WAP mobile, you can only display text and characters and a few symbols or icons (all in black and white) while on a PDA pictures in colours are also possible. Some automated translators from the HTML for PCs to WML for mobile phones exist, but imagine the long time it would take to display the full content of a PC website on the small screen of a mobile phone. So, you had better design your websites specifically for the targeted device.

Let us recap what you need to have in mind when designing the website – it is summarised in Table 8 (see my website for a softcopy).

Then, let us see what not to do. According to Patricia Seybold, the well-known US consultant for creating a customer-centric approach, the top ten mistakes when designing a website are:

❏ imposing a penalty for shopping online, for example, worse response times than in a physical branch;

❏ no call to action, such as 'order now', 'click here for obtaining our services';

❏ no phone number to contact the call centre or help desk;

❏ not enough relevant information;

❏ mixed messages;

❏ difficult to find from search engines;

❏ inconsistent look and feel;

Table 8   Drivers of website contents and design

Driver	Characteristics of contents	Impact on Design
Customer Segment	Products, services and packaged bundles for the segment. Availability of product and service options. Discounts or special features for the segment. Coverage against specific risks of the segment.	Style (e.g. young/mature). Navigation support. Availability of entertainment and infotainment. Community features and topics/mailing lists.
Region / Country	Local variation of product or service, e.g. special regulations, taxes, warranties.	Language. Local entertainment and infotainment.
Product	Product information. Order forms. Links to service partners	Customers' goals and expectations when using the product should be highlighted.
Channel	**Full-size branch:** full availability of paper brochures, products, experienced staff. **Small POS branch/'kiosk':** day-to-day transactions performed by a few clerks. Immediate confirmation of transactions or pick-up of standard products. No or little consulting on the service offerings. **Call centre:** prospective customers can obtain general information and request printed brochures. Customers with a pre-agreed contract can execute day-to-day transactions. No consulting. **PC-based Internet:** full availability of online brochures, entry of transactions, confirmations with little delay, access to online help or call centre for support, value-added services (e.g. infotainment), maintenance of customer profiles. **Mobile Internet:** favourite transactions (according to pre-defined profiles). The products, services and prices of all channels above must be synchronised – there may be discounts for using a specific channel (such as online order entry), but the policies must be explicit for customers and staff.	Paper brochures have a long shelf-life, so only ongoing information should be printed; flexible information (such as current prices) can be provided via an intranet and a hard-copy should be made available upon request. The terminals used in the branches have to use the same terminology (e.g. for product names or for entries on the order/transaction forms) as the call-centre screens and the website. The design should be tailored for the customer segment, region and product. This is easier the more virtual the channel is – a full-size branch will reflect a compromise in design, a small kiosk can reflect some local characteristics, the call-centre agent can use the customer profile for a specific approach and the Internet services (in particular mobile services) can additionally reflect very specific situations. For all channels, a thorough test has to be performed, in particular all the different browsers (in their various releases) have to be checked.
One-to-one marketing	All the above.	All the above.

❏ letting the customer get away, that is, too few attractive links and hotspots that make the customer stick to the website;

❏ promises, empty promises;

❏ too many ads, too little content.

Enough words now; let me share some more screen shots with you exemplifying these recommendations. You can see the various brands and home pages of the Bank of Montreal, namely their mortgage centre targeted at the more mature customers, the mbanx Direct mainly focused on younger customers and students, and Competix for professional users. The designs have a different 'look and feel' for each target group and have a look on page 121 for a mobile portal example.

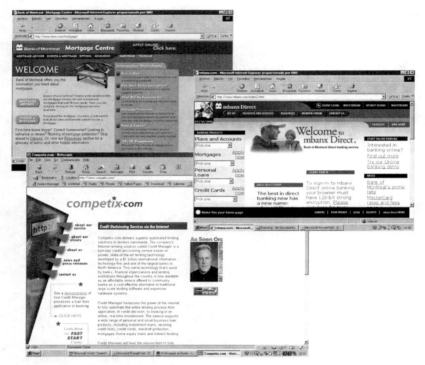

Figure 18   Different brands for banking target segments

Let us wrap up this important section by highlighting the key points to check when you have drafted your website:

❏ Ensure a high speed of downloading the website – particularly for customers with slow dial-in modems. Texts should be downloaded first, pictures should be built up, getting sharper during transmission. And make sure you transmit the contents the customer is interested in first, before assaulting him or her with unsolicited advertising.

❏ Design a high speed of interaction, for example, a small number of mouse clicks to find information or to submit a transaction, supportive user guidance or help functions. Use the 'max 3' rule: a maximum of three clicks until the visitor arrives at the information he or she wants; a maximum of three seconds until the contents of the website can be seen; and a maximum of three forms to fill in on the mobile phone (via SMS or WAP).

❏ Provide completeness and robustness, for example, test your website with different browser types (and different generations of browsers, for example, Java browsers or HTML browsers); include the option of getting the necessary update for browsers or plug-in players downloaded when needed to view or listen to the contents. Ensure that no transactions are lost and that the website is permanently available.

❏ Provide secure transmission of private information such as payment data.

7.3 Call centre

For customers who have problems with Web interactions, or currently without access to the Web, the call centre will be the point of contact. For your e-nitiative, operational excellence in the call centre should be the target. The key aspects* are:

Intelligent interactions – any customer interaction should reflect the latest knowledge you have on the customer's preferences and values.

Personalised service – service should be personal both in style and content. CRM (customer relationship management) solutions used effectively can help providers understand individual customer needs, and this can be reflected in both reactive (for example, when the customer calls with a complaint) and pro-active (for example, for direct marketing activities) interaction handling.

Marketing based on known customer preferences – marketing can be customised on a one-to-one basis to reflect individual customer targets and values. Preferences may include types of product, frequency and time of purchase, and channel use. By designing marketing in this way selling becomes valued not intrusive.

Rapid response to requests – an integrated CRM solution will provide accurate 'one touch' resolution to customer requests. This provides cost-effective and satisfying service.

* Source: Sue Faure, AMSCAT research director, customer operations, The Hague.

To implement this strategy, customer approaches have to be defined, the organisation needs to be set up and software systems need to be integrated, in particular:

❏ CRM solutions for the call-centre staff: this software displays the customer profile, the history of his or her transactions, the specific approach (for example, sales suggestions or risk warnings) and the appropriate entry forms. It should accelerate the speed of the communication of the agent with the customer.

❏ CTI (computer telephony integration): these systems allow automatic outbound dialling, for example, for direct marketing activities, and, for inbound calls, they route the calls to the nearest available call-centre agent. Smarter implementations even allow different service levels (in particular waiting times on the phone) for different customers, provided that the customer can be identified by the number he or she is calling from or by entering his or her customer number. In such a way at the time when the agent picks up the phone with an inbound call, customer information is simultaneously displayed on the agent's PC screen.

❏ DMS (document management system): in the DMS scanned papers are archived, for example, the original contract, amendments, invoices and account statements, complaints and other formal information that have been exchanged between the customer and the enterprise.

These systems not only support your staff, but also allow you to monitor the performance of the operation and the efficiency of your customer interactions. You can continue to fine-tune both the operations and the interactions. For example, the peak-time service level performance can be improved, customers who regularly complain without reason can be blacklisted (and those who were hit by bad luck can receive some bonus), interaction patterns can be used for cross-selling – and overall efficiency should grow by having the necessary information at the right time at your fingertips.

7.4 Partners and field force

We have discussed the approaches relevant for marketing and sales – but there is one more important area, namely partners of all kinds, including the field force. Relations with partners are currently shifting towards a closer co-operation, reflecting a shift from the past focus on cost cuts to today's priority on effectiveness and to the upcoming overall value proposition. Outsourcing and partnerships may cover a range of activities, from the simple tasks of office cleaning or mail handling, to a strategic asset like field service and maintenance, external IT services and even outsourced research and development. If you have physical products to be delivered, your delivery and logistics partner should carry your marketing messages. If your products need configuration or support, your staff in the field should be fully informed about your goods or services, pursue cross-selling opportunities and be ready to take additional orders. If third-party sales partners also offer products from your competitors, you should support the needs of partners in a way that puts your goods or services in a most visible position, for example, by providing a partner portal.

With strategic partners, with whom you may even have an exclusive agreement, you should integrate tightly, for example by using enterprise application integration approaches as discussed in the last chapter. Tactical partners who supply you with some commodity products or services can work with you more loosely – co-operation may be supported by an electronic marketplace, where many sellers and buyers exchange their goods at daily market prices.

Most of the partners offer additional opportunities for establishing customer touch points – no matter if the partner is a sales agent, a delivery organisation, or a technician fixing problems at the customer site. To provide partners and field staff with the appropriate information, you have to let them access your customer profile information from the data warehouse, and integrate them in your CRM approach. Not surprisingly, it is a bit more complicated than linking call-centre staff, because your field force travels a lot, so you cannot use normal computer terminals or intranet PCs. With the growing power of mobile terminals, though, technical communication is becoming less of an issue. The big delivery companies such as UPS, FedEx, Deutsche Post, are all equipped now with mobile devices where even the signatures of the recipients of the parcels can be scanned. These data are transferred back to the data centres at the end of a tour. Likewise, you can download customer profiles and specific order forms to the mobile devices of your field staff when they are preparing their tour or you can use next generation PDAs and build up a mobile intranet with the new UMTS standard. So you can enable your outside staff and partners to become a large sales force.

Your field staff and partners are also an important source of market research data. Specific questions can be raised, such as: how often do customers have problems with the configuration of your products, where do they have questions and what missing features do they complain about? Very precise answers can be kept in your CRM and CTI databases.

Be careful with your partners, though, not to cannibalise your sales channels too early. Those who help you sell will see your online services as competition to their sales activities – and in the long run you are indeed interested in cutting their sales commissions. In order to gain their acceptance and support, you need to slowly change the commissioning scheme. First, subsidise their commissions during the initial phase of your online offerings – see, for example, how airlines still subsidise travel agents. The customer relationship is maintained by the travel agency and they get 'their' commission even if the customer purchased the ticket online. But travel agents have to accept a general cut of the commission percentage. At later stages, the very sales channel that closed the transaction will get the commission, which means that in the case of transactions closed online directly between the airline and customer, the airline saves the commission costs. But if you try commission cutting immediately, you risk an important sales channel being discontinued abruptly.

7.5 Specific services for mobile users

Designing a portal and creating new services for Internet users meant primarily looking at young, higher educated professionals who either had a PC with Web access at home or could use the Internet from work. But access was still restricted; it ranged in most Western countries between 10 per cent and 30 per cent of the population, which was not enough for mass marketing. Only Scandinavia and the US top those figures with a PC penetration (not necessarily with Web access) in the neighbourhood of 50 per cent. Therefore online sales for most businesses are disappointingly low.

Mobile commerce is going to change the situation soon! A very large and very quickly growing number of people have a mobile phone. In most European and Asian countries more than half of the population can be reached via mobile phones. Mobile commerce can be handled by SMS (short message service), by WAP (wireless access protocol) and by UMTS. SMS has the advantage that (apart from the very first generation), almost all mobile phones can handle it. The downside is that services are restricted and secure transmissions cannot be guaranteed. WAP is the method most of the large providers have now implemented. Content providers such as Amazon have adjusted their service to the limitations of small 'screens' with a small bandwidth – see *www.amazon.com* (on your WAP phone). But it still takes a disappointingly long time to find and order a certain book or music title. This will only get better with higher bandwidth services. The launch of UMTS in the next few years will allow this to happen and screen contents will then resemble those of today's PCs. So currently mobile services are rather interesting from the point of view of key niche applications and for the early adopters. You can gain your experience of mobile services now in order to be ready for the boom to be expected once UMTS is widely accepted.

Meta Group expects 100 million users of WAP phones in 2001; IDC expects that the value of mobile transactions in Western Europe will be more than 37 million Euros by 2004. The actual market penetration indicates that users are starting to be sensitive to the costs of communication and hardware: in the countries where WAP services are offered, the user-base after twelve months is usually around 2 per cent of all mobile users, while the much cheaper Japanese DoCoMo/i-mode service that can be used with all SMS capable phones has achieved six times the market penetration (12 per cent) in the same time! One important reason is that during the (sometimes long and tedious) time of punching in the i-mode message no telecom connection exists; thus this time is free of charge, while with a WAP phone the meter keeps running.

But no matter, if you plan to use SMS or WAP technologies, the user numbers will soon outnumber those of PC-based Internet. Already in 1999 25 million Europeans were sending and receiving SMS messages.* With one exception, all countries checked by the European Information Technology Observatory (*www.eito.com*) showed in the year 2000 a higher number of people able to be reached via mobile phone (and SMS) than by PC: Italy with 58 per cent mobile penetration, Japan with 46 per cent, US (the exception due to high PC penetration) with 36 per cent and the main European countries with 32 to 37 per cent of the population mobile phone users. Ericsson estimates that in the second half of 2002 the

* Source: IDC/Computer Zeitung 34/2000.

global number of mobile users will be larger than the PC-based Internet — by that time one billion users or one sixth of the globe's population will be online!

With the current SMS or WAP implementations, the service provided by mobile phones has to be focused or condensed on the core of the value proposition, as not much space is available on the tiny 'screens'. The upside of such interactions is that they have a very high visibility for the customer. If you implement your service right, you can create some kind of loyalty — as long as you provide the information customers need for performing transactions at their fingertips (and at a reasonable cost), they have no reason to change their provider. Actually, the good news is that 'surfing' the Web is so inconvenient on a WAP phone, that people would rather use their 'favourite' page with their favourite services where all the relevant providers are summarised (see example in the next section). So you do have the opportunity to build up a client base of frequent users.

In addition to condensing your current mobile service, you can also offer specific services for people on the move by exploiting a particular feature of mobile phones: customer location can be exactly identified. This is useful for all types of travelling and traveller support: traffic routing, restaurant/hotel recommendations, plane/train reservations, tracking down the person you are supposed to meet in a foreign environment, dating. Most of these transactions can earn you a commission from the referred partner company — and you can make sure that payment (with its related fees) is made by you.

What services are currently available? Let me give you a summary:

❑ e-mail service/SMS, downloading special ringing signals and logos;

❑ news and weather;

❑ mobile banking: funds transfer, balance check, stock transactions;

❑ credit card bill enquiry and recharging mobile phone payment card;

❑ ticket service: sports, music, show (including payment via mobile phone);

❑ travel: air transport, train reservation, taxi request;

❑ dining guide and reservation;

❏ book and CD sales;

❏ directory services;

❏ dictionaries;

❏ classified ads: for example, jobs, real estate;

❏ entertainment: games, horoscopes, recipes, downloading music;

❏ photo transmission (from digitised cameras).

This list (compiled from DoCoMo's current services in Japan and some European services) should give you an indication of what is available in the marketplace, but by its nature it cannot be complete. So add to this list by looking at what fits your value proposition best – and by checking what your competitors are doing.

The mobile e-business market is currently dominated by telecom operators, as they own the link between the customer and the content providers. Vodafone/Vivendi, one of the international telecom conglomerates, for example, implement their WAP service and use their brand 'VIZZAVI' throughout user-countries as a standard portal for their mobile Internet users. They expect 70 million users in the near future. The best strategy for you to adopt is partnership with one of the telecom operators – the larger the better.

Partnership is actually the biggest issue for such a mobile service. Due to restrictions in communication and display, and the time necessary to navigate to specific services, the consumers will turn away disappointed if your services are too incomplete (for example, connected to hotels only in the biggest cities). This is the greatest risk for acceptance of mobile services – so the co-operation of big partners is advisable such as telecom operators + banks + travel agencies. These services then need to be integrated into some well-defined packages – and the appropriately localised and personalised selection must be presented to customers without forcing them to enter too many parameters while they are on the move.

7.6 Mobile portals

Once marketing messages and specific product services for mobile customers have been defined, portals have to be set up. In addition to the considerations discussed, you need to restrict navigation to very few mouse clicks.

Some examples can be found on the WAP. A good one is that of the *Financial Times* (*wap.ft.com*) – not only have they a good short name to enter easily on the tiny mobile phone keypad, but also their service is useful for the professional on the road (recent articles, an archive, the 'market pulse' with alerts and quotes for example) and the navigation is good to use. Other examples show good ideas – see the cash flow calculator of *wap.dit.de* (a fund investment company). Localised service examples for travel and entertainment can be seen at *www.geodiscovery.com* and an airline check-in at *wap. lufthansa.com*. In many of the WAP sites, the implementation is not robust enough in all operational environments – the 'Internal server error' message is still to be seen too frequently. Some have cumbersome entry forms, which is currently the weakest area of all mobile portals. And access to the WAP services is often restricted to the home country of the customer, because roaming agreements do not yet incorporate WAP services. So start early gaining experience of the set-up of mobile portals.

In order to optimise navigation, you have to pre-define a variety of parameters, customer favourites in particular. There are favourites at different times during the interaction: overall, there are favourite providers, for example, the telecom operator, the stockbroker, the travel agency, the credit card company, the employer's intranet, the preferred book seller. This profile is better maintained by the customer, and the telecom operator should provide for this maintenance.

Then, for each of the related content providers, the specific favourites need to be shown, for example a stockbroker will immediately display the overall portfolio value plus the current buy and sell recommendations according to the customer's strategy as defined in his or her profile.* For an example of how such a dialogue looks, please refer to Figure 19, which shows a WAP implementation (on a relatively large Nokia screen).

For those customers who do not currently include you in their favourites list, you may want to rethink your website URL. Long names are good for the PC-based Internet user, but mobile phones

---

* Please note that profiles have two parts – one is the area the customer maintains by selecting his or her favourites, the other area reflects the strategies you define for each selection. Customer access has to be protected with passwords agreed between the customer and you, the update of strategies will be a combination of workflow adjustments that your system administrators will perform together with specific activities from call-centre staff.

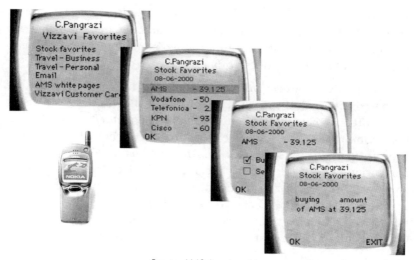

Source: AMS American Management Systems, Prototype Studio

Figure 19   WAP navigation example

with their cumbersome entry requiring multiple hits of each number key to create letters, are better suited to abbreviations of your name, that can be keyed in more quickly.

For a complete design of customer interactions, you have to consider the use of the various channels and how the customers may want to mix this use. You have to ensure that the services are accessible via the full range of virtual channels: PC-based Internet, WAP and of course via phone and the call centre. Practitioners have a good view of pragmatic approaches:

> The phone might be regarded as a good device to quick balance checks, basic transaction requests and as a messaging service, whilst the PC morphs into a channel for more considered purchasing of products, account reconciliation and window-shopping.

Source: *CRM as Strategy*, PeopleSoft Whitepaper, 2000

But there are more mobile portals to consider. Look at the car industry. They have started to equip cars with broadband communication. The 'basics' include a navigation system with online warning of traffic jams and help with orienting yourself in a foreign city, emergency systems that will make an SOS call when the sensors recognise that you have had an accident and additional features allowing you to be connected with the Internet or intranet, and enabling travelling employees (such as sales staff) to look at client profiles, exchange the latest contact updates and contract amendments or even participate in video conferences from the car, which thus becomes a rolling office.

And finally, whatever you implement, test to see if it works. For PC-based interactions, it is sufficient to test the various versions of Microsoft Internet Explorer and Netscape Navigator/Communicator. For mobile Internet, you also need to check how you can use shorter words and sentences on the screens in order to avoid truncations or long scrolling. For special devices (such as built-in hardware into the car), additional tests have to be performed. In addition to this basic check, you should also measure how long it takes to complete the transactions on the various channels. Continue to optimise, that is, reduce the time needed!

7.7 The impact of UMTS

UMTS is now licensed in most European countries. The launch of the first consumer services is expected in the different countries between the years 2002 and 2004. For the consumer market, services can be envisioned as the combination of the current PC-based Internet with localised mobile services. Assuming that the cost of the services will be significantly higher than today's PC and mobile Web services, due to the high costs for the licences and for the technical infrastructure, UMTS will not replace SMS and WAP, but will be just another way to present information. SMS and WAP will be maintained as low-cost alternatives, so UMTS will be the third mobile delivery channel you have to think about.

What applications can be expected for UMTS? We will probably see more and more-high value services, such as stockbroker transactions with intensive support with analyses of data such as stock charts and performance evaluations, and the opportunity to have a video conference with the stockbroker. UMTS may lead to individual weather forecasts with an online simulation of the weather situation at particular places for a selected time of the day, again with the opportunity to talk to the weatherman or weatherwoman. Important, pre-selected news updates can be delivered on demand, when the customer (a business customer in rush, in this case) has some time available, like in a taxi or in a train. Maybe a mail order company will provide a high-profile catalogue and allow for shopping (and delivery to any place) when the customer is on the road and runs out of clean clothes.

Currently, the goals for the UMTS consumer market are still vague, but several business applications are already in preparation. These are primarily intranet applications, such as systems to allow company field staff full access to internal databases, data entry forms and workflow tools. So, travelling employees can be fully integrated into the internal procedures. For example, calendar entries can be updated while the service person is with the customer, and he or she can immediately be directed to the next urgent customer needing support. Another business application is the remote control of machines with high bandwidth need, for example, when pictures from a camera need to be transferred to the person remotely controlling the machine, or when huge volumes of telemetric data are to be transmitted.

The cost of UMTS licences and infrastructure will force providers to co-operate even further. And the payment models for value-added services may lead to interesting revenue splits between the different active partners, such as the weather studio, the video provider, the telco provider transmitting the information and the bank ensuring the secure online payment. For these payment models, some early implementations can be seen in the Anglo-Saxon countries, namely online bill presentment combined with bill and payment consolidation, see Section 1.2.

7.8 Summary

My recommendations for the set-up of your portal:

❑ create a good image for your online brand and create sub-brands for different target markets;

❑ organise customer communities within each market segment;

❑ tailor the website contents and design to each customer segment;

❑ provide entertaining navigation and interaction options appropriate for the targeted customer segments;

❑ use the first mover advantages for mobile commerce services;

❑ distinguish contents and design by user device (such as PC, mobile phone, UMTS equipment, TV set);

❑ complement the specific strengths of the channels to achieve a full service coverage: an online presence for browsing, submitting orders and defining the customer preference profile, a call centre for service requests too complex to handle oneself, and a mobile service for the quick transaction to be done when 'on the road'.

8

Empower your employees for pro-active customer service

@@@ Guide your staff to draw the right conclusions for the different customer situations and to take the action responding to the customer need that is most appropriate for the customer and your enterprise. @@@ Set rules that accommodate the different experience of your staff and empower them to exploit their potential. @@@

People make the difference – even in the Internet world. As customers do not want to feel like robots in cyberworld, they appreciate every opportunity to interact through a 'virtual' interface with real people. The better you are organised to deliver a smile on the phone and a smile on the Web, the easier you can defend your customer relationships against attacks from your competitors.

Based on the analysis we have discussed, you should implement customer strategy approaches throughout the customer touch points that allow your staff to deliver the most appropriate service. Rules and competencies have to be set centrally, dependent on the performance track record of the particular staff; the local execution should be made flexible in order to maximise the human interaction and creativity of the people involved.

8.1 Customer relationships

If you do not want to let your service or goods erode into a commodity that could be challenged by any other provider, you need to work against the trend of fragmenting all services into single components. Actually, many of the services that created a large part of the Western countries' wealth are very close to becoming a commodity. Most traditional products in the business-to-business market such as steel, cars, office supplies, transportation, communication are put out on online bidding processes in 'electronic marketplaces' to force suppliers to cut prices (look at the car supply marketplace *www.covisint.com*). Consumers start to get used to auctions and reverse auctions, where they can put out a similar bid to companies that accept that customers, not themselves, define prices – as for airline 'last minute' tickets (for example, *www.flights.com*, formerly *www.tiss.com*), for hotel reservations, for TV sets or hi-fi equipment (for example, *www.letsbuyit.com*). Also, service markets are under pressure. As examples: interest rates for loans can be easily compared on the Web, or telephone charges are transparent and the cheapest provider can be selected on each occasion, by using call-by-call.

How can you get out of this situation? Well, there is a bit of hope. First, you can augment what you offer, in particular by adding services to your 'standard' products. Next, you can keep your customers happy enough to prevent them from shopping around. Most people do not like to continuously analyse the market, anyway, because it takes energy to go through intense price comparisons again and again, and check if the providers offer good quality over and over again. Moreover, each new decision is a moment of uncertainty, because you do not know if the new vendor is worth your trust. Therefore people change their standard provider only occasionally. They read the same newspaper every day, because they are used to it. They use the same telecom provider (or maybe group of providers). And they do not usually change their bank account.

So, why bother? Even if your existing customers are loyal to you, you need to win new customers to prevent erosion of your market share. And there are situations (in traditional customer relationships) when customers do change their provider, namely:

❏ when they are frustrated about lack of support;

❏ when their community or opinion makers change as well;

❏ when they go through a major personal change (such as moving house, marriage, birth of a child);

❏ when price differences are very significant and they have a similar amount of trust in another provider as they have in you.

Additionally, on the Web, visitors are still curious to experiment with the various providers; therefore, loyalty on the web does not exist (yet). All the new services challenge initial relationships and familiarities, so Web visitors still like to check if the grass is greener at the other site of the Web.

In the case of such situations that might trigger the customer to stop buying from you, do not let them pass without notice! Look at complaint letters, ask your call-centre staff about customer frustrations, monitor when the customer requests an address change. Prevent the customer pro-actively from terminating his or her custom. Additionally, use such situations to encourage prospective customers to leave your competitor and use your services instead. Each of these situations is too complex to leave customers alone with it, or to let them get rid of their frustration via 'self-service'. That just does not work. They need a human person they can complain to, or someone they can trust, with whom to discuss the impact of the changes in their private life on their 'suppliers', and they need to get an empathically listening ear plus possibly some guidance. Only then business as usual can continue – or new business can be closed. So, the staff in your call centre have the challenging task of convincing these customers to stay with you, and they need to get the support from the systems you implement that indicate what might be an attractive approach or offer for the customer in the specific situation.

8.2 Teams and skills

To be pro-active, you have to guide your staff through values and culture as well as with examples of how customer experience should be. Take an example from the retailers Wal-Mart or McDonalds. These enterprises:

❏ post their values and service level commitments at places where the customers and the staff see them regularly (doors, cashiers, toilets);

❏ provide instruction in corporate values in briefing sessions, trainings and role-play for all staff;

❏ communicate a clear expression of corporate identity: the

environment 'look and feel', colours of the premises, the dress-code for the employees;*

❑ have clear rules for employee behaviour and enforce rules through incentives and penalties. Incentives include money and recognition (for example, employee of the month, inclusion in highly visible task forces); penalties can be as forceful as termination of contract.

To increase a team's speed of operation, you have to assess how the current staff would support new ideas and how they can deal with additional features the new front-office systems you are about to implement provide. Unfortunately, many big enterprises are burdened with an inherited attitude of slowness. The older staff do not accept the need for change, because they have always done business as they do now. And the younger staff members with a high energy potential are demotivated, because their effectiveness is stifled if procedures kill creativity. So this is an issue to be addressed as a priority.

So check what it is that you would most dislike your competitor to know. Once you have identified this area, you can start protecting that point of vulnerability. Where are the areas where you could not continue your business, if an employee or a group of people should leave? That is another area for taking priority action. Then, once these defence issues are covered, get started on pursuing new opportunities – in particular to revive the initial pioneer spirit.

Re-establish the pioneer spirit – your new 'A' teams

Do you still remember the days when your company was founded and everybody was full of energy and enthusiasm? Now you have experience of many years in business. Combine this experience with the pioneer spirit and form the new winning teams. Let me underline some key characteristics of such winning teams:

❑ clear and unambiguous *goals* are established and understood by all team members;

❑ everybody works together in a positive *co-operative* spirit;

❑ the priority is on *getting the job done* – not on cliques, intrigues or hierarchy considerations or jealousies;

---

* Psychologists even recommend having the call-centre staff show up in business attire. They behave less casually than if hanging around in jeans and sneakers.

❏ the team shares an openness for *constructive criticism*;

❏ *change is readily accepted* and 'routines' are few; new situations are not seen as a threat, but as opportunities to excel;

❏ high awareness of risks that might endanger attaining goals, *risks are early identified* and mitigation activities quickly executed;

❏ everybody feels the *entrepreneurial* attitude.

A good vision, is it not? So, how do you get there pragmatically from your existing organisational legacy? How can you a) leverage and b) improve your biggest asset, your employees? Give your teams and individuals incentives to contribute to the achievement of your targets through financial and non-financial benefits, such as more competencies, additional learning opportunities and more decision power – in other words, implement a meritocracy.

Meritocracy based on A/B/C analysis

First of all, keep in mind that your staff are an asset that no competitor can copy – he only could 'steal' it from you by hiring them out of your enterprise. Well, of course you need to do all the homework for defining a less hierarchical organisation with small, but concise target definitions for the incentive compensations that are about to replace job descriptions. But more importantly, you need to look at your people. As for your customers, do an A/B/C analysis regarding your teams using the key factors you want to assess – take the areas reflected in the balanced scorecard already discussed as an example: ability to maintain customer loyalty, service quality and responsiveness, and the will and the ability to learn and adapt. The A performers are those people who have managed to provide an excellent and pro-active service to the customer while maintaining a good financial contribution for your company. Here are the stars or champions you should encourage to work closely together to make the changes happen. Now let us not fall into the trap of promoting them to be the new managers – do you not want to keep your organisation non-hierarchical? Instead, include A performers in task forces to work on improving customer experience, creating new innovative products and services, or fine-tuning the operational processes. Additionally, A performers should support the other staff with their everyday decisions, for example, by being the point of contact for resolving some difficult client issues.

The B performers are the solid workers – you should identify training activities that can help them to become more effective. In many cases, a clearer guidance (by the target definition process and by regularly communicated goals) will give them the focus they need to generate a good contribution. And for C performers, you may still have some routine tasks they can complete to your and your customers' satisfaction. Only you should not overpay them! Between the various contribution ranks, both the fixed salary and incentive payments should be significantly different – with incentive making up a bigger fraction of overall remuneration for the A rank than for the C rank, but everybody should be part of the incentive scheme in order to refocus on the company's goals. For an example, refer to Section 9.1 where we describe how a big bank translated this A/B/C analysis into green/yellow/red ranks regarding the credit handling quality of their various teams.

The initial A/B/C analysis can then be refined into staff profiles where contribution generated, knowledge acquired, together with the customer network, can be reflected and used for setting thresholds for employee empowerment, such as the authorisation to approve transactions, to grant discounts or to change delivery priorities.

Organise small flexible teams and make their experience grow

Your teams should also get the room and time for informal exchanges of the experience they jointly acquire and to help them improve over time. In the beginning, such meetings may require the help of a professional facilitator, but soon the team will appreciate the importance of its own creative ideas. You should build small teams and measure their respective contributions. Soon you will realise that performance is different – then you can combine an informal internal knowledge transfer, for example, by staff rotation between the units, with formal guidance from a central, more experienced team that the less experienced customer service staff can call upon in case of doubt. Identifying when there are such 'cases of doubt' is an ideal application for decision support and knowledge management systems. The data of customer interactions can be screened for behavioural information, for example:

❏ from your Web applications: the frequency of using your website, preferred contents, past buying decisions;

❏ from external data providers: the buying power of the customer's regional environment, blacklists on payment defaults;

❏ from CRM applications: the frequency and reasons of contact, the number of complaints, the recommended treatment strategy for this type of customer;

❏ from your legacy applications: financial contribution of customer, applicable price and discount schemes, his or her most recent transactions.

These data are then condensed in the data warehouse and are summarised as assigned customer segments with related profile information. For each segment, the treatment strategy indicates what should be done when certain trigger events happen. Trigger events might be the desire to extend an expiring agreement, the demand for a discount, a complaint, or a change in customer situation such as a move. So, the customer service staff should present the customer with an appropriate pre-defined proposal and configure it according to customer needs. For most of these proposals, all the necessary checks should have been done in the background before discussing with the customer – it would look odd if the customer service staff offered some credit facility and in the end the credit check prohibited any more loans.

Figure 20 summarises the information to be compiled into a central warehouse from which decisions can be derived. This compilation of data then needs to be analysed in order to apply the right treatment strategy for each customer situation. We will discuss this in detail in the next chapter – and the raw data will be complemented by the results obtained from the warehouse and decision support system.

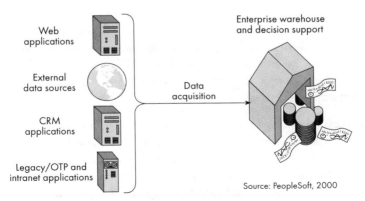

Figure 20   Automated knowledge management and decision support

8.3 Human resources management

The management of human resources needs also to focus on the consequences of e-business velocity. Staff development from a quality and quantity perspective, as well as hiring versus subcontracting options (or insourcing versus outsourcing) in a bigger context, needs to be revisited. Salary and incentive systems need to be adjusted as well. It may be necessary to hire a 'guru' for specific areas in order to get a head start in a new business field and to coach the team in getting up to speed, too. This guru might get a salary inconsistent with existing remuneration structures, and the human resources (HR) section should define new guidelines on maintaining fair treatment.

Industry best practices show how the maturity of a company for HR management can emerge. Here are the evolutionary layers:

Transact: with current ERP technology, reporting is limited to historical transactional data, which supports the tactical aspect of the human resources function. These systems are designed to provide efficient transactional processing and statutory compliance. Transactional systems, however, are less capable of measuring organisational effectiveness. Some efficiency is lost because analytical reporting from transactional systems is cumbersome and impinges on system resources.

Measure: measuring the performance of the human resources function is similar to measuring the performance of the organisation. There are methodologies that can assess the human resources function but the availability of tools to aggregate data around these methodologies is limited. An application that can link key performance indicators to an enterprise, at departmental and individual level, is necessary to further assess the effectiveness of the organisation in meeting stated business objectives. Not only should a tool be able to assess an individual critical success factor, but it should also be able to illustrate the cause and effect relationship of one measure upon another.

Analyse: today, financial, human resources and external information rarely reside in one transactional system. As a result, the human resources department often requires full-time employees dedicated to manually extracting data from these multiple sources of transactional data. Data warehousing helps provide a central repository of human resources, and financial and external data for more comprehensive reporting. The Internet can also be used to streamline the distribution of these reports, thus increasing the efficiency of communication. Multi-dimensional reporting tools over the Internet or intranet allow real-time 'slicing and dicing' of information to provide line managers with the insights necessary for effective strategic decision-making. After gaining a complete historical view and analysing future scenarios, the human resources executive can better make decisions to enhance organisational performance. Additionally, he or she will have more accurate intelligence about the workforce to provide the organisation's executive management committee.

Plan: typically, when human resources departments address future business plans, they do so manually through spreadsheets, sacrificing both flexibility and timelines. For more robust planning, human resources analysts need to use corporate-wide data to simulate user-defined scenarios. This approach can provide a more comprehensive projection of the impact of strategic decisions. By streamlining the typical manual process, organisations can also react more quickly to marketplace and labour relations' changes.

Source: *PeopleSoft Workforce Analytics*, White Paper, July 2000

Those new approaches need to be implemented stepwise in order to improve your current balance of staff costs versus skill level.

8.4 Knowledge management

Let us briefly discuss here how you can use Internet technology for accumulating and leveraging your experience. Good knowledge management requires organisational set-up plus personal interactions, in particular:

❏ Knowledge centres: one or several employees compile repositories of experience gained on specific subjects, for example, on campaign responsiveness, telephone marketing, complaint management, customer behaviour models, partnership and alliance handling, or the various aspects of front-office system development. They should distil currently best experience and make the information available to everybody in your organisation who needs it.

❏ Internal conferences: occasional or regular events where key experiences are presented. During such conferences, the measured service levels should also be presented and ideas on how to improve further can be discussed.

❑ Learning resources: you should make the latest books and research available to your staff in order to help them extend their knowledge. Additionally, concrete problems someone in your organisation has been confronted with, should be presented. Actual case studies of, for example, how people dealt differently with customer complaints (with the actual audio tape of the conversation) and what the results were, are often more informative than abstract explanations.

The main topic for knowledge management is communication. Communication and personal interaction do not need to be face to face. Instead, you can use electronic media. To get in touch with knowledge centre representatives or contact individuals, you should have at least voice mail and e-mail systems in place that your staff can use for tapping into knowledge centres – and of course you need to tell them which centres exist and who the contact people are. An even better tool is to establish an intranet where the best practice examples are stored and can be individually accessed by your staff. The more diffuse your organisation is, and particularly if people cannot go to a central physical library with all the best practice materials, the more you need such a virtual learning environment.

You should also implement discussion forums on specific subjects. In a forum, people can post their questions and describe their experience and get advice from more experienced colleagues. Each knowledge centre can have its own forum where all the little things that compose the corporate knowledge can be stored. They can be used for topics and issues that have just recently appeared, for example, a change in your pricing strategy. You can announce the visit of an expert on the subject who will respond to questions from some of your staff – and the questions and answers can be viewed by your whole staff. The big advantage over a get-together conference or over a video conference is not only that it is cheaper, but also that the discussion is documented. So, people who were not able to attend in person can check the areas they are interested in later; moreover, people do not waste their time, because they can just select those subjects about which they wish to know.

Some companies have started telelearning, too. There are two parts to it: computer based training (CBT) and tele-teaching. CBT is very useful for formal training, such as for call-centre staff learning their new scripts, and it does not require lots of effort to prepare

CBT materials. Tele-teaching on the other hand is still in its infancy. The significant point is that a teacher is available remotely and that the teaching is organised as in a classroom. There are online lectures (by audio or video for providing information) and discussions or audio conferences. Homework and case studies have to be done remotely, the results are sent to the teacher and he or she checks the results and returns comments and corrections. This requires a bigger commitment to staff development, the organisation of curriculum and career patterns and the set-up of an internal school or university with the appropriate faculty members.

8.5   Service levels and processes

As you aim to accelerate the speed of your services appropriate to e-business, you need to define those service levels up front – and you need to measure them, as the traditional statement 'You don't get what you don't measure' still holds true in the Web world. Such service levels should monitor the customer transaction end to end, for example, by asking, 'how long does it take for a customer to find your service on the Web, select and configure it and to receive it?' or 'how long does it take to respond to a complaint in a way that the customer is satisfied again?'

As you can imagine, such complex questions have to be broken down into the various steps appropriate to your organisation and systems environment to actually handle the interaction. For each of the steps, you then can define the level of service you are targeting. This could include the following targets:

❏ order entry is possible with just three mouse clicks;

❏ 80 per cent of credit applications will be decided within thirty seconds;

❏ a confirmation on a transaction will be sent back within two minutes;

❏ gold-card members will reach a member of the call-centre staff within ten seconds, 90 per cent of the other customers will get through within one minute;

❏ complaints are handled within twenty-four hours;

❏ marketing campaigns hit at least a 10 per cent response rate;

❏ launches of new products can be done within seven days.

Service level achievement has to be included in your regular reporting and it should also be reflected in the balanced scorecard approach.

You probably do have most of the steps for processes already in place and the service level definitions will help you to get an integrated perspective of end-to-end interactions. Ideally, this should be expressed in workflows that describe cross-departmental co-operations – a workflow tool can even support your measurement initiative, because for each transaction it stores the information concerning when and by who the transaction was initiated, how long it was waiting in a queue and when it was finally completed.

There is one more thing to change in your traditional organisation. You should implement the correct responsibility cycles that allow you to learn from experience and to fine-tune the achievement of the service levels. Existing departmental boundaries and hierarchy levels should not be driving (or constraining) the handling of a transaction, but collective knowledge should be used to process customer interaction as quickly and in as friendly a manner as possible. Let us take a closer look at this.

Your people have to be challenged and supported to improve performance permanently. Each of their activities has to be part of a feedback loop, that is they should be structured in such a way that at the end of a transaction your staff and your organisation have learned something for the next transaction. For this continuous improvement let us take a look at the various responsibility cycles

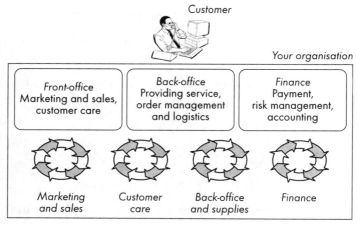

Figure 21   Responsibility cycles

as they emerge for sales and marketing, customer care, back-office operations and finance.

Compared with your traditional organisation, there is more emphasis now on customer-oriented processes. And the customer-oriented units in your organisation have to ensure that the processes are completed quickly. To initiate change in your organisation, if it would require too much energy to change reporting lines and career aspirations, it is often just easier and more pragmatic to overlay the existing static organisation with the appropriate process cycles. Let us discuss the activities within each of the responsibility cycles now.

8.6 Marketing and sales

Marketing has to raise awareness, inform prospective customers of goods and services and get them interested. Sales, on the other hand, has to identify those prospective customers that are ready to buy, and to actually make them buy.

As the marketing campaigns eat up a lot of money – consider TV advertisements or paper mailings – campaigns should be as concise as possible, that is, as much focused on the target segments as possible. The purpose of such campaigns may be to cross-sell additional services to your customers or to prevent them from terminating their purchases with you and shopping with the competitor instead. It may be to push them into an additional usage of such of your products or services they have already been using or to refer you to relatives and friends.

The campaigns have to be clearly defined:

❏ targeted customers or prospective customers;

❏ the messages to put across;

❏ the channels to use for the various targets (for example, e-mail, SMS, personalised web-site, mailing, call from sales force);

❏ expected outcome.

At each of the interaction steps, the results should be closely monitored. You may find out that some of the customers like to make a verbal order, but do not return the written contract. Check if they do not like the hassle of paper mail – then you may look for electronic delivery of the order forms. Or did they just forget to return it? In that case, a reminder might be the right approach. Moreover, you should monitor the responses of the customers to your different types of services and analyse customer behaviour probabilities and segments. Once you can identify what characterises a customer who is about to make a referral rather than buying again versus a customer who will never recommend you, but is loyal in buying more and more from you, you can save a lot of unnecessary mails and e-mails.

Key measurements for the feedback loop are the response and closure rates.

Customer care

Customer care is the second client-oriented area. They are in charge of providing the human touch at the customer touch points. Customer care is handled separately from marketing and sales because those people who 'hunt' for new customers have a different attitude from those who have a deep understanding of an ongoing customer relationship, care for the customer's concerns and give him or her advice. Additionally, interaction cycles with the market are different before and after closure of a transaction: before closure, every activity is focused on getting the deal, that is, contact increases in frequency until closure, while after sales occasional contact is appropriate, even if no particular events have happened. Thirdly, you can outsource marketing/sales independently from customer care to different third-party call centres. However, you need to maintain overall control and you need to get detailed data on customer responsiveness in order to implement the behaviour modelling and measurement programme and improve on a one-to-one marketing capability as discussed in Chapter 4.

But there are also many reasons why customer care should not be split from sales and marketing. First, it is the trend to try to achieve customer loyalty. If you want your customer to be loyal and to contribute a high profitability, you need to treat him or her nicely unless you want a competitor to pull him or her away. So, efficient customer care, well-organised support and anticipation of customer needs will support this sensitive approach to the customer. Customer care representatives are actually closing deals with customers in this scenario. Another reason in favour of joining the two units is synergy: the same information about services and about customers is needed in both groups, both units have to sell and the tools they use to do their activities are the same.

Here is my advice. For those customers who purchase your products and services like a commodity a forceful sales approach is appropriate with massive marketing efforts and ongoing contacts initiated by you – these interactions can be outsourced to a third party. For the high value and loyal customers you have to maintain an empathy and an environment where they can call you and you fully support them – this should be done by your own staff. You may even need two separate brands for commodity sales versus high-value sales with separate delivery channels, not to risk a high-value customer being put off by the sleaziness of your salesmen.

Key measurements for the feedback loop are interaction durations, complaint closure rate and speed, customer retention and cross-selling ratios.

Back-office operations

In your back-office you have the biggest remainders of your traditional production. There are some key differences between e-businesses and traditional businesses, though. The brick and mortar side of your enterprise will get smaller over time and often a large part of your production facilities will be outsourced to third parties. Instead, you should focus on creating new services, that is, focus on knowledge-heavy products and services rather than on heavy-materials products. A good part of the 'production' will be covered by information systems or by teams co-operating across organisational and regional boundaries and even working together across different companies – just as the computer 'manufacturer' Cisco is managing its suppliers rather than running its own production. You should be permanently challenging approaches and inviting ongoing improvements. Those improvements have to be implemented within weeks or a few months (rather than years in the traditional brick and mortar business).

The key measurement for the feedback loop is speed of innovations.

Human resources

The key point is that development plans and incentive systems are in line with the service level target that you are working to achieve.

Key measurements for the feedback loop are staff experience levels (for example, expressed in the A/B/C categories).

Finance

Let me make a few comments on what additional aspects have to be covered in a company running at e-speed.

Budgets and accounting: on top of financial planning, you have to monitor the achievement of your balanced scorecard targets. Make sure that these can be reflected in your system and are monitored regularly. Also make sure that trends can be easily and flexibly shown.

Payable items: in your e-nitiative you will have more business partners than in normal business. And you may be allowed to offset payable items with receivable items when you have partnerships which include mutual business exchanges. Make sure to cover all partnerships with your payment approaches.

Receivable items: you should avoid creating hurdles for your customers by not providing the 'right' payment method. Credit card payment via SET (secure electronic transaction, see Figure 22) is the most common form of payment, but not all consumers like it. At least for those customers other payment possibilities need to be foreseen, bank transfer for example (for customers with solid credit worthiness).

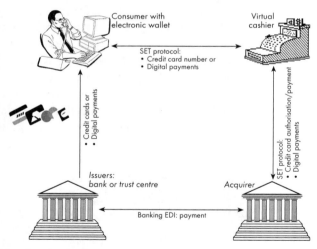

Figure 22   Credit card payment via SET

An additional option for online and mobile business will be that the customers send you digital money. This would be handled in a very similar way to credit card transactions (only instead of the credit card number, the customer would send you a digital payment), but the banking and trust centre infrastructure necessary to support digital cash is not fully implemented yet.

Risk management: if everybody paid by credit card and you always requested an authorisation from the credit card processor, then no additional risk management would be necessary. Usually, though, you also offer other means of payment, because either your customers do not like credit card transactions or because you want to avoid credit card processing fees. Therefore you need to check which of your customers is good for deferred payments and you need to enforce the collection of all receivable items that were not paid on time.

Practically, the people responsible for risk management will also deal with credit card authorisations and the definition of credit policies, that is, who can get goods on a credit basis.

Implementation of process architecture

For further details of this process architecture and cross-departmental co-operations, please refer to my book *Success @ e-business* or to my website *www.success-at-e-business.com*. The key areas to cover are:

Marketing and sales:	Product management
	Segmentation
	Treatment strategy management
	Results review
Customer care:	Client feedback
	Customer relationship management
	Suggestions/improvements
Back-office operations:	Order management
	Supplies
	Packaging and delivery
	Enterprise resource planning

Let me highlight again the need to measure your success. I mentioned that feedback based on measurements has to be used for building up know-how. In the Figure 23 we see response rates from a marketing campaign. If you compare campaigns, you should ask questions leading to additional knowledge, for example 'which of the attributes used for qualifying leads has a strong correlation with an actual response/purchase?' With those findings, you can run your next campaign in an even more targeted way.

Measuring and comparing your results is the only way for you to drive your enterprise to higher and higher performance levels, to

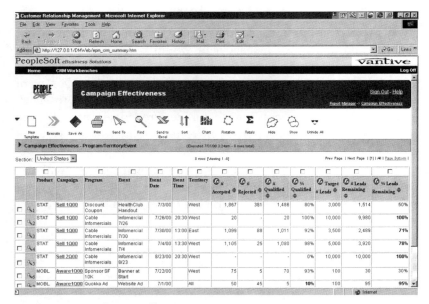

Figure 23   Marketing effectiveness measurement

check fulfilment of the commitments of your various departments –
and the only way you can inform your customers about your service
level achievement.

Front-office components supporting successful customer interactions

Pro-active customer service will require you to implement quite a
few systems in your organisation that allow the customer to visit
your service, provide various interaction channels and allow call-
centre staff access to the profiles and treatment strategies. Figure 24
is focused on the front-office components necessary for customer
interaction. The components presented are relevant for all sizes of
companies; the sophistication of particular components will be
different, though, depending on the size and focus of a company.

Let us go through the components from the outside in, starting at
the top left.

Customer access via Internet portals: we have discussed this in
the last chapter. Let me add here the recommendation of a single
sign-on. This means that the customer can identify himself or herself
only once, no matter which particular application he or she wants to
use, so a sequence of several log-ins can be avoided.

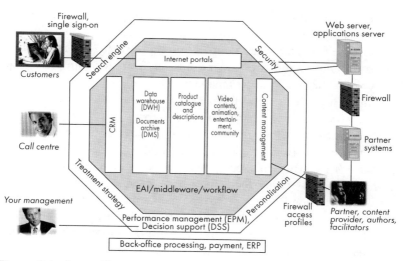

Figure 24 Front-office components

Firewalls: the different types of applications need to be shielded from each other by a firewall. The outer firewall, that is, the one closest to the customer, has to ensure that Web users only access those areas of your website they are entitled to. No hacker should be able to change the website contents you have reserved for maintenance by your staff. And nobody must be able to overwrite customer transaction data or to read confidential, personalised information. Additionally, firewalls are necessary at all places where external people or companies have access to your IT environment, such as your marketing agency, content providers, external consultants or authors for your website contents.

Search engine and security: in addition to using the navigation options you have provided on your website such as selection options or links, you should provide a search facility that allows the customer to request certain information or services directly and in his or her own words. Setting up this search function requires anticipating the customers' terminology in order to link their requests to specific services. Again, you should organise the search so that it is a learning process. Enquiries that cannot be linked to one of your services should be logged in order to add terms subsequently to the dictionary and to provide the necessary link to your website contents. In a smart implementation, you may even be able to dynamically reconfigure search engine contents depending on the customer profile – if you do not want to show the customer your discount schemes for example, you can disable that selection in the search engine and prevent him or her from accessing the page with your security and access management tool.

Security includes several features. We have already discussed the firewall. Additionally, encryption may be appropriate for some or all data transmissions, for the execution of payments for example. Products for SSL (secure socket layer) and SET (secure electronic transaction) covering the secure transmission of data are available off the shelf. So let us focus here on authentication and access restrictions. Depending on security needs, one or several different identification options can be used. The most convenient (but least secure) is to place a cookie on the PC or on the mobile phone of the customer. This cookie contains the customer specific data such as account number or payment preferences. However, everybody with access to the PC or mobile phone can execute transactions on behalf of the customer. A more secure, but less convenient approach is to have the customer define a user-id and password. As such data can be intercepted and fraudulent activities can take place, you can add TANs (transaction identification numbers). Those are generated in your computer centre, sent to the customer by certified mail and have to be used for executing transactions or even for viewing customer-specific data. Even more secure, but most expensive, is to protect the customer-specific data with a smart card the customer has to swipe on his PC. The cost of this security approach is to equip the customer PC with the appropriate card reader.

Web server and application server: your website with the portal is stored in an environment physically and technically separate from your in-house systems. These servers handle transactions, provide security mechanisms (such as the aforementioned access control and encrypted data transmission). Thus, Web interactions do not have a direct impact on your in-house production systems. A good part of the applications is even available when your production systems have some down time, because the Web server provides preliminary storage of transactions until they can be further processed by production systems. Separating the Web server from your production systems also provides additional security to prevent hackers from interfering with your internal day-to-day operations. The Web server and application server can be run in your computer centre or they can be outsourced to an ISP (Internet service provider).

Call-centre support with a customer relationship management (CRM) component: your call-centre staff have to have access to more information than the online customers do. Stored contractual agreements, transaction histories and interaction logs including marketing activities or complaints, have to be available to provide an efficient service to customers. Therefore, the CRM system has to provide an integrated view of this information and it has to recommend how to deal with specific customer situations. These can be reflected in scripts the call-centre staff can follow or even read out to the customer.

Product catalogue/data warehouse/document management: the online product catalogue can be well supported by off-the-shelf solutions that allow the maintenance of your product descriptions and usually have built-in order handling functions such as the shopping cart as well as a range of payment methods.

The data warehouse has been addressed various times in the book – the key point is to store the customer segment and profile information and use them appropriately. In addition, history information of customer transactions has to be stored to allow the call-centre staff to retrieve the data should the customer have questions or complaints about some past transactions.

A document management system is probably already in place for archiving an electronic copy of key paper documents. You should make it accessible by the call centre to allow a search of contractual agreements, invoices and other significant mail from and to the customer.

Video contents/animation/entertainment/community: probably you are not used to seeing yourself in the entertainment industry. The fact is, though, that the Internet is the first medium that significantly eats into the daily television viewing time. So you are competing against a lot of entertainment. That is the reason why many serious providers add infotainment and entertainment. Serious contents should also be presented in an appealing format. Look at mass media communications like the Weather Channel, CNN or Bloomberg News – and at online auctions where entertainers encourage customers to make higher bids. A video can show customers how nice it would be to live in their own house, to get a loan for a yacht, to travel. And they can watch when their car is built in the factory at the other end of the globe. Think of similar examples for your industry; think how customer experience can be personalised; prepare some video clips; and allow your customers to enjoy your new relaxed attitude. We have already talked about animating your service – at the very least you should highlight your special offers by putting them on the top of the website and attracting customer attention with some special visual effects. Additionally, avatars should be used to guide the customer through your website – and website communities can entertain themselves by discussing topics on which they feel strongly.

Content management: the contents of your website have to be updated regularly. There will be different areas to be maintained and different people will be in charge of them. Let us go through some of the contents in the sequence of their update frequency.

Tickers for news or stock prices: you need to link with a content provider that automatically streams the new data on your Web server, that is, news agencies or financial information providers such as Bloomberg or Reuters.

Community news and forum maintenance: if you decide to establish customer communities, you should encourage them to discuss specific issues – and you need to have an eye on what people are contributing to the forums. Misleading, outdated or obscene contributions to the forum have to be deleted. Discussion groups should be opened, merged or closed depending on usage activities. This requires a forum facilitator checking messages daily. The facilitator should also seek to have your company culture portrayed in the contributions posted in the forum.

Press releases of your company: your corporate marketing group has to make them available simultaneously with the release through the traditional channels for an inclusion on the website.

Product and price updates: your product managers have to describe new features for the Web and a web designer should dress them up to attract customers' attention to the key characteristics.

Third-party and partner advertising: if you include banner advertising for some of your partners, they have to take care of updating it as needed.

Updates to the overall website: service extensions need to be planned in co-ordination with the back-office systems. Once the added services are tested, they can be included in the updated website.

Enterprise application integration (EAI)/middleware/workflow: we have already discussed this approach in the section 'Level three objectives' on page 95. Let me highlight here once again the important benefit of a workflow system. It can log all customer interactions, measure how long is needed for handling and escalate in the case of over-long waiting times. This is the most logical way to monitor the efficiency of your business processes.

Treatment strategy and personalisation: customers profiles should correspond with a high-level classification, such as VIP, member of the gold club, standard, termination risk, or high default risk. Depending on this classification, different service levels and treatment strategies should be configured. The treatment strategies include the type of services the customer is entitled to view; they identify applicable pricing schemes; and assign the appropriate marketing campaign. Some of those treatment strategies are relevant for self-service functions (such as pricing schemes); some will be used in the call centre (such as marketing offerings).

In addition to that, personalisation reflects customer preferences such as what customers purchased last time, their standing orders, relevant events such as birthdays or seasonal events that might interest them.

Enterprise performance management (EPM) and decision support (DSS): you and your management colleagues need to have an integrated view of your company's performance, that is, on the achievements of your goals with regard to all the defined measurements. EPM distinguishes itself from the classic ERP approach by reflecting not only financial performance (actual versus plan), but also process performance (such as achievement of service levels), customer satisfaction (such as customer retention and new acquisitions) and staff situation (for example, staff retention, skill development, new product pipeline). For measuring all these different dimensions, the EPM has to be neatly integrated with the various front-office and back-office systems.

To support day-to-day decisions, the analytical framework, customer profiles and the treatment strategies are handled by the decision support system. This system assesses customer history, classifies customers accordingly, selects and awaits the relevant triggers for initiating treatment and executes the treatment through customer-initiated Web interactions, through discussions with the call-centre staff or traditional mailing/e-mailing activities.

8.7 Summary: activities to initiate

Here is my list of key activities to initiate:

❏ establish hungry, powerful teams of entrepreneurial pioneers serving their customers;

❏ have the teams co-operate on customer-oriented processes instead of focusing on organisational units;

❏ help your teams to learn by using knowledge management and decision support systems.

Value-based business execution: apply the right treatment at the right time

@@@ Steer your enterprise better than on 'gut instinct' and reduce decision times by complementing instincts with quantitative analysis of customer behaviour. @@@ Support the day-to-day operational decisions with treatment strategies for customer behaviour profiles. @@@ Send convincing messages to interested customers at the time it triggers them to buy. @@@

You have to avoid running into the same problems as a bank before it decided to implement a CRM solution. They were

'offering loans to customers that hadn't paid their credit card bills. Alternatively, and more damagingly, a customer that had loyally avoided missing payments at the bank was rudely stung for one outstanding debt – and then only because they were on holiday.'

Reasons for that included that

'decision makers were left unsupported and had to rely more or less on intuition. Hard facts that at worst would prove their case, and at best could highlight significant new trends that had not been anticipated at all, played a minority part. Some executives' sense was right. Others was not. Today even for these decision makers with an excellent feeling for what is going on, the pace of change and complexity of change inevitably increases the chances that they will make errors. ... Traditional executive information systems and the like could not speak to executives, let alone respond directly to their requests, without compromising on the multiple sources of information across the enterprise. It was too complex.'

Source: *CRM as Strategy*, PeopleSoft Whitepaper, 2000

What a waste of your staff's time, your customers' patience and what a destruction of shareholder value! KPMG research from 1999 indicates that many companies still struggle to answer basic questions upon which CRM depends: only 49 per cent of businesses can identify which customers are at risk of payment defaults and only 22 per cent realise in time when the actual default starts. These types of mistakes happen when you do not have the tools in place to analyse customer performance, to translate analysis into actionable and profitable knowledge, to make this knowledge available to your staff in charge and to increase that knowledge by a feedback loop looking at the results of the actions.

You will want to come up with efficient leadership for your enterprise that is based on measurements and facts instead of gut instinct. In this chapter, we first discuss how customer interactions based on such 'intelligent' processes can be built using the approaches discussed in previous chapters. We then refine the underlying analysis and monitoring that is necessary to implement such an individual treatment.

9.1 Effective customer treatment

For improving the effectiveness of your operations, that is, for increasing shareholder value, you have to look carefully at the details of customer situations. One-to-one marketing is one example where customers and prospective customers are not seen as an amorphous group, but where individual needs are addressed to achieve better response and closure rates.

Minimum requirements are:

❏ accelerating decisions with standardised procedures and DSS in order to come up with immediate responses to the customer instead of a long series of calls back or papers to be shuffled around;

❏ 'smiling' on the phone – that is valid for all customers; even if you have to collect money or terminate a relationship you should do so in a constructive way in order not to prohibit possible future business and not to create a bad reputation;

❏ prioritising the responsiveness of your call centre and the amount of time your call-centre staff spend with a customer depending on the customer's individual value contribution – the first suggestion, that is, the priority for the call centre, can be easily implemented if every customer has a category that the CTI can evaluate in order to pull him or her forward when he or she has waited long enough in your inbound call queue; the time assignment for discussions with your staff is more tricky, but basically the same concept can be followed, in this case by highlighting the recommended remaining time on the staff CRM screen;

❏ 'smiling' on the Web – this is a bit more difficult because your Web presence needs to be smart enough to be personalised in a way to offer lots of guidance and support to people who need it (no matter how time-consuming it is) and to have a speedy order entry and sophisticated analytical tools for customers familiar with the interactions.

Let me share with you an example of how a large European bank implemented pro-active customer support for loan approvals. When they started the project, each loan required a minimum of six and a maximum of twelve checks and signatures. The approval process took between a week and a month. The staff did not like it and the customers felt they were being treated like beggars. The bank had defined some statistical risk models reflecting the probability of default, appropriate risk cost assignments and the appropriate write-off policies. But that did not help the people dealing with loan applications. Based on the experience that you need to translate analytical findings into easy-to-use recommendations, they adopted the KISS principle ('keep it short and simple') and created a 'traffic light model'. This model expressed in clear terms what the statisticians had found out. Red, yellow, green, the well-understood traffic light codes were assigned to customers (representing their risk profile) and to branches (representing their performance profile). In essence the credit policy was expressed in a decision matrix as summarised in Table 9.

In fact, for defining the exact amounts of the competency, some analysis combined with a systematic trial and error was applied.

After the initial amounts were set, some regions were allowed to experiment with slightly adjusted limits. The performance of those regions was then compared with that of the other regions and the better performing model was then activated for all regions – a champion/challenger approach to have different treatment strategies compete against each other.

Needless to say, the risk profiles for the customers and the branches were regularly checked – for the customer based on rating algorithms and for the branches based on the actual contribution (after risk adjustments). And of course, the incentives for staff to be in a 'green' team were higher than those in 'yellow' or 'red' teams.

This approach implemented two breakthrough concepts: the day-to-day operations were drastically accelerated and a learning culture was created. Standard loan approvals are now processed within minutes instead of days and more complicated cases treated within days instead of weeks.

Table 9   Decision Matrix reflecting credit approval process*

Customer risk profile	Branch risk experience	Approval competency
Green	Green	Up to 10 million Euros Discounts possible up to a zero margin
Green	Yellow	Up to 5 million Euros Discounts only after approval from central risk team
Green	Red	Up to 100,000 Euros Discounts only after approval from central risk team
Yellow	Green	Up to 1 million Euros Discounts only after approval from central risk team
Yellow	Yellow	Up to 100,000 Euros Discounts only after approval from central risk team
Yellow	Red	Check from central risk team required
Red	Green	Up to 500,000 Euros (provided a risk premium will be agreed and collateral is available) No discount
Red	Yellow	Check from central risk team required
Red	Red	Check from central risk team required

* Note that the figures are illustrative examples.

Such combinations of human decisions and automated screenings of the transaction in a well-designed data warehouse and decision support system are a prerequisite for processing customer interactions at Internet speed – the trick is to come up with a 'KISS' representation of your overall business model and competency model. And this representation has to be bullet-proof from an operational perspective, that is, provide guidance to the staff (or in a self-service environment, directly authorise the customer to execute a transaction), *and* must provide performance monitoring. This performance monitoring is necessary to check not only your customers' contribution and your staff's capabilities, but also the performance of your treatment strategy! You have to be able to adjust some components of the strategy in a test segment (like the credit limit in the example above), watch the result and then implement the appropriate change in your overall strategy. Without this performance monitoring, you would not be able to perform top-down steering of your organisation. One brief note on playing with the parameters of your strategy: do not change everything at once, because you will not be able to tell which key factor made the difference; rather test the impact of the various factors step by step. Only then can you improve your performance gradually.

The self-learning organisation was built on the decision support system as discussed above plus a knowledge management environment. People cooperate across the units by using the specified contact points and decision criteria for getting issues resolved; experience could be exchanged within the groups, and the staff now share their insight in regular formal and informal meetings. Knowledge management is also supported by systems, namely by the risk controlling system and the teams' intranet. The risk controlling system takes care of statistical analysis, for translating it into the traffic light colours, and for reviewing credit policies regularly. In addition, the team intranet provides a learning environment for new team members describing the approach, highlighting lessons learned, identifying the contact persons for key topics and providing a discussion forum where the staff can individually exchange their concerns and ideas.

Altogether this is a new understanding of the hierarchies: the management defines the rules of the game and leaves the teams on a pretty long leash − as long as they show a good contribution. The teams can flexibly create their business and shape their customer relationships − as long as they perform well. Those teams that fall below standard get guidance from more experienced colleagues in order to help them catch up − and become self-sufficient and mature in dealing with their customer relationships. Of course, it is slightly more complicated to monitor such sophisticated policies, but once you have replaced your paper-based processes with an integrated CRM and workflow solution, it can be easily traced (and automatically monitored), who entered and who authorised a transaction. Even approval can be automatically checked by reflecting the appropriate competency matrix in the system – or the transaction can be forwarded to a person with enough competencies for the transaction size and characteristics.

Let us take a systematic view on the various kinds of 'treatments'. What you are about to implement is the translation of customer categories into actionable, workflow-oriented recommendations for each business field.

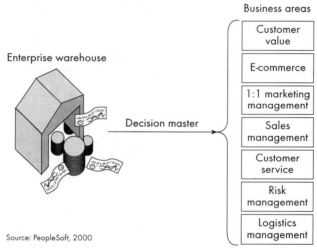

Source: PeopleSoft, 2000

Figure 25   Customer treatments defined by business area

Figure 25 is the complement to Figure 20. The business areas shown on the right hand side can work more effectively, based on a decision tool's recommendation to support your staff in taking action specific to the customer situation:

Planning and improving the *customer value* and relationship: how much contribution do you expect per customer and per customer segment? What are the actions you want to trigger if the contribution falls below expectation? What do you want to do if the market share does not reach your targets? Which of the actions taken in the past show the best impact on customer contribution?

Personalising *e-commerce* interactions and Web presence: which products address customer needs best and what should be available for which customers? When are discounts applicable? Can customers adjust the fees you are invoicing (for example, wrong interest or fee calculations, disputed credit card transactions, invalid telephone bill items) themselves in case of complaints? Up to which amounts? How frequently? Which attributes do you want them to maintain in preference profiles and in concrete product configurations and how does this influence your back-office operations?

One-to-one marketing: how frequently do you approach the customer with cross-/up-/and deep-selling opportunities? Which customer events trigger specific marketing campaigns?

Sales management: which customers are to be excluded from specific marketing campaigns in order to reduce the number of wasted stamps? How aggressive is your follow-up for closing deals after a response to a marketing campaign – and in which cases is it worth your time?

Customer service: when are discounts applicable and which of them can be selected by customers themselves, which only from call-centre staff (and in which cases)? What benefits (for example, reverse call-charges) can be offered in case of complaints? Which offers should be made when a customer terminates the relationship, for example, a free contractual period? To which customers?

Risk management: what risk premium is applicable for which customer? What products or services is he or she not entitled to subscribe to? Up to which limit does he or she have a pre-approved credit line?

Logistics management: which of the delivery channels and at what speed is the one to select for the customer? What is the priority of fixing a defect?

9.2 Analytical framework: the decision master

You have seen now how your operations can be improved by using smart decisioning tools and we have talked about the necessary input into that 'black box' such as frequency of customer interactions and the base data from your operational systems and from your ERP system. But how does that black box, the 'decision master' work? It includes the classics, that is, financial performance monitoring, but in an advanced form, it uses statistical analysis on financial results and on non-financial data such as behaviour patterns, it reflects process efficiency and it monitors the overall effectiveness of the strategy. Let us discuss that in a bit more detail now.

Advanced analysis of financial performance

The key for an advanced analysis is to be able to identify the costs and the profits per transaction and per customer. Table 10 shows the evolution of controlling methodologies. Cost assignment, for example, is most advanced if you apply activity-based measurement. If you do not want to look only in the rear-view mirror, you have to reflect future expectations such as assessment of the customer potential. For some industries or business areas, specific measurements exist such as RAROC (risk adjusted return on capital, deducting risk costs from the returns – like an insurance premium) for loans or option pricing for stock derivatives.

Table 10 Customer value measurement

Measurement	Customer value		
	Simple	Intermediate	Advanced
Assigning unit activity costs	Industry standards (FFCA)	Industry standards Some internal measures	Activity-based measurement
Assigning fee income	Distribute evenly across customer base	Allocate across customer base	Based on actual transactions
Reconcile to accounting systems	No	Yes	Yes
Frequency of calculation	Annually	Semi-annually or quarterly	Monthly or shorter
Summary data vs actuals	Summarised data	Some summary and some transaction-level data	Primarily transaction-level data
Time to implement	1–3 months	3–6 months	6+ months
Key metrics	Relative profitability	Current profitability	Future customer potential or lifetime value

Source: The Tower Group, 1999

The other prerequisite for an advanced analysis is the existence of a proper data structure throughout your applications or a data warehouse with quality data.

Statistical analysis and modelling

Based on detailed transaction-level information, you then can do lots of number crunching for different purposes. You can check how key characteristics of your customers correspond to their buying behaviour and contribution. How is your per capita contribution in certain regions? What are the preferences of age groups and of genders? At which time of the month or year do your customers make their buying decisions?

Questions like that traditionally lead to tons of useless paper – unless you have a smart group of statisticians in your organisation who are capable of handling data mining tools and can interpret the results. They should also be able to formulate hypotheses that can be tested against the actual data situation such as 'females between twenty and twenty-nine years of age have an x per cent higher probability of requesting a loan in the period thirty to sixty days prior to their birthday'. The best way to formulate such hypotheses is by defining a concise model where you can express and monitor such probabilities according to the characteristics or attributes that have been shown to be the most important for your situation, for example, gender, age, education, home address, time of the year, time of the month.

Such models can reflect various cases or profiles for:

❏ acquisition of new customers;

❏ retention of existing customers for preventing terminations;

❏ propensity to buy different product areas for cross-selling;

❏ payment default and risk probabilities;

❏ customer relationship cycle from acquisition through ongoing business to the termination phase;

❏ customer life-cycle from 'cradle to grave';

❏ seasonal cycles;

with specific events for each of the models. Please refer to the outline of such models in Section 4.3. Each customer then is assigned to a variety of segments, for example, gender segment, age segment, socio-demographic segment, birthday, risk situation *et cetera*.

For each segment, a treatment approach is defined for various situations and events, for example, marketing campaigns for young customers, or contract extension campaigns for risky customers. The closure rate or success rate of each of those treatments has to be monitored and stored.

When a particular event happens, for example, the day sixty days prior to a birthday, the decision master assigns the appropriate strategy. This assignment is done based on experienced success probabilities, so all possible treatments can be ranked by probability – and the one with the highest success expectation should be activated.

To tell you the truth, people are talking about one-to-one marketing a lot, and the decision master with its detailed analysis as described will eventually break your treatment down into small customer groups. The current stage in most enterprises, though, is still at a level where maybe four to five traditional segments exist (such as corporate, SOHO,* private, mass market). The vision of one-to-one marketing is still a great idea to pursue. You will probably never exactly get there (as with the data warehouse idea framing the dream of perfectly integrated and documented data repositories), but those who begin now to add the first refinements of the segments by behaviour components can make significant improvements compared with their competitors. So, do not wait until everybody hops on the train!

Customer profiles

In order to ensure that customers appreciate the value of the treatment they receive and the information they obtain, you have to allow them to specify their preferences. There are two good examples that might create some ideas for your design. A private life example are the 'flirt pages' such as *www.matchmaker.com* where people searching for a partner can indicate their preferences and then a decision master looks for the closest match for a date. A business example is the recently announced AUI (attentional user interface) from Microsoft that allows users to define when they want to get which types of messages. This definition can be done by content (for example, keywords) by channel (for example, e-mail or SMS), and by sender (for example, customers, bosses, team members, peers, friends, family).

Efficiency of processes

The next area to watch is the efficiency of processes. Efficiency is to be measured in time invested against the result achieved. For example: how many staff hours were necessary to close the deal? How many days did it take to respond to a complaint? How long have waiting times been between departments that are involved? What is the achievement rate of service level commitments with

---

* SOHO = Small office/home office, for example, accountants, lawyers, freelance programmers.

existing staff and procedures? Where are bottlenecks in the end-to-end processing of the transactions?

A prerequisite for this type of reporting is the time-stamping of all transactions at the various stages of their processing. Some IT applications provide that feature, but in most cases it will be necessary to embed the various applications into a workflow tool. Such workflow tools reflect the time when a transaction was handed over to a system or to a person and when the processing was completed.

Effectiveness of strategy

The effectiveness of your strategy finally indicates which business strategy and treatment strategy is better suited for achieving your targets. For implementing this comparison, you have to create permanently new 'challenger' strategies that compete against your current 'champion' strategy. This competition has to be organised in comparable segments, for example, in distinct regions that have been showing a similar buying behaviour before, or in distinct age groups that do not differ too much in their contribution.

Items you should measure for this effectiveness are: how many customers responded to your marketing campaign? Which referral programme created the biggest number of new customers? Which type of price increasing propositions was able to gain the best acceptance? Which collections strategy allowed you to get the most money back from defaulting customers?

Once a challenger treatment or strategy shows a significantly better result, you should implement it for all the appropriate segments.

9.3   Analytical tools

Remember the discussion of command and control and the maintenance of oversight we had in Chapter 5.6. You should now see what types of analysis and decisioning you should perform to replace traditional command and control approaches with treatment policies and strategies for an up-to-date, personalised approach to the customers. This is an ideal way to influence everyday decisions by very clear directives – without needing a micro-management that would require your personal decision every time. Instead, your experience and your guidelines are to be expressed and implemented in the policies and the related treatments. And the employees are empowered with higher competencies to take action and to interact with the customers at a much higher velocity.

We have discussed some aspects of quantifying experience, making it measurable and including it into feedback loops to systematically increase that experience. There is one thing still missing, namely the infrastructure for actually analysing your data. This infrastructure has to include a proper data structure and the appropriate reporting tools.

Data structures and data warehouse

Depending on the size and complexity of your IT environment, a proper data structure may be embedded in your primary IT system (provided you have only one and it is well enough documented), or you will have to build up a data warehouse. In either case, you need to be able to:

❑ identify all transactions that belong to a particular customer;

❑ cluster customers in groups by region, responsible customer care units, socio-demographic attributes;

❑ find out trends, that is, you need to store historical transactions either on a detailed level or as summarised information you need for your analysis purposes.

With these data, you can monitor your own performance and compare the various segments (customer groups, regions, sales representatives) against each other and check evolution over time. If you add external information, you can benchmark yourself and can check how your actual market share evolves against your anticipated market share.

Monitoring instead of reporting

In earlier days, those managers who really wanted to use adequate information had to programme some analytical applications themselves (or have it done within their staff). Today, easy-to-use applications exist, where Internet-like navigations or even touch screens support intuitive analysis and allow even top managers to slice and dice problems with *ad hoc* questions to view the issue at hand from various perspectives. These applications have evolved from reporting tools (first generation) analytical processing tools (second generation) and enterprise performance management tools (latest generation).

First-generation reporting tools were based on the underlying data structures and were implemented by programmers in SQL – or SAS – code, and were good for reporting and formatting data such as sales histories or contribution details. So they supported department directors in their planning and execution tasks.

Second-generation OLAP (online analytical processing), ROLAP (relational OLAP), and MOLAP (multidimensional OLAP) tools are in place today that allow to slice and dice in the 'cubes' that have been defined – as mentioned before such as by regions, by organisational units, by product, by time *et cetera*. This is good for eggheads working in the various statistical departments, for product managers and marketing people experienced in interpreting the many dimensions of those cubes. Some reports even help managers and leaders of the company drive the analysis of some critical business issues at hand. But they are still too 'bulky' to be useful for everyday communication.

The latest tools are shaped for strategic communication: all these data are condensed into information from which clear actions can be triggered – as in the example on the call-centre workload in Figure 26. All bars are green (the workload in all call centres is within the defined service level targets and sufficient staff are

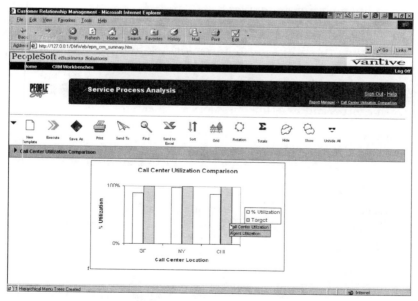

Figure 26   Monitoring instead of reporting

available to handle the calls), so no emergency action is necessary. On the other hand, as utilisation is below target, some staff can be made available for other tasks.

To define the contents of such easy-to-use monitors, reporting workbenches are necessary which will:

❑ help define the contents of the attributes to be monitored and how to make them roll up to the overall balanced scorecard;

❑ 'translate' detailed data records and statistical analysis;

❑ provide management with reporting in an easy-to-use way.

9.4 Summary: actions to take

❑ Measure customer interactions with CRM, CTI and DWH solutions (for example, frequency of interaction, duration, responsiveness of your organisation and systems, closure rate).

❑ Model your customer behaviour based on statistical analysis of transaction level data.

❑ Define rules and policies with different levels of empowerment depending on the demonstrated performance of the staff or unit.

❑ Maintain rules and policies centrally and give freedom of execution within those rules.

❑ Assign treatment strategies depending on customer profiles reflecting the value of the transaction and of the customer relationship versus the cost of treatment.

❑ Express strategies in scenarios and reflect them in scripts for your call centres and in online messages and banners.

❑ Support your teams with an information system environment providing the history of customer interactions, actionable analysis of customer behaviour, and supporting the staff's treatment decisions.

❑ Measure and monitor process efficiency and strategy effectiveness.

❑ Base your analysis on a data warehouse, and condense the results by using performance and reporting tools into easy-to-understand overviews such as the balanced scorecard.

❑ Keep it short, simple and actionable.

Part 3

Transformation concept and programme for a modernised, quickly adaptable enterprise

10

Your e-business 'factory'

@@@ Follow a 'factory' concept to refine your e-business strategy and to implement your new organisation by focusing on the most important recurrent customer interactions that have to be made excellent. @@@ Create regularly and frequently a new 'release' of your enterprise's process and system capabilities. @@@

Each business initiative has a number of disciplines. In traditional organisations, dealing with these disciplines is assigned to different units or departments. Only a few people have an overview of markets, processes and technologies. Due to the speed of change in the Internet world, holistic thinking is necessary. To prepare your restructuring along the lines of customer interactions, you need to build a task force to create an e-business factory. The factory has to produce new releases of your strategy and business approach at the e-speed of changes.

In your e-business factory, similar disciplines as in traditional enterprises will be found, but the clear focus is on customer-oriented processes such as marketing, sales, order handling, delivery, service and complaint management. These should be organised outside the boundaries and restrictions of your traditional hierarchy. It will lead the way to new attitudes and approaches such as openness for change, new schemes for incentive compensation, time-oriented project management and different, quicker implementation cycles.

10.1 Recipe for success

To outline the disciplines of your e-business factory, I have presented them in Figure 27 next to each other. I am not using a top-down picture to avoid suggesting a traditional kind of hierarchy and command structure. Actually, the disciplines mentioned are the 'horizontal' underpinnings of your new business, so if you want to show some verticals on top of it, you should do that for your different lines of business, that is, for the particular customer segments such as corporate customers, consumers or different regional customer orientations.

One key to success is to take the factory idea seriously, that is, to look for recurrent tasks, and execute them regularly. Traditional projects are defined by their scope and implementation time is the result of their complexity. E-business projects work differently. In your factory, you have to set time rules for the development cycles, for example, three or four months. At the end of each cycle, the results of all the disciplines need to be looked at together to allow you to release the next stage of your product or service. All the parts must be in place in a 'just in time' fashion, as in an automobile factory where the body, the wheels, the engine, the seats, the electric equipment are supplied to the assembly line when they are needed, in order to get a car ready every few minutes. We are not yet down to a release from the e-factory every minute, but I hope you see the similarities.

Let us discuss the disciplines of the factory now:

Strategy: a small group of leaders has to provide the focus for the whole e-business factory. What is the specific value proposition for the online business? Which customers are to be connected via the Web? What products and services should be offered at which stage of the implementation and for which price? What areas of business will be covered in-house and where should outsourcing partners be engaged? Are there areas for spinning off subsidiaries or merging with other companies? The result of those considerations is a strategic roadmap reflecting all those considerations (see the next chapter).

Business redesign: as defined by the strategic roadmap, the business processes for the particular area have to be streamlined, based on appropriate competencies and policies. For each implementation step:

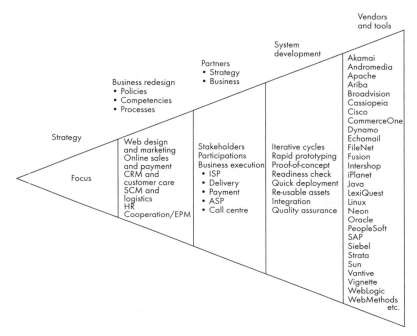

Figure 27   E-business 'factory' concept

❑ the contents and design of the website and the marketing messages need to be defined;

❑ online interactions with the customer, authentication, risk management and payments have to be described;

❑ the customer segments have to be identified, the appropriate treatment strategies and workflows outlined;

❑ production, supplies and logistics need to be organised;

❑ and the success criteria and measurements, in particular the service levels have to be agreed.

Partners: based on the strategic insourcing and outsourcing fields, the partners for executing the day-to-day operations have to be selected. Key partners include:

❑ the ISP hosting your website and performing the Web traffic analysis;

❑ the call-centre provider providing customer support by telephone as well as hotline services for technical and operational questions;

❏ the logistics partner or partner(s) for delivering products to customers, obtaining supplies when they are needed (for example, with just-in-time approaches), and performing the field support for fixing customer problems;

❏ payment partners such as authentication providers and issuers of digital certificates as well as banks, credit card companies or payment consolidators;

❏ the ASP for running one or several of your applications in their computer centres, such as an outsourced letter shop for printing your invoices or mailing marketing materials, or for an outsourced ERP solution.

System development: the identified system components that are to be provided internally need to be built or bought. The system developers need to document the requirements in cooperation with the business redesign team, with future users and in co-ordination with the development strategy. Selection criteria for software and hardware purchases need to be identified and the actual selection, purchase and implementation be done. For internal development, the necessary teams need to be built up and trained, and development has to be done. All these components have to be tested in co-operation with the business redesign team and future users. For each of the developments, iterative development cycles have to be envisioned and an early feedback on the design ideas has to be obtained by joint application design workshops and rapid prototyping.

Vendors and tools: for all the development and implementation work, you will have to rely heavily on a broad set of vendors and tool providers. In general, you can follow either the strategy of using pre-integrated applications from large vendors or you can buy a variety of small tools from a broad set of providers. For each of the tools, you need to build up the know-how internally for operations, extensions and maintenance. So, each tool should be evaluated not only with functional requirements in mind, but also these ongoing considerations. Selection criteria for the different tools and key features of the various vendors are listed in Chapter 14.

In each of the teams, you should seek to pull together those of your staff who think in possibilities and opportunities, capable of looking beyond the horizon, understanding the full picture of the end-to-end processes and interactions with customers and suppliers, and who are committed to creating the future, that is, to making your changes happen. To make the creation of something new a reality, you should also have different procedures from your existing enterprise. If you had Monday morning status meetings, change them (at least to another day); if your dress code requires formal outfits, set a colourful example with fancy ties; organise regular creative sessions in offsite locations where it may be that your creativity task force use finger colours for documenting their best ideas on flipcharts.

Let me wrap this section up by sharing with you the considerations of IBM for creating their e-business factory to produce 'Fast Blue'. As Steve Ward, the CIO has put it, fast teams need:

❑ a strong leader keeping the staff on course;

❑ a good mix of talent;

❑ clearly defined measurable targets, like 'we want to generate 2 billion revenues online monthly';

❑ quick internal communication via voice-mail, e-mail, intranet and video conferences;

❑ to follow the targets defined in the plan, but flexibly realign the specific tasks;

❑ quick cycles with teams pulled together (and dis-assembling) as needed.

10.2 What is different in e-projects?

We have discussed the customer online experience in Part 1 of the book. Table 11 summarises where e-business differs from traditional exchanges with the customer and highlights the impact of the differences on your organisation. This summary helps your transformation task force to focus on those aspects which are most relevant.

So, the differences are speed and end-to-end integration. Regarding speed, a perfect service would deliver results immediately. But do not kill yourself; you just need to be slightly ahead of your competitors.

In the banking industry, there is an example of how strategic decisions are revisited regularly: the banks have been pushed by the regulators (in order not to risk their own capital and that of their investors) to regularly review the capital they invest in certain

Table 11 Impact of e-business on your organisation

E-business challenge	Impact on your organisation
Customer online interactions (for details see Part 1 and Chapter 12.1)	End-to-end integration of all business processes Transparency of internal process steps to customers and competitors The customer interaction architecture needs to be defined and maintained Responses to local settings have to be reflected in overall design
Frequent adjustments of positioning and value proposition	Innovation speed has to be accelerated Separate e-business group implementing the changes
Online orders require quick confirmations and execution (for details see Chapter 12.2)	Operational systems, production, supplies and delivery logistics need to exchange service requests and update on the execution progress frequently The importance of hierarchies and departmental borders diminishes Customer need and the value proposition to the customer have to be the common focus
New tools and products, often from small vendors, are on the market (for details see Chapter 14)	The right combination of application components needs to be found and integrated Key components are ordering and complaint management for consumers and corporate customers, self-service for profiles and preferences, electronic marketplaces and supply chain management The internal users and operational staff must be trained to use selected tools
The end-to-end value proposition requires the operational integration of business partners (for details see Chapter 12.3)	People must work together across departmental and company boundaries A framework must be established and service level agreements need to be monitored
Mergers and acquisitions as well as spin-off situations need to be organised (for details see Chapter 12.3)	Organisational changes will be the rule, not the exception Business process redesign is an ongoing task The value proposition will be permanently adjusted Innovation needs to be driven and managed
The players are on different levels of e-business maturity (for details see Chapter 11)	The balance of investments and pay-off has to be revisited regularly in the light of the maturity level competitors have reached at each particular time
Personalised services and one-to-one marketing are necessary (for details see Chapter 9)	Customer value models have to be defined The customers need to be segmented and the appropriate profiles and treatment strategies per segment need to be defined The treatment strategies have to be implemented in the call centre and customer self-service
Speed of innovation (for details see Chapter 10.1)	The e-factory needs to be managed by time targets, not by scope targets Customer feedback has to be reflected in a learning and improving organisation The e-factory has to be organised in design and development cycles; the exact targets have to be set cycle by cycle

trading areas, for example, stock derivatives. In order to do this, the capital at risk is calculated daily, taking into account each and every open deal in the books of a bank around the globe. This actual use of capital at risk is allocated to the various risk categories and checked against the limits set for the respective category. With the usage and limit information, the ALM committee (asset and liability management) has to convene regularly, check if usage in the various categories is still appropriate or if a re-allocation of limits should be made. So, an integrated view of risks and performance is provided and the board and ALM are able to optimise the performance of the risk bearing activities. That is an early implementation of the shareholder value idea! It does not come for free, though. The bankers still experience the huge efforts that were necessary to integrate all the different systems to get all transactions together centrally and to have the same systematic view on risk and performance. And the non-bankers probably can also imagine what it meant to interface dozens of systems running in different time zones, where different local regulations have to be reflected and a central steering of the various business units in trading has to be achieved.

So, end-to-end integration is the real issue requiring a change in the mentality of your staff and a significant investment in your IT systems. The mentality change means that your staff must not be looking any more to their department-internal objectives, but need to focus on their contribution to the cross-departmental process of providing for a superior customer experience. The IT investment is necessary for integrating all your (and your partners') stand-alone applications, in particular in a way which still maintains your flexibility. But you should not rewrite all your procedures and systems in one huge project, because the competitive environment and the customer requirements would change more quickly than you can adjust your project plans. Instead, you need to improve integration in many little steps, each with a clear value to your customers and a clear contribution to your business performance. In order not to make your projects too complex, look for the quick win that allows you to gain a significant improvement at reasonable cost.

What is it now that your e-factory should produce? Let me highlight that whatever they produce, they need to produce it regularly and in short cycles. And their overall product is your e-business organisation with its:

❑ value proposition;

❑ integrated processes and people focusing on customer experience;

❑ partners joining you in providing your value proposition; and

❑ an integrated, flexible, efficiently performing, highly available, secure and scalable IT solution

based on a business component architecture and according to a strategic roadmap.

10.3 Summary

E-business forces your organisation to get acquainted with two new perspectives: one is speed, the other one is end-to-end integration. Your e-business factory continually has to produce a renewal of your enterprise. Fine-tune strategy, make the organisation more flexible and check and improve the performance of your overall business in the light of the trends of your customer interactions.

The e-business factory's 'product' releases are renewals of:

❏ your business strategy with your value propositions;

❏ your business design with your concrete services, streamlined processes for these services, and people working together across the organisation;

❏ agreements with your partner companies; when necessary the preparation of outsourcing decisions or mergers;

❏ the online interaction capabilities and the end-to-end integration of your IT systems;

❏ the best of breed selection of tools and vendors for particular e-business applications.

11

Strategy-based execution

@@@ Create a strategy 'think tank' with champions from marketing, customer care and IT. @@@ Have them extend and adjust the strategy, express the strategy in an evolution roadmap with measurable targets, trigger the necessary activities and monitor the success. @@@

Strategy is a way to define what you want to achieve relative to your environment such as competitors and customers. Ideally, you should be able to create a monopoly of services where your customers appreciate being locked in (or positively speaking: loyal) as was the case for example for Microsoft. Due to ongoing innovations, your positioning on the market and your competitive advantages need to be regularly revisited and documented in your strategy and targets. But as Michael Porter highlights, strategy is also 'to decide what not to do'. Let me extend that thought by its time dimension, that is, deciding what not to do *now*. Also, let us be clear that it is necessary to *decide* what not to do. It is no good reason not to do something, just because it was never done before. Look for the reasons if a new idea is not immediately accepted. It may well be that it will develop into to a big revenue generator after you have it fine-tuned a bit.

As a start, your strategists need to see the situation you are in; namely, they should understand:

❏ the trends and cycles and your unique competencies applicable for various channels and segments, for example, PC-based Internet, mobile business, professional/business users, high-profile consumers, mass market;

❏ customer motives, demands and service needs, as well as the challenges for commoditising aspects of your services;

❏ the dynamics of your supply market and the respective electronic marketplaces, to identify possible dependencies;

❏ the key security issues by identifying the weakest part of the chain.

This situation is the baseline for the first draft of your strategy definition. It needs to be reviewed and updated regularly and the targets derived from the current situation have to be expressed as releases for your e-business organisation, with each release clearly stating what to achieve for the specific point in time, and what to postpone. In this chapter we will discuss the tools you can use for developing, documenting and communicating your strategy.

11.1 The strategy 'think tank'

The strategists can be either a small group of senior experts who only work on defining strategy, or they can be a committee of managers who convene regularly to step away from their day-to-day business and agree on long-term development. In both cases, the strategists have to coordinate their recommendations with the board in order to achieve their buy-in and support. The two approaches mentioned have their particular strengths and weaknesses.

The dedicated team has the benefit of working full time on the strategy and solutions, so there is a clear point of contact for defining and improving methodology and architecture. Companies that have decided on this approach include financial service providers such as Bayerische Vereinsbank, when they went through their merger with Bayerische Hypobank, or consulting companies such as KPMG, when they launched their e-business solution centre. With the central hub for your e-business activities, you have a clear point of reference, where all your e-business assets can be compiled, refined and leveraged. The disadvantage of this approach is that a separate 'cost centre' is created and sometimes its value contribution is challenged. Moreover, you need to avoid an ivory-tower attitude by making sure you keep the team working on day-to-day issues and maintaining and extending their understanding of the latest development in methodologies, processes, tools and architectures.

The management committee approach has the strength of being very well anchored in the operational units, so the decisions of the committee do not need an additional translation into the various lines of business. Companies using that approach include software vendors such as Microsoft with their regular manager 'retreats' or consulting companies such as AMS with their virtualisation of globally dispersed interest groups held together by knowledge centre contact points and distributed team environments such as Lotus Notes and an intranet. The disadvantage the management committee often face is that they can only dedicate a small amount of time to e-business work. To build up a real e-business factory, they have to create a separate management structure, deal with the everyday conflicts of their dispersed staff as well as the conflicting demands of urgent, client-exposed projects and work on the internal e-business progress. Therefore, the production speed in the factory tends to be slower than with the first approach and planning of releases for the e-business assets is much more difficult.

In either case, the members of the group or committee have to represent the aspects of marketing, customer care and IT. Marketing 'owns' the customer experience and will be inclined to improve it constantly. Customer care has first-hand information of customer concerns and IT has all the tools and systems necessary to make improvements (or they have to get them). Ideally, there should be a champion in each of those units who adopts the e-business topic. This person will not necessarily be at the top of the organisation in that unit, but he or she has to be very capable of networking in order to put all the requirements and concerns of his or her colleagues into a concise framework. This person also needs the backing of your top managers to execute the decisions the strategy group or committee has agreed upon. The best choice is a young fast tracker with high energy who has won the trust of the respective department heads. With a small group of empowered and active people, you can create miracles of change in your organisation – in particular they have to be quick in their decisions to stick to the release intervals in your e-business factory. Allow them to make mistakes; this is an advantage of the short cycles. In the worst case, you will have wasted three or four months and the costs related to that period. If you compare that with how much time and money is currently wasted by not being pro-active, the choice should be easy. Avoid sending 'empty suits' to the meetings unless you want to kill e-business initiatives!

Let us look at how well-known companies have identified which changes might become relevant for them:

> General Motors launched a number of initiatives aimed at getting everyone plugged into the future. In one, a diverse cross-section of individuals identified 19 broad change categories (e.g. global urban culture, entertainment in everything) that encompassed more than 100 discontinuities.* Every discontinuity was illustrated by a visual image in order to help individuals connect with what's changing. The goal was to use this inventory as the backdrop for every serious strategy discussions. ... GM is learning that you have to pay close attention to the discontinuities if you're going to get anywhere close to the bleeding edge of change.
>
> Source: Gary Hamel, *Leading the Revolution*

Similarly David S. Pottruck, president of Charles Schwab reports: 'It took ten months, the input of eighty executives and a million-dollar communication project to realise what we wanted – the commitment of the entire company to continue to grow in new directions.' This experience shows that change requires significant investment and energy to be successful, but these examples also highlight the fact that it is worth the effort.

We talked about innovation and some tricks for finding creative new ideas for your services in Chapter 5 – one of the tasks of the strategy think tank is to organise creativity sessions and to maintain a portfolio of innovative ideas with their success track record. Take a venture capitalist approach: it is OK to discard seven or eight out of ten ideas, if only one or two give you a boost in earnings and another one or two provide some incremental improvements. Only make sure through regular reviews that you always know which of the ideas have been bad (stop their roll-out quickly) and which are champions (push them as much as you can).

My recommendation for all of you whose operations are not too much geographically dispersed is to implement a central strategist

---

* 'Discontinuities' is the concept Hamel uses for highlighting changes; we need to become explicitly aware of the attitudes that are discontinued. For example, what in the customer environment does not exist any more? What are the new things the customers are exposed to? What old forms of enterprises are challenged/what new forms show success?

group that also triggers the other disciplines of the e-business factory. In either case, the strategists need to look out for competitive challenges and to fine-tune the value proposition of your company. Make it required reading for them to identify a business or leisure magazine nobody in your company has read before and to report to the think tank what interesting opportunities this may lead to.

To give you some ideas of different strategies focusing on a particular enterprise's strength, let us look at examples from the banking industry again* — other industries can use respective analogue strategies.

Defensive strategy, labelled 'everybank.com'; the focus is on e-banking to complement other channels:

❑ the primary aim is to protect the existing franchise;

❑ some secondary aims include: to reduce costs, improve cross-sales, generate new revenue streams and to achieve limited gains in market share.

Offensive strategies: proprietary e-banking focused on content, providing the opportunity to:

❑ sell own banking services in an Internet-only strategy;

❑ target new customers and gain market share from a start-up or existing position.

Open e-banking/aggregator, focused on *distribution*. The aim is to:

❑ develop a distribution franchise as aggregator selling products from other institutions;

❑ derive revenues from distribution of Internet applications rather than from the provision of banking products.

Partnering with aggregators, focused on content with the aim of:

❑ providing product content to other aggregators' Web sites;

❑ accepting price-based competition, aiming for large volumes and scale economies.

* Source: PeopleSoft Essential Document, *Managing Change in the e-World*.

Geographic expansion, focused on content. The aim is to:

❑ enter new geographies relying wholly upon e-banking.

Product line expansion, focused on content. The aim is to:

❑ use the Internet to break into other product and service areas such as insurance, travel services or information services;

❑ cross-sell from banking relationships or launch as a stand-alone venture.

e-Payments, focused on content. The aim is to:

❑ develop new payment solutions, and capture volumes by targeting the e-commerce market sector.

11.2 Evolution roadmap

The strategic roadmap establishes a concise summary of the change projects in your e-factory and in your whole enterprise. It has to address the 'magic cube' of time, time and time:

❑ when will which customers get Web access?

❑ when will which products be offered?

❑ when will which types of interaction be available?

The settings for each customer group need to be reflected according to the maturity levels of e-business we have discussed. Once your brochureware is available on the Web, you need to consider what orders and transactions can be entered online. Can a new customer be created online or are there some prerequisites for a 'traditional' set-up of a contractual master agreement before Web transactions can take place? Can new products be subscribed to or are there some risk assessments with traditional approaches necessary up front? Can the transactions be entered online and is an immediate confirmation available via the Web? Which cross-selling offers are made to existing customers? Which communities are open for which customers? What loyalty programmes are offered? On a high level, your roadmap can look like Figure 28.

On this high level for presentation purposes, the key areas have to be highlighted and summarised to communicate the targets of the project. To plan activities in more detail, we need to look closely

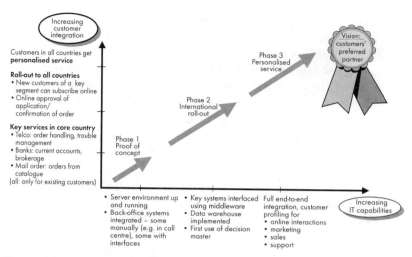

Figure 28   Strategic roadmap (illustrative example)

into the various dimensions, namely customers, regions, products, processes and IT. First of all, let us recap our assumptions concerning which e-business maturity the company currently has reached and what the targets are.

Let us assume that the basic online features like brochureware are already available on the Web, and that key interactions can be handled in the home country via the call centre or by online form entry, but that the front-office applications are not completely integrated with all back-office processing.

The first new step, Phase 1, has to prove that the targeted online interaction concepts actually work. It also has to highlight where in the operational processes bottlenecks exist that require additional fine-tuning in order to improve customer experience on the next level of e-business maturity. For a telecom provider, this can mean providing online order handling with (almost) immediate confirmation when new or changed services will be available – such as an additional telephone connection, the change in a subscribed number, call forwarding, or a change in the selected tariff model. A bank might want to offer all routine dealings for current accounts and brokerage online – such as bank transfers (domestic and abroad/in local and foreign currency), stopping cheques, requesting new cheques, account reconciliation, purchasing and selling of stocks and derivatives with online pricing. For a mail order provider, online order entry with immediate confirmation of availability of products or the recommendation of an alternative can be the target of this phase.

Phase 2 then, should push the Web experience to the next level of e-business maturity, namely to level three of the maturity model discussed in Section 6.2. New customers should be attracted via the Web, their subscription or application be checked for risk profile, applicable price plans should only be shown for the specific customer profile and key events should be used for retention programs and cross-selling activities.

In Phase 3, the segments have to be more refined, and one-to-one marketing has to be applied. Instead of the marketing campaigns that were executed occasionally, each customer has to be subject to a particular campaign (for example, up-selling, deep-selling, cross-selling, particular loyalty activities, referral, win-back) at each point in time. The performance of each campaign in each segment has to be monitored systematically and the treatment strategies need to be fine-tuned permanently.

Each of the phases may require various design and development cycles for implementation. We will discuss the development tasks for those cycles in Chapter 13.

11.3 Service quality targets per cycle

For each of your targeted phases, you should have the various dimensions clearly defined. Here we construct the example that will be used in our worksheets below – as you will define your dimensions when you go through the transformation exercise:

❏ Customer segments: corporate customers, SOHO (single office and home office), high-profile private customers, consumers. *Note: these customer segments are included in our example because we hope to have the highest profitability here. You should focus on the currently best performing segments (as identified by the A/B/C analysis discussed in Section 1.3).*

❏ Countries: UK, Germany, France, Italy. *Note: these countries are included in our example because we hope to have the highest probability of success here, based on an assessment of the existing market share, the competitive situation of other online services, and the likelihood of adapting our service to the specific needs of the local market. You should focus on those countries where you have the highest expectation of success.*

❏ Products: as indicated above, specific for each industry.

❏ Processes: order entry, complaint management, new customer application and administration, customer care, cross-selling, community service. *Note: the focus should be on those customer-oriented processes that improve customer experience the most and help you save transaction handling costs.*

❏ IT (as discussed in Section 8.4): Web front end and portal, CRM (customer relationship management) system, CTI (computer telephone interface)/DMS (document management system)/ workflow, CMS (content management system), decision support system (DSS), to support dedicated marketing activities and to assign specific treatments. *Note: with the focus on customer-oriented activities, the sequence of the list above reflects my recommendation for the implementation of IT systems.*

For each combination of these dimensions, the targeted service level per phase has to be defined. This definition is to be used to commit your team members to the results – but it is a different type of commitment than a 'zero defect' software delivery commitment. We are all gaining experience Web business, so the targeted results are an orientation for benchmarking and of course they are the baseline for incentives to the team. Actually, the team should seek ways to achieve results with a reasonably low effort. Pareto's rule that 80 per cent of the results can be achieved with 20 per cent of the effort is valid in this area, too. So do not try too hard to get the last increment of additional revenue, but watch the balance with costs as well. It is better to go for ratios or indicators to be achieved.

Let us look at the list of dimensions again and come up with some indicators. We have a total of six dimensions including time. Unfortunately, the two-dimensional display of these combinations requires many repetitions overlaying the pattern of the project roadmap. I will show you how we can line up these dimensions in a comprehensive way. First, the processes and the IT support can be squeezed into one dimension, because the IT components are very closely related to the processes they support. So we are down to five dimensions. In my example, we would create a separate table per country, each with the same structure. We assume that the processes are very similar for the various customer segments, so I have bundled some of the customer groups together; if that is not the case with you, it may be more appropriate to do things the other way round, that is, you should use customer groups as primary line item, and then as a secondary item you should list all the necessary processes.

Finally, you may use colours to represent the time dimension, thus you can make the project pattern visible – in Table 12 I have replaced colours by shades of grey (the darker the later) and use P1 for Phase 1, P2 for Phase 2 etc.

The details of your actual roadmap have to reflect all the dimensions properly. In a project I undertook with a client, we produced a wall chart measuring one meter by two meters (still in relatively small print) to show all the products, processes, countries and customer segments with their anticipated online interactions. The tool to create it was a standard spreadsheet program (where you do not have to worry if you need to insert a row or a column), the phase assignment was marked with various colours and then the sheet was printed on a large plotter.

11.4 Summary

Create your strategy 'think tank' with a small group of high-energy decision-makers. Have them agree on the duration of each factory cycle and clearly define the intensity of your customer interactions for each cycle:

❏ when will which customers get Web access?

❏ when will which products be offered?

❏ when will which types of interaction be available?

❏ what are the measurable indicators of success?

Express the strategy and the execution targets in a visual roadmap summarising the focus of each of the cycles, and break it down to the targeted service quality for the specific products, customers and processes per cycle.

Table 12 Sample service levels per phase for home country

Process	IT component	Customer segment	Product A	Product B	Product C
Order entry	Web front-end	Corporate	P1: confirm within 24 hours	P2: confirm within 2 hours	Not offered
			P2: confirm within 2 hours		
		SOHO, high profile private	P1: confirm within 2 hours	P2: confirm within 2 hours	P2: confirm within 2 hours
		Consumers	Not offered	P2: confirm within 2 hours	P3: immediate execution
Complaint management	CRM	Corporate, SOHO		P2: call centre	
		High-profile private, consumers		P3: self-service account adjustment	P3: call centre
New customer application/ administration	DSS	Corporate, SOHO	P2: decision in 24 hours	P2: decision in 24 hours	
			P3: decision in 2 hours	P3: decision in 2 hours	
		High-profile private, consumers	P2: decision in 2 hours	P2: decision in 2 hours	P3: decision in 5 minutes
				P3: decision in 5 minutes	
Customer care	CTI, DMS, Workflow, CRM	Corporate, SOHO, high-profile private, consumers	P1: resolution in 1 week	P2: resolution in 2 days	P3: resolution in 2 hours
			P2: resolution in 2 days		
Cross-selling	Marketing and campaign support, EPM	Corporate	P3: 80% retention	P3: 90% retention + 20% x-sell from product A	
		SOHO	P3: 70% retention	P3: 80% retention + 20% x-sell + 30% new customers	
		High-profile private	P3: 60% retention	P3: 70% retention + 40% new customers	
		Consumers			
Community service	CMS, EPM	Corporate			
		SOHO	P3: forum for two sub-segments		
		High-profile private			
		Consumers	P3: chat room		

12

Business (re-)engineering

@@@ Re-architect business units to provide customer-focused services integrated across all earlier departmental borders. @@@ In a quick look assessment of the current service levels, identify the targeted leap to the next level of e-business maturity. @@@

To implement touch points we have discussed for customer interaction, flexible process configuration and personalised customer treatment, I will equip you with an important tool to assess the e-interaction quality of your front-office and back-office operations: worksheets which allow you a quick look assessment of the key areas of e-business described in the e-business factory earlier. The worksheets* highlight possible measurements of success, and indicate frequently observed organisational weaknesses. You should also compare these with targeted shareholder value improvements. With these findings, you can create your e-business organisation based on architecture templates for several key industries.

12.1 Quick look assessment

You should perform a quick look assessment (QLA) of the current status of your key processes. What is it the staff do not like? What is the core of the customer complaints you receive? How can you distinguish yourself from your competitors? How would your customers like interactions with you to improve?

---

* You can request a softcopy of all the worksheets from my website, *www.success-at-e-business.com*.

For the various fields of redesign defined in Section 10.1, I have created outline worksheets for the quick look assessment. My recommendation is to define the key measurements at this early stage. Remember, you won't get what you don't measure. Therefore, the definition of measurements is a highly strategic activity. As a side effect of this definition, you will see what on the one hand can already be easily measured in your organisation and just needs to be compiled in a proper way, and on the other hand where you need to implement additional measurement tools. This should be the start of your EPM, your enterprise performance management!

The areas, each with suggested related measurements, are listed in the worksheets. In some cases, I have included weaknesses I have seen in many of the projects I have conducted with my clients, for you to check if a similar situation exists with you. You can use these worksheets directly, have your strategy think tank to assess the current situation and to define the target for future development cycles.

Web design and marketing

Web design and marketing responsibilities include product management, providing online product descriptions, defining and refining the value proposition for the different customer segments, segmentation and campaigning.

The worksheet in Table 13 addresses the primary objectives that often require extensions for the online Web presence and online customer interactions.

Online sales and payment

For sales, the picture gets a bit more complex than for marketing. The reason is that you need to check a variety of customer interaction types. And you need to support the various behaviour models to allow an improvement of your proposition to and interaction with the customers.

For this reason, two worksheets are necessary; one for interactions, the other for behaviour models (see Table 14 and 15, respectively). The customer interaction worksheet reflects:

❏ order or transaction entry for each particular customer segment and product;

❏ change of an order or transaction, for example, additions, reductions, prolongations;

Table 13 Worksheet for re-engineering the marketing activities

Area	Measurement	Now	Target	Frequently observed weaknesses/ your observation
Product management	Number of new products launched per month			
	Number of price plans per product			
	Discount policies (which, how refined)			Policies are not defined, discounts are given *ad hoc* without contribution and value considerations
Product description	Percentage of product descriptions available on website			On the Web, only standard brochures can be found The contents are not distilled and directed to the various market segments Design features attracting attention are infrequently used Full legal descriptions are complicated
Value proposition	Areas of strength identified (compared with competition)			
	Areas of weakness identified (compared with competition)			
	Customer benefits identified, formulated and quantified			Benefit descriptions exist only on a high level Focus is on cost comparison instead of on value comparison
Segmenta-tion and campaigns	Market share (per segment)			
	Number of customer segments identified			One-to-one marketing is desired, but only very few customer segments with their respective buying preferences are identified
	Number of campaigns defined			
	Number of different campaigns executed			One-to-one marketing is desired, but campaigns are global rather than specific for customer situation
	Response rate of campaigns (per campaign and segment)			No systematic measurement of responses is implemented No models to forecast response rates and closure rates are used
	Performance of loyalty programs (cross-/up-/deep-sell percentage)			No systematic measurement of the loyalty programme's constituencies takes place No models of customer behaviour (life-cycle, relationship cycle, seasonal cycles) are used

❏ termination of a standing order or cancellation of a transaction;

❏ payment for the service or product;

❏ defaulting payment and triggering of collections activities.

In addition to your internal assessment during the QLA you have to listen to your customer. Show him or her early prototypes of what you want to change, get his or her feedback and reflect it in one of the forthcoming coming e-business cycles.

Table 14 Worksheet for engineering the online sales interactions

Customer Interaction	Measurement	Now	Target	Frequently observed weaknesses/ your observation
Order or transaction entry	Number of products in the online catalogue			
	Number of online order forms			Online forms are just an implementation of the traditional paper order form instead of using information already available from the customer (e.g. address information, payment preferences)
	Duration of completing a form (per product)			
	Selection of different price plans per product			
	Discount volumes requested from customers			Should decrease over time and be replaced by price plans allowing a pro-active support of customer retention
	Discount price plans offered by you to increase customer loyalty			Discounts are not used to increase customer retention and loyalty Flat discounts should be replaced by bonus point schemes.
Order or transaction change	Percentage of products consistent in front-office and back-office			Often, the data in the front-office are not integrated with the back-office. Thus, changes need to be applied in various systems and lead to errors.
	Number of supported change types			Should be supported for most frequently used changes, e.g. date change, amount change, price plan change
Order or transaction termination/ cancellation	Number of customers won back			No pro-active win back campaign exists such as offering a special re-enrolment discount
Payment set up	Number of payment options			
	Number of credit profiles			Depending on the credit profile, only specific payment options should be allowed, e.g. only 'good' customers should get a credit line from you. Others have to pay up front or by credit card.

The results obtained through the assessment should be cross-checked against the current state and the target for your traditional sales channels, for example, transactions executed in one of your branches, orders accepted from your travelling sales force or from sales partners, orders handled by telephone, orders received by mail or fax. You also need to come up with the product selection and the price plans that are appropriate for the specific channel.

Consumers should be motivated to use the online channel by more attractive prices or by bonus points (like the award winning American Express airmiles programme where each credit card transaction adds up bonus points that can be transferred to travel or purchases of goods) – they save and you save, because your handling effort is smaller. Business customers should get added value through faster confirmations and better execution of their transactions.

Next, you need to check your customer behaviour models describing buying decisions as we discussed in Section 4.3. This check should be done by marketing and sales in close co-operation. The key models to consider are related to:

❏ controlling, that is, the relative classic discipline;

❏ customer life-cycle;

❏ customer relationship cycle.

Table 15 Worksheet for checking customer behaviour models

Model	Measurement	Now	Target	Recommendations/your observation
Controlling	Percentage of customer attrition (per segment)			
	Volume (amount) of sales			
	Margin/contribution			
Customer life-cycle	Number of events identified as key for buying decisions (per customer)			Consider the different need of your products at various life stages and the events of transition from one stage to another (e.g. start of university, start of first job, change of job, marriage, birth of child, moving, children growing up, retirement)
	Number of relatives (per customer) identified as possible referrals			
Customer relationship cycle	Events identified as key for buying decisions			Monitor, for example, first and subsequent successful cross-/up-/deep-sell, Analyse the patterns (probability of repeated interactions)
	Loyalty			Check the impact of different loyalty approaches (points, discounts, prizes) for retention per segment
Statistical foundation	Completeness of data warehouse			
	Availability of data-mining tools			

Additionally, the foundation for these models has to be assessed, namely the data warehouse and the analytical tools.

CRM and customer care

Let us look at what customer interactions mean for CRM and customer care. Their responsibilities and activities include:

❏ Supporting customers during their online order entry. In this role, customer care staff provide a hotline function.

❏ Entering orders for customers who cannot access the Internet when on the phone, as in a home banking setting.

❏ Entering transactions from other sources such as customer letters or faxes. In this function, customer care has a back-office and quality assurance responsibility.

❏ Servicing the customer with requests that are beyond the capability of the Internet application, such as complaint handling, or research of particular enquiries. These activities can be triggered by phone where an immediate response is expected, or by e-mail or fax.

❏ Organising the personal visit of either a sales representative or service people where appropriate.

❏ Making outbound calls to execute direct marketing campaigns, in particular win-back campaigns.

❏ Collecting payments from customers who have happened to disregard due dates.

To assess the current state of your customer care operations, you will find an outline for key measurements in the worksheet in Table 16.

As you can probably see from this worksheet, the borders between sales and customer care, that is, between front-office functions and back-office functions are becoming transparent. Actually, the customer care organisation you are running should be set up in such a way that they can 'test' new products and services and new sales approaches. When such new products and services are accepted by the market and the processes are settled and can be performed with good response times, you can reduce the workload of customer care by letting the customers care for themselves with a Web front-end. So customer care has moving targets in terms of the

Table 16 Worksheet for re-engineering customer care

Area	Measurement	Now	Target	Frequently observed weaknesses/ your observation
Customer support/ hotline	Number of requests handled			
	Duration for answering the request			
Order or transaction entry and processing (new, change, termination)	Number of orders or transactions processed daily			
	Number of new customers set up daily			
	Duration of order completion			Integration issues, for example, banks could inform their customers when a stock price stays close to a limit but has not reached it and offer to change the limit; telecom operators need to implement automatic provisioning systems and link them with order handling
	Number of early cancellations of orders			Reasons given by customers should be assessed to identify the weak points in the order handling
Customer requests	Number of enquiries answered			Lack of integrated view of customer (different customer IDs in different systems, no access to contractual agreements, enquiries into other departments cannot be followed through) Contents of conversation with customer cannot be recorded and forwarded to next colleague dealing with the case Frequently asked questions should be answered via self-access (online or from tape recorded messages)
	Number of complaints processed			
	Duration for solving a complaint			
	Number of visits (e.g. sales force, repair service), organised by customer care			Planning tool for field service should be accessible by customer care Cost impact of visit has to be reflected in guidelines to assess when visits are appropriate
Outbound calls	Number of marketing calls made			
	Closure rate of marketing calls			
	Number of outstanding payment collection activities (calls, letters) performed			Lack of workflow and CTI tool to focus on the most promising collection cases
	Amount of payments collected			

products they are supporting – but they do have the consistent objective of optimising the processing time of orders, speeding-up the handling of customer requests and gaining high response rates for their outbound activities. And they need to deliver the feedback they obtain first-hand from the customers back to marketing and to sales to allow them to improve the overall product or service.

Supply chain management and logistics

Supply chain management (SCM) and logistics has three key roles. First, it needs to provide the 'indirect' supplies such as office materials, desks, computers or cars. Indirect supplies are relevant for all enterprises. Secondly, it has to support the business transactions by having 'direct' materials available that are necessary to execute specific customer transactions, such as the goods to sell in an online shop, the telephone equipment for telecom operators, the steel for producing cars. Direct supplies in the strict sense only exist when you are dealing with physical goods. Similar interaction concepts, though, can also be applied service enterprises. So far, SCM focuses on identifying the vendors of the supplies, agreeing on terms and conditions and (in leading enterprises) on automatically supported procurement.

Logistics has to ensure that the purchased goods are available in time, when they are needed and at the right place – both for items received from suppliers and for goods and services delivered to the customer. And there must be pro-active information supported to the customer: the Web world has learned from Amazon how to keep customers informed about the delivery progress of an ordered book with messages such as:

❏ 'usually available in 24 hours' when the customer is browsing through the catalogue;

❏ 'we have received your order and will ship the book tomorrow' when Amazon has received the order and checked the actual availability;

❏ 'we have now sent the book, you should receive it on the next business day' when Amazon has handed over the parcel to its logistics partner.

A similar information policy can be adopted in other business fields. If you also look at 'supplies' such as money funds, telephone lines or available resources and skills, you can engage in new ways of dealing with your customers. We have already talked about new ways in which stockbrokers can make sure that the customers' orders can be processed by making them aware when the stock price is getting close to the limit the customer has set. Similar examples are:

❏ online information to customers when the telephone line they have ordered will be implemented and be available;

❏ conversion of a loan with floating interest rate to one with a fixed-rate agreement when market rates reach certain ceilings the customer can specify and adjust online;

Table 17 Worksheet for re-engineering SCM

Area	Measurement	Now	Target	Recommendation/your observation
Supply availability	Number of supply items monitored in supply database			The most frequently needed supplies have to be reflected in a supplies database
	Percentage of products offered mapped to supply items			Supplies necessary for the most demanded products have to be reflected in a supplies database
Status information	Percentage of product availability information accessible via Web front end			Availability information should be shown in the online catalogue
	Number of logistic chain events reflected in order status			Key events have to be identified to keep the customer informed (see Amazon example)
	Products supported with an order-completion forecast			Customers should be informed when they can expect to get what they have ordered
	Order status available to customers on request (pull information)			
	Order status communicated actively to customer (push information)			
Procurement	Agreements with suppliers available online			
	Price quotes available online			
	Percentage of staff entitled to order supplies via electronic procurement			Effort and cost to execute price comparisons is often higher than the value of the purchased good. In such cases, the staff should directly order from preselected suppliers.
	Value of supplies ordered via electronic procurement			
	Number of suppliers participating in electronic marketplace			For commodities, suppliers should be invited for making bids online. Then, purchases can be made at the best available market terms.

❑ offering surplus resources on electronic markets; for example, utilities companies are now starting to sell energy on an options and future market.

The key responsibilities for indirect and direct supplies are:

❑ checking availability of supplies;

❑ integrating the status of availability with the front-office to inform the customer, and with the logistics components for supply and delivery;

❑ organising procurement with supplier agreements, price arrangements or bidding processes.

The respective measurements are listed in the worksheet in Table 17.

Human resources

All the details outlined above imply that the focus of your staff should shift from an internal perspective looking primarily at procedures and dealing primarily with their peers in their own unit to a more mature understanding of the overall processes and interactions with your customers. To attain this maturity your staff must be supported by pro-active support from your human resources department (HR).

They need to help develop the new policies and guidelines that empower current staff to make far-reaching decisions – as in the example discussed where multi-million loan approvals can now be made by the clerk in the bank branch. This additional empowerment, responsibility and value contribution on the part of individual staff members has to be reflected in an incentive policy in line with the enterprise's business objectives.

HR has to develop training programmes and put them into practice to make the staff ready for the new approaches and to use the new systems effectively. Where necessary, some additional know-how has to be injected by hiring key employees with experience in the new type of pro-active customer interactions.

You need to focus on HR responsibilities for:

❑ defining policies for empowering staff and for remunerating them in line with their value contribution to the enterprise;

❏ developing skills to enable them to pro-actively service your customers by setting up training programmes and knowledge centres;

❏ attracting and keeping staff (and keeping them happy);

❏ defining incentive schemes in line with overall targets, and based on individual contribution.

The HR worksheet can be constructed like the ones for the operational units discussed earlier.

Table 18 Worksheet for re-engineering the HR activities

Area	Measurement	Now	Target	Recommendation/your observation
Policies	Percentage of staff guided by policies for value-based empowerment and competencies			
	Percentage of staff eligible to incentive remuneration based on contribution and service level achievement			
Skill development	Percentage of staff trained in pro-active customer service			
	Number of identified focal areas for knowledge development			Contact points for increasing corporate knowledge should be established Discussion forums on the intranet for documenting and communicating day-to-day experience to be created
Staff attraction and retention	Staff size targets (per responsibility and skill area)			
	Staff attrition (percentage of staff leaving)			
	Barometer of staff satisfaction			

Co-operation/EPM

We have been reflecting numbers throughout this chapter. They include counts (such as number of orders, or number of customers), amounts (such as volume of closed orders, or size of contribution) and percentages (such as percentage of customer responsiveness to campaigns). Can you imagine the tons of paper with detailed figures that possibly do not even help you to steer your business? If you just compile the numbers as outlined above, you may actually end up with a data graveyard.

Instead you need to design your reporting properly. The raw materials we have outlined above need to be condensed to a meaningful, easy to understand, crisp and short report. That is one of the traditional tasks of controlling. Such a report has to be the baseline for communicating your progress to stock analysts and customers. And it should indicate the areas where the co-operation between your various departments and with your business partners has to be improved. With those measurable objectives, your service level agreements can be monitored and managed.

How can this be done? Well, the best way is to come up with a ranking system for relative achievement of goals. So, you need to add to the worksheets the commitment of the particular department by the end of each reporting period (for example, by the end of every month). When you then measure the actual results and compare them with the commitment, you see either:

❏ achievement or over-achievement of the plan;

❏ a slight deviation from the plan, say up to 10 per cent;

❏ a significant deviation from the plan.

If all the measurements in a business unit show an achievement, your strategy group and the top managers of the company do not need to worry, so the report from that business unit can be summarised by a green symbol. If most aspects of a business unit show an achievement, or if there are only slight deviations from the plan, the strategy group and the top managers should be alerted by a yellow symbol. In-depth reports have to allow a more detailed assessment of where problematic areas are and you can provide some guidance for the business unit to get back on track. And finally, if a business unit is significantly off track, very active help in fixing the problems is necessary. In this case, the standard reports will not suffice, but you should organise a task force to analyse the situation and organise an improvement. To indicate the colours in black and white hard copies, traffic lights are a good symbol (upper light on = red, middle light on = yellow, lower light on = green).

In this way, you will not have lots of numbers, but a clear one-view summary indicating traffic light conditions. In the online display you can get details by clicking on the area in which you are interested. You can look in depth at data from various perspectives, for example, according to products, regions, evolution over time, actual figures or planned figures as defined by your measurement programme. Please refer to the example of the enterprise performance management in Section 5.6.

On the subject of online interactions, I should also mention that this 'report' should not be delivered in paper form, but on the screen of the strategy group and top managers. Your strategy group and the top managers do not have a computer with access to those numbers? Well, that is something you should change before the other areas of the project start. It is your responsibility to set a good example and you should familiarise yourself with current Internet possibilities. If you have implemented a leading-edge system, you should even be able to forward a screenshot of a page where you have questions or recommendations with your annotations to the people in charge.

The acceptance of this internal reporting and controlling system is, by the way, another thing you may want to measure, for example, by the number of managers using it actively.

12.2 E-business architecture

To help you define customer-oriented processes supporting the co-operation we have discussed across your traditional business units, we will go through sample organisation configurations from the finance industry, from telecom and from retailing. What these examples have in common is the way in which their architecture is broken down into customer support, operational support and business management. In addition to the focus represented by the new grouping of responsibilities, the close co-operation between the units has to be expressed in end-to-end processes as discussed in the section above.

Customer support: if you have one, this is the 'classic' front-office. These are the people in contact with your customers, accepting their orders, negotiating the details of the transactions, taking care of upcoming problems in customer relations and getting the product delivered or the service provided to the customer. The difference in e-business is the number of different channels customers can decide to use: not only are they talking to your staff in their branch, but they may want to use another branch, contact the call centre, or do transactions online via the Web. And transactions issued in either of the channels must be accessible from all other channels. The messages sent to the customer via either of the channels must be consistent, and price plans including discounts for using a particular channel must be aligned.

Operational support: yes, that is the back-office, but with the new customer-oriented attitude we have discussed. In the past it was enough to develop a particular product or to provide a particular service, but that has to be extended now. The back-office organisation has to see and constantly improve their overall impact on customer relations, customer satisfaction and service quality. Managers and staff have to be very active in understanding customer needs and in refining and extending services to get a better response to customer demand and they have to watch service level commitments and seek ongoing improvement. Back-offices have often been structured with many hierarchical layers. This should change as well; instead of reporting to a boss, the staff should see the customer-oriented units as their clients, that is, understand their demands, how to respond quickly and at a reasonable cost to their demands, commit themselves to a result and deliver on time. And what if the services of a particular back-office unit are not in demand at all? Guess what, they may not be needed and you had better close the unit down, sell it or re-assign the staff to other units working at full steam.

Business management: beyond the new holistic measuring activities discussed in the last sections with related planning, controlling and EPM activities, we find here traditional business management tasks.

For components (or units) in the subsequent architecture templates, I will highlight what is different in e-business from your current activities. Your strategy group should use the architecture recommendations to map the responsibilities of the outlined units with your specific value proposition. If your industry is not included, you can still find enough indicators because most of the customer-oriented units as well as the necessary back-office integration should have a similar nature. You can obtain soft copies of all the following tables from my website.

And do not forget — your uniqueness comes from being different, and your market success comes from being entertaining. Did anybody say that your business should not be fun?

Retail banking objectives and solution template

Table 19 Key e-business objectives for retail bank departments

Unit	Key e-business objective
Touch point coordination	Set-up of new touch points/delivery channels: call centre, Internet, banking kiosk Allocation of specific products and services to the respective touch point/delivery channel(s) Ensuring accessibility of transaction and profile data and consistent messages across the different touch points/channels Design of different pricing schemes per touch point/channel Effective design of entry forms depending on channel, e.g. pre-configured forms for frequent transactions
Treatment management (marketing and sales)	Frequent update of information on website Design of infotainment components on website Consistency of Web approach with ongoing traditional business, if necessary creation of new brand Effective use of 'virtual' media for campaigns: outbound calls, e-mail, personalised contents of website Use of customer profiles and pricing policies, for selecting products, price plans, risk premiums, discounts
Treatment management (customer service)	Definition of critical business scenarios with related service level commitments Quick responses in customer interactions Availability 24 hours a day, 365 days per year Development of customer-buying behaviour models with respective customer treatment strategies
Customer profiles and segmentation	All customer information accessible using one unique code (e.g. enterprise-wide customer ID) Good coverage of customer data in data warehouse Data mining tools in place and used for behaviour modelling
Checking/ deposit account processing	Intraday processing instead of nightly batch runs Customer self-service capabilities, e.g. standing order administration, request of chequebooks, blocking of cheques, savings plan administration Self-service administration of frequently used transactions, e.g. beneficiary and accounting data for money transfers
Loan origination	Credit worthiness checking automatically supported Online approval for loan applications New product and service features, e.g. pre-approved credit lines that can be activated by customer self-service
Credit/debit card processing	Online presentment of credit card bills Online handling of complaints about incorrectly debited amounts New product and service offerings, e.g. bill consolidation for various vendors (electronic shops, utility provider, telecom bill), digital cash
Mortgages	Credit worthiness checking automatically supported Online approval for mortgage applications New product and service features, e.g. support for buying and selling real estate online, evaluation of real estate value
Private banking and investment management	Online entry for brokerage transactions Automatic cash management New product and service features, e.g. automatic saving plans, alerts for buy/sell opportunities that might interest the customer according to investment profile, day trading
Treasury and risk management	Position update and risk monitoring close to real time (should be already implemented for capital adequacy guideline) Development of customer treatment approaches depending on risk profile

The business management units and objectives will be discussed on page 205.

Source: PeopleSoft, 2000

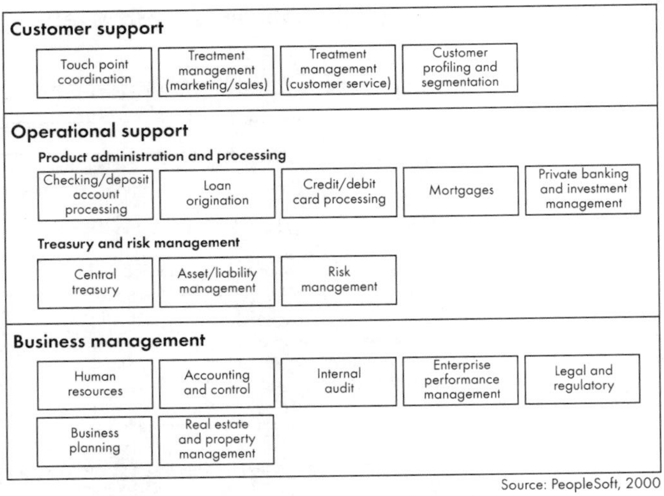

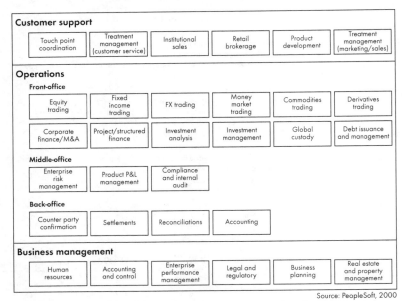

Figure 29 E-business architecture for retail banks

Investment banking and brokerage template and objectives

Source: PeopleSoft, 2000

Figure 30 E-business architecture for investment banks and brokerage

Table 20 Key e-business objectives for departments of investment banks and brokerages

Unit	Key e-business objective
Touch point management	Set-up of new touch points/delivery channels: call centre, Internet – with options for PC interaction, mobile phone interaction, UMTS interaction, multi-language features
	Allocation of specific products and services to respective touch point(s)/delivery channel(s)
	Ensuring accessibility of transaction and profile data and consistent messages across the touch points/channels
	Design of different pricing schemes per touch point/channel
	Effective design of order forms depending on channel, e.g. pre-configured forms for frequent transactions, easy to use screens for mobile phones
Treatment management (customer service)	Definition of critical business scenarios with related service level commitments
	Quick responses in customer interactions
	Availability 24 hours a day, 365 days per year
	Access to international stock exchanges
	Development of customer buying behaviour models with respective customer treatment strategies
Institutional sales	Sophisticated online performance analysis for customer investment
	Structure of portfolio and buying profiles maintainable online
	Online order entry
	Day-trading
	Online problem handling
Retail brokerage	Personalised information regarding stocks owned by the customer
	Online performance analysis
	Online order entry
Product management	Definition of new services exploiting the interactive capabilities, e.g. day-trading for private customers, investment profile maintenance triggering automatic buy/sell transactions, customer alerts for buy/sell opportunities, online invitation to shareholder meeting
Treatment management (marketing and sales)	Frequent update of information on website
	Design of infotainment components on the website, e.g. news feeds from the stock exchange, games with dummy stock portfolio, analysis function for customers' portfolio
	Consistency of Web approach with ongoing traditional business, if necessary creation of new brand
Operations	As traders, middle-office and execution in the back-office are already highly automated and integrated, no change in responsibility is to be expected.
	The number of transactions will increase drastically with e-brokerage, so the systems performance needs to be significantly increased

The business management units and objectives will be discussed on page 205.

Insurance solution template and objectives

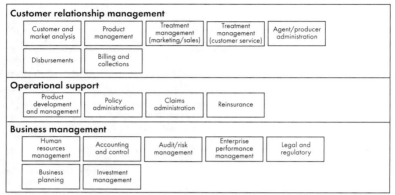

Source: PeopleSoft, 2000

Figure 31   E-business architecture for insurance companies

Table 21 Key e-business objectives for insurance departments

Unit	Key e-business objective
Customer and market analysis	Extension of customer risk profiles by buying behaviour models and life-cycle models Loyalty and referral models, win back approaches
Product management	Definition of new services exploiting the interactive capabilities, e.g. life insurance combined with investment portfolio management self-service, brokerage of insurances Value-added services for segments such as education service supported by saving plans, real estate communities for house insurance customers, traffic services for car insurance customers, health community for senior citizens
Treatment management (marketing and sales)	Effective use of 'virtual' media for campaigns: outbound calls, e-mail, personalisation Use of available data for cross-selling to family members and of products of additional insurance branches (life, health, car, house) Frequent update of information on website Design of infotainment components on the website, e.g. games Consistency of Web approach with ongoing traditional business, if necessary creation of new brand
Treatment management (customer service)	Online self-service submission of claims, extension of existing contracts by self-service Information to the customer by e-mail or personalised Web contents before policies expire to allow an extension Definition of critical business scenarios with related service level commitments Quick responses in customer interactions, availability 24 hours a day, 365 days per year
Staff administration	Availability of customer information via intranet Application forms and claims forms available for staff on their laptops Commission calculation available online Premium calculation available online Online bill presentment
Disbursement	Claims forms available online Automatic approval of standard claims depending on customer and product profile
Billing and collections	Online bill presentment
Operational support	In the short run, no change in responsibilities is to be expected. In the future, policies on claim handling can be developed, allowing approved customer claims. Then, an online handling of standard claims will be possible.

The business management units and objectives will be discussed on page 205.

Telco solution template and objectives

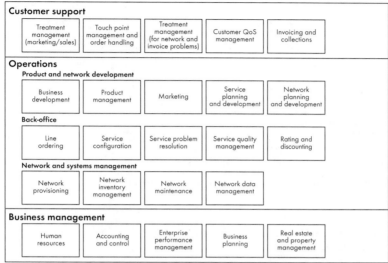

Source: Telecom Operations Management, Tele Management Forum, 1999

Figure 32   E-business architecture for telecom providers

Table 22 Key e-business objectives for departments of telecoms

Unit	Key e-business objective
Treatment management (marketing and sales)	Effective use of 'virtual' media for campaigns: outbound calls, e-mail, personalisation Use of customer profiles and pricing policies, for selecting products, price plans, discounts Reflection of local availability of service (e.g. ISDN, DSL, on-/off-net) for Web orders
Touch point management and order handling	Online order entry for additional lines to existing customers, change of features such as ISDN upgrade, or new standard package such as DSL Online status updates on progress of installation and activation Service configuration, e.g. call forwarding, request of new telephone number Ensuring accessibility of transaction and profile data and consistent messages across the touch points/channels
Treatment management (network and invoice issues)	Online entry of problem reports Online status updates on progress of trouble resolution
Quality of service management	Online availability of line quality, call pattern analysis, service level commitments of customer care organisation
Invoicing and collections	Online Bill Presentment Bill consolidation including bills from third parties, e.g. online shops, online payments
Operations	Back-office, network management and field service planning, customer service systems and the Web front end have to be neatly integrated in order to allow end-to-end support for the transactions submitted by the customer. The current focus at many telecom operators is the integration of network provisioning and service activation; subsequently additional services such as selection of specific telephone numbers, administration of call forwarding (e.g. depending on time of day, caller, holding duration), display of service availability and service quality can become relevant

The business management units and objectives will be discussed on page 205.

Retail sales solution template and objectives

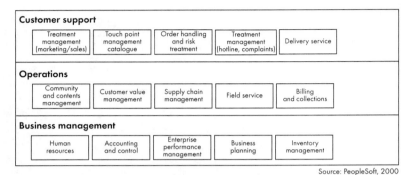

Figure 33   E-business architecture for sales retailers

Table 23 Key e-business objectives for retail sales departments

Unit	Key e-business objective
Treatment management (marketing and sales)	Effective use of 'virtual' media for campaigns: outbound calls, e-mail, personalisation Use of customer profiles and pricing policies, for selecting products, price plans, discounts
Touch point management and catalogue	Set-up of new touch points: call centre, Internet – with options for PC interaction, mobile phone interaction, UMTS interaction, multi-language features Allocation of specific products and services to respective touch point(s)/delivery channel(s) Ensuring accessibility of transaction and profile data and consistent messages across the touch points/channels Design of different pricing schemes per touch point/channel Multimedia contents in catalogue (videos, audios) Availability of products and delivery options (e.g. same day delivery) Embedding of customer contents into community services and infotainment, e.g. on fashion, children, sports
Order handling and risk treatment	Online order entry with confirmed delivery date and time Pricing and payment methods (e.g. immediate cash versus credit lines) depending on customer risk profile
Treatment management (hotline and complaints)	Access to customer transactions and availability of repair service updates Definition of critical business scenarios with related service level commitments Quick responses in customer interactions Availability 24 hours per day, 365 days per year Development of customer- buying behaviour models with respective customer treatment strategies
Delivery service	Tangible information on production progress, e.g. video from facilities producing the goods Online availability of delivery status (location of shipment, expected time of arrival)
Community and contents management	Online communities for various customer segments, e.g. fashion, music, sports, children News, entertainment, games and facilitated discussion forums for communities Extensions to catalogue contents and highlighting of special offers aligned with the communities' interests (e.g. special edition CD after a concert, early orders after fashion show, promotion on merchandising goods after sports championship)
Customer-value management	Analysis of customer-buying behaviour Definition of models and identification of events triggering buying decisions Design of personalised marketing campaigns

Table 23 Key e-business objectives for retail sales departments (cont.)

Supply chain management	Order forecasts based on customer behaviour models and planned marketing campaigns Online ordering from suppliers integrated with delivery logistics (just in time approach) Electronic marketplace
Field service	Automatic and reliable scheduling for delivery, installation and repair activities Accessibility of field service schedule for customers and call centre Availability of customer profile Cross-selling objectives
Billing and collections	Online bill presentment Bill consolidation including bills from third parties, e.g. telecom provider Online payments

The business management units and objectives will be discussed on page 205.

Business management objectives

Business management objectives are very similar throughout the different industries. Below you will find the additional objectives induced by your transition to an e-business.

Table 24 Key e-business management objectives

Unit	Key e-business objective
Human resources	Development of customer focus on the part of staff Policies and empowerment/competencies allowing quick decisions in customer-oriented units Incentives based on value contribution, service quality and speed
Accounting and control	Non-financial measurements to be included in reporting Implementation of balanced scorecard
Internal audit and risk management	Service quality and speed Soundness of data encryption approaches for online transactions to be checked Check of performance of policies and guidelines Check of compliance to policies and guidelines
Enterprise performance management	Condensation of reporting figures into easy to understand information Definition of corrective actions in case of unfavourable performance
Legal and regulatory	Customer contracts need to reflect online business (validity of electronic transactions, PIN/TAN approach, digital signatures) Access restrictions and data privacy to be checked
Business planning	The releases of the e-business factory have to be planned In addition to financial figures, customer interaction targets and service quality levels have to be planned
Real estate/ property/ investment management	Electronic marketplace can be established

And do not forget, speed is the most important objective:

❏ **time to market** – speed of innovation and the frequency of new products and services;

❏ **service levels** – speed of transaction execution and frequency of keeping the customer informed about progress;

❏ **releases of the e-business factory** – speed of change to redirect the orientation of the whole enterprise.

12.3 Partners

You may think that you are already experienced in partnership concepts. Sales partnerships are common, and parts of your operations may be outsourced to some service provider. E-business now adds some important impetus to your partnership considerations:

❏ the speed of innovations and the increased transparency on the market with its related intensified cost pressures forces you to stick to your core competencies;

❏ the focus on fulfilling and increasing service level commitments demands small units that are capable of pro-actively improving customer service and increasing specific skills for their contribution to the value chain;

❏ the global trend of mergers and mega-mergers may lead to one of your traditional partners suddenly not being available any more because the company has suddenly become a member of a competing conglomerate.

So, leave all areas where partnership reaps excellent benefits – in order to be able to offer partners' excellent services in a great package to your customers. Many traditional enterprises have started a shopping tour to acquire the pioneers of e-business – or the e-pioneers merge with each other. Why not do a similar deal as the Italian directory service Seat Pagine Gialle (online yellow pages, *www.paginegialle.it*) investing 150 million Euros into the electronic marketplace Mondus (*www.mondus.de*) to get immediate access to several hundred solid business customers?

But there is more leverage to gain than just access to customers: many aspects of your operations can be outsourced. What does that mean now for you in practice? Let me show you an extreme example of a start-up providing a mobile payment service. You can use your mobile phone for example, when riding in a taxi to pay the taxi driver. Actually you can trigger a payment to be executed, and the taxi driver obtains a confirmation number from the payment provider that guarantees the payment. Or you can pay for mobile ticket reservations by providing your mobile telephone number like a credit card number. This start-up, *www.paybox.de,* with only twenty-two employees, has no less than a dozen partner companies – see the screenshot of their website in Figure 34. Can you imagine what it means for twenty-two people to handle all the customer relations, the day-to-day operations and on top deal with more than a dozen partners? On the other hand, without all those partners, how could such a small team come up with such a good value proposition and a decent market coverage? What a difference from the current relationship you have with some vendors or service partners! That is the new paradigm we are talking about.

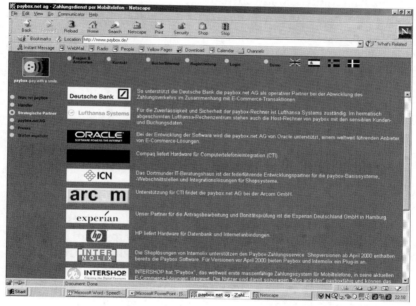

Figure 34   Some partners for launching a new e-business offering

Paybox is partnering with a bank for actual payments, with service providers to run the computer centre to host the applications, with hardware vendors and integrators for the e-commerce solution, for the CTI, and for database and Internet connectivity, with an overall systems integrator, with external services for credit scoring and with a handful of connected online catalogue and shop providers.

Intensive partnerships between earlier competing traditional companies are now the rule, no matter how unthinkable they would have been a few years ago. We mentioned Bank of Montreal's ownership of specific interaction channels and their dominance in some market segments. Their turnaround was supported by creating several new brands: Bank of Montreal Online/BMO as their online channel, mbanx with a particular focus on students, competix for business-to-business credit decisioning services and now even TradeLC.com for the international trade finance. Why am I telling you this here? Well, to show you the stepwise evolution from a local bank to a leading global financial service provider.

BMO has quite a few good features exploiting the interactivity of the Web such as mortgage calculators – but they just use the Web channel for quite traditional banking. Mbanx takes the next step: they partner with their customers, the students, intensively through community services and service providers linked to topics and benefits the students are interested in, such as partnering with a mobile communication provider for mobile banking, earning free airmiles, accessing research pools and news archives. With competix Bank of Montreal goes a step further: this is a joint venture between themselves and the provider of the analytical and decisions software, namely American Management Systems (AMS). And now the current TradeLC.com service is really positioning the players in the joint venture, that is, the three participating banks from the various corners of the world, on the leading edge of global Web business execution.

Hurry up, strategic alliances are being formed now that will be the drivers of business evolution in the next few years! And you need a new model for engaging in partnerships and monitoring their performance. First of all, you should distinguish between strategic partners and partners that just fulfil one of your operational requirements. Operational partners need to be primarily evaluated on the ratio of cost versus performance. You should be ready to change such partners from time to time, either if another provider offers the services at a better cost/performance ratio or if new competitive situations arise. Usually, your computer centre operator, your Internet service provider, the delivery and logistics partner, or payment clearing facilities are such operational partners.

Some areas of high strategic value require a different approach. With them, you need to consider mutual participation or mergers; stakeholders may have dual roles in the boards of both companies; and you should seek a long-term commitment for support and non-competitive activities. Typically, the call-centre operations and sales partnerships are of such a strategic nature. Some joint services may require close strategic partnerships, too. We discussed, for example, the idea of bill consolidation, where different companies provide joint invoices to their customers, such as an online shop with customers' banks, or a telco operator together with customers' building societies. Such joint services require good balancing of the mutual dependencies and commitments.

There is also an ongoing movement between partnership types as well as insourcing and outsourcing considerations. Initially in your e-business transition, you may need to push your organisation through a rapid adjustment process by spinning off some key departments – such as the field service or the delivery team. At that stage, you may need to keep control by maintaining the majority stake in the new company. While guiding them to become more pro-active and to improve their service levels, you need to protect your participation by allowing them higher prices than from a third-party provider. At later stages, when they have started on their own to generate new business with other companies, you can keep them on a longer leash by reducing your participation. In successful cases, you can even make additional profits by having your subsidiary go public. At that point, though, they have evolved from being a strategic partner to being an operational partner, and you need to treat them like your other operational partners, that is, negotiate hard on their prices, or even replace their services with those of a better and cheaper provider.

The contrary movement is possible, too. One of your operational partners may become better and better integrated in your end-to-end processes and thus provide excellent service for you. In such a case you may want to prevent competitors getting these excellent services and you should seek participation or even merger with the provider.

For all partners, you have to regularly check benefits and risks according to the following parameters:

❏ Strategic importance: how unique is the service provided by the partner and what would it mean if a competitor had the same quality of service that you get?

❏ Risk: what would it mean to your market position, market penetration and profitability, if the partner should stop supporting you, for example, due to a hostile take-over?

❏ Integration: how well does this type of service need to be integrated in your customer-oriented and operational processes, and how well is it actually integrated?

❏ Innovation: how flexible is the partner in the process and service changes you need to implement and how pro-actively does he or she come up with new leading-edge approaches for his or her activities?

❏ Cost: how expensive are the partner's services and the particular service qualities compared with competitors?

In any case, you must never outsource the core of your business, you need to agree on unambiguous service levels and notification periods for terminating the services that allow you to engage with another partner and you have to have a fall-back plan ready in case the partner fails to deliver.

12.4 EPM based on collaborative systems

All the various bits and pieces get together in your enterprise performance management. Here, your targets are expressed and actual development is monitored against planned development. An automated EPM means that not only do your people have to work together, but also your IT systems need to collaborate. Make sure

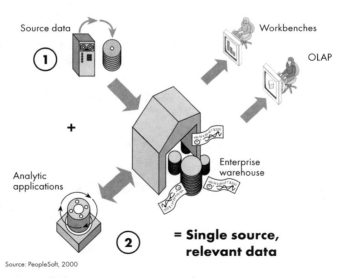

Figure 35   Collaborative enterprise performance management systems

that all the components are embedded in one common strategic measurement and steering approach. Figure 35 summarises the key components from a system perspective. Make the data from the source systems available to your data warehouse in a defined way and with a defined content, apply the analysis we have discussed, and you will get your single source of relevant data, from which you can trigger internal actions and customer treatments.

12.5 Summary

Many details have been given in this chapter on how to do a quick look assessment and how to create your own e-business architecture. As a summary:

❑ focus on customer-oriented processes;

❑ use the worksheets appropriate to your industry and define the service levels you want to achieve;

❑ define your e-business based on the template provided for your industry;

❑ partner with third parties wherever you cannot come up with excellent services yourself; equip your partners and your field force to further your sales;

❑ implement a measuring programme to come up with your enterprise performance management based on a balanced scorecard monitoring of your service quality, extending current financial control.

13

System development

@@@ Develop your systems in iterative cycles. @@@ For each cycle, on-time delivery is more important than full compliance with all requirements. @@@ In each cycle, enforce co-operation across the organisation, rapid prototyping, early deployment and measurement of service quality. @@@

The development tasks discussed in the following sections are based on various e-business development methodologies. Usually, though, these methodologies have two disadvantages in common. The first one is that due to their completeness they are complex: key points are scattered over several hundred pages, and it would take you a long time to distil the success factors out of them. The second disadvantage is that they are constructed to help development teams that strive for excellence in building systems rather than provide excellent services for their customers.

Is it your core competency to build complex systems? Probably not, so *buy* your solution instead of *making* it! And for those areas you need to make anyway, because you have not found appropriate packages available on the market, implement a solution by rapid prototyping and deployment as described below.

The contrast and extension to traditional development approaches is highlighted below. Now the overruling priorities for development are customer benefits, quick implementation and an early opportunity to gain operational experience with the new processes. The tasks discussed in the following pages allow you to frame integration activities, set objectives for your teams and monitor their success. And if you want to grow your competency in building huge systems, you still can adhere to tight methodologies at a later stage.

13.1 Optimise time instead of scope

In traditional development, the focus was on compliance with design (usually balanced against cost and effort considerations). This led to projects that often ran late, it induced fights regarding 'scope creep' when vendors, system integrators and the client had different perspectives on contributions from various players to the project – and thus created even more delays. Some systems were often over-engineered and had great flexibility built in, but unfortunately in areas not actually needed in the everyday business, while adding unnecessary operational overhead when using and running the system. And even worse, when the system was eventually compliant with the initial requirements, the actual business and market requirements had changed in the mean time, leading to formal change requests and a permanent process of catching up with reality.

At today's Internet speed, this attempt to catch up would never be successful and competitors would beat your slow time to market. Even worse, if it takes too long for your project to deliver its return on investment, you will lock yourself into an approach that may already be outdated. You understand that the focus has to be on the timely delivery of improved customer interaction capabilities. So what can you do?

There are three tricks. The first is actually what not to do – do not start by describing the required result in detailed handbooks, requirement definitions or design documents. Instead, agree on measurable benefits that the new release of your organisation has to create. Once you start defining measurement processes, you will find out what the real issues in business execution are. How long should it take a customer to enter a transaction? The possible target of 'two clicks' will need some pretty smart design, so you may need to accept a 'four click' implementation as the first step. How long should it take a member of the call-centre staff to de-activate a customer in all relevant sub-systems? One minute may be the target, but if it takes you one hour today, half an hour would be a great improvement.

The second trick, again something not to do, is not to stick to the traditional sequence of:

1. user expresses functional requirements and throws them over the wall to development;

2. technical designer interprets functional requirements, adds technical requirements, documents them in a thick requirement manual and throws it back to the users;

3. user reviews the manual, marks his comments, throws it back to development;

4. repeat steps 2 and 3 until formal acceptance of requirements is achieved;

5. develop according to documentation;

6. test the system against the documentation;

7. put it into operation and realise the operational impact;

8. fine-tune the system to get better response times and quicker interactions.

Instead, marketing, users, developers and operational staff have to work together. This co-operation has to start from a better understanding of mutual objectives and responsibilities. In joint work groups, they have to express their measurable targets – and then they need to create the solution jointly. The definition of business processes should happen at the same time as the developers define the system. Performance forecasts with anticipated architecture need to be made by operational staff at the same time, based on the initial business and technical architecture. With this approach, unnecessary efforts of investing too much in features of only limited benefit can be avoided.

The third, and last, trick is to manage the project by input rather than by output. Yes, you have read that right! Maybe you are proud of all the quality instruments you have created, and it is correct, they are good tools to use in a big software factory, but be honest – they have led to long timespans for your projects, so they are good for brick and mortar, but not for click and mortar! Therefore, to manage wisely by input, do not ask developers (or a third party) at the end of the many requirement iterations discussed above, how expensive the whole process may end up being. Instead, decide how much of the expected benefit of, say, the first phase, you want to invest into the implementation of this very phase. This decision defines the size of the team and the amount they have available for purchasing components from external sources. So, the joint team can act like entrepreneurs and optimise the outcome of the budget they have been allocated. And they had better be quick with their implementation by adjusting the tasks discussed above to a task plan such as in the following list:

1. identify targeted overall improvements for customers, call-centre staff, process execution and operations;

2. identify best solutions available on the market;

3. design extensions to the best available solutions specifically for your business; use tools for the design that allow you to prototype key interactions during the design sessions so that you have a running prototype available at the end of the design sessions;

4. implement the solution (with as few extensions as possible) as a proof of concept for a small test group and integrate it into a preliminary system environment; check compliance with performance objectives;

5. extend the proof of concept to an operational pilot for the first group of 'friendly' customers; obtain their feedback for improving the next release;

6. roll the next improved release out to a larger group of customers.

Just compare how long alone the steps 1 through 4 would take you in the traditional approach, with the anticipated length of steps 1 through 4 in the new approach. At step 4 of the new approach you have a solution in your hands – instead of the paperwork produced traditionally by that time – at approximately the same investment. You may argue that the repetitions are more costly in the long run, because there is no defined end. But consider that each system release should achieve a payback by itself, and you can repeat all the steps as long as they are successful, that is, as long as they produce a positive return on investment. In case of a negative return on investment, you can stop the activity or look for a better approach – in this case you have saved a lot of money compared to what you wasted when sinking a huge traditional, monolithic project.

13.2 Iterative development cycles

Let us now look more closely at iterative development cycles. The objective is to deploy new system releases within short, pre-defined time frames. Each release has to achieve the service level commitments for this cycle. In addition to changing the managerial focus from scope to time, cross-departmental co-operation has to be intensified and new types of success measurement (for example, on service level achievement) have to be implemented to support cross-departmental co-operation.

Each cycle contains the tasks subsequently described, and one cycle follows after another. In some cases, it may even be appropriate to have overlapping cycles with the business strategy definition and the first assessment of available approaches of the new cycle commencing while the implementation and deployment of the earlier cycle still continues. For each task, we will discuss objectives, success criteria, dependencies, risks and mitigation strategy. You should use these definitions to come up with your project definition document and a detailed task plan.

Figure 36 is a graphical representation of the key tasks for each cycle.

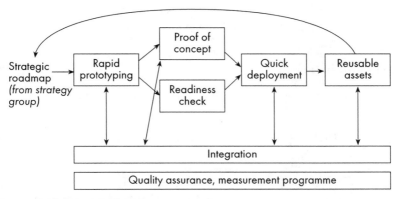

Figure 36   Iterative development cycles

Rapid prototyping/tool selection

Objective: design the website sitemap and contents, the 'look and feel' with the appropriate navigation and the customer interactions. For the priority components of the respective cycle (according to the component lists in Section 8.4 and Chapter 14): identify which solutions are available on the market. For the functions not covered by them: design screens and functions with tools allowing a quick and ideally automatically supported generation of the executable code. For an e-cycle with a three-month duration, you should aim to complete design workshops within the first month.

Success criteria: design is accepted by marketing, users, developers and operational staff after completing workshop sessions. Where necessary, the preferred tools and vendors are identified. Briefly after design completion, first mock-ups are given to customers and users to gain their feedback on navigation, interaction and contents.

Responsibilities and dependencies: the functional design has to be driven by marketing and user departments (for example, call centre), and the technical architecture has to be supported by developers and operations. In each of the departments, sub-projects may be necessary to assess specific aspects of the programme. In case of third-party software to be licensed, procurement activities need to be undertaken.

The members of the workshop team should convene regularly and frequently, for example, every day for three to four hours, or twice a week the whole day with an open-ended finishing time. They need to still oversee their day-to-day responsibilities the rest of the time, and trigger supporting activities in their respective departments.

Risks and issues:

a) The activities necessary in the various departments may not be supported.

b) The existing procurement processes may not support the necessary e-speed.

c) The design team may be stretched too thin to drive the e-development activities on top of their day-to-day responsibilities.

Mitigation strategy:

a) A programme management should be implemented to focus upon the contribution to be expected from the various groups and to keep track of slippages. In case of delays, early escalations have to be triggered and trade-offs (if necessary functionality reductions) should be suggested to meet the deadline.

b) Challenge procurement approaches and apply quick fixes such as flexible arrangements with vendors, for example, a trial licence for initial tests.

c) Assess the value of the e-offerings in term of their future. If this does not work: look for replacements. If this does not work either and if it happens with a larger number of the design team members do not try to kill yourself and your staff – it may well be that you need to educate the people in your organisation more thoroughly about the threats posed by your e-competitors and about the opportunities for your enterprise, first. In other words, revisit and adjust your strategic roadmap.

Pre-decessing task: once the overall roadmap has been agreed, rapid prototyping workshops should start. Design and tool identification should be completed quickly, for example, after one month.

Subsequent tasks: proof of concept and readiness check (going on simultaneously).

Proof of concept

Objective: implementation of key components with an end-to-end integration. For components to be developed from scratch, a framework has to be developed, but possibly with only a subset of functionality. The key components have to be testable by some test users. The focus should be on key transactions and on 'good weather flying', that is, error handling may still be non-existent or with just a little guidance given to users. The proof of concept has to indicate if the overall targets such as performance and business process support are achievable.

Success criteria: end-to-end processing of key transactions in line with targeted service levels.

Responsibilities and dependencies: the website contents have to be pulled together by marketing, the user departments have to crank out the new end-to-end business process based on targeted business scenarios and the IT department needs to provide and set up the computers on which the new software can run. The necessary access restrictions and security have to be set up and the security administration needs to be organised.

This task is executed in parallel with the readiness check. The proof of concept will indicate a variety of activities that have to be performed once the system is in production; these activities need to be recorded and the conclusion has to be recorded in the readiness check.

Risks and issues: at this time, you may realise that you have been asking more than is feasible in the remaining time frame. You have the choice between two bad options: delaying the project or cutting back scope. Unless it drastically hurts your business case, you should decide to cut back scope. That is not only because I was preaching that doctrine earlier, but also to allow your organisation to learn to become more realistic in defining targets – and to experience your new commitment to manage by time objectives instead of managing by compliance with a requirement paper.

Mitigation strategy: make very small steps in the first e-cycles. Most of the surprises will happen when all your staff have gained a little experience with the new time-oriented project approach. Experiencing the lead times on decisions, identifying possibilities to cut back on overhead times, finding flexible ways for procurement and co-operating across department boundaries are all a big step forward in themselves! Subsequent cycles then can be more demanding, once your e-factory operates at high speed.

Pre-decessing task: rapid prototyping.

Subsequent task: quick deployment.

Readiness check/gap analysis

Objective: identify what is missing in the organisation for running and using the new system.

Success criteria: complete recommendations available on what activities to perform once the new system is in place. Key 'suspects' include

❏ marketing: regular updates of website contents (for example, press releases, new product announcements, catalogue entries, forum administration);

❏ customer care: 24 × 7 availability, e-mail correspondence, access maintenance (for example, Web user activation, password administration, PIN/TAN administration);

❏ system administration: security (for example, firewalls, secure transactions and payments, virus checking, encryption);

❏ system operations: separate physical environment for Web server, 24 × 7 availability, hardware and software maintenance;

❏ training needs for the various departments.

Responsibilities and dependencies: this task is going on in parallel with the proof of concept. The results of the proof of concept should be closely monitored to identify all readiness gaps.

Risks and issues: this task is to assure the quality of the resulting organisation. If it is not executed thoroughly, it may lead to delays during deployment.

Mitigation strategy: compare the results of the readiness check with the results of traditional projects. Most of the gaps materialising in traditional projects should also be identified for your e-cycle. Additionally, the impact of the online customer experience has to be factored in.

Pre-decessing task: rapid prototyping.

Subsequent task: quick deployment.

Quick deployment

Objective: making the new system available to customers on the Web and to internal users.

The quick deployment should happen in two stages: first, a small group of 'friendly' users, for example, the employees who are customers of your company or close business partners, get access to perform their daily customer transactions with the system and to obtain feedback. Depending on the quality of the feedback, you then can allow all users access – or it will take you another cycle to refine the solution for fulfilling customer service expectations.

Success criteria: compliance with the committed service levels.

Responsibilities and dependencies: now everything really needs to come together right: components delivered from (probably various) third-party vendors, newly developed software, business processes, the people trained in operating and using the system – and the parallel marketing campaign to make customers and prospective customers aware of the improved services.

Risks and issues:

a) A hiccup in any of the underlying activities will lead to delays in the overall project.

b) The performance and service level figures from the test runs may not be as good as the targeted commitment.

Mitigation strategy:

a) An overall programme management has to closely monitor the timing of all sub-projects. In case of delays, early escalations have to be triggered and trade-offs (if necessary functionality reductions) should be suggested to meet the deadline.

b) If performance and service levels are still better than the earlier release, switch to the new version and fine-tune the running system. Those aspects that cannot be fine-tuned can be optimised in the next e-cycle.

Pre-decessing task: proof of concept and readiness check.

Subsequent task: re-usable assets.

Re-usable assets/lessons learned

Objective: once deployment is complete, the lessons learned have to be documented. The results will be a list of things not to do in the next cycle, and things to do instead. Also, experiences gained have to be documented as an asset for re-use during the next cycle. Such assets may include (for example) design templates, programme progress-monitoring templates, new order forms for procurement, issue escalation procedures.

This task is at the transition stage from one cycle to the next, so the strategic roadmap should also be reviewed, if the next targets still look feasible and desirable.

Success criteria: the strategic roadmap is updated and agreed, lessons learned are documented, re-usable assets are made available for the next cycle.

Responsibilities and dependencies: the strategy group has to trigger discussions on lessons learned and has to organise the review of the last cycle.

Risks and issues: none – except if you do not revisit the performance of the last cycle, you will lose a lot of speed and waste energy in the next cycle.

Mitigation strategy: just do it.

Pre-decessing task: all the above (from the last cycle).

Subsequent task: all the above (for the next cycle).

Integration

Objective: have the currently available components run smoothly together.

For this objective, it is advisable to prepare a detailed component integration plan (like a refinement of a release plan). New hardware, new software modules, extensions to existing modules, error fixes and changes in the business processes need to be reflected. This integration is necessary to support the operations of the system as it is in actual production (with a focus on error fixes) and to support testing activities (with a focus on the extensions and new modules resulting from development). You should try to prepare a small set of test data that allow a regular retesting of the system after each change. There will be many times when extensions to the system (in particular to the test system) happen daily; during these times the system should be re-integrated daily to ensure that the user tests at the various stages of the cycle.

Success criteria: test system and production system are up and running with the agreed service quality.

Responsibilities and dependencies: the integration team has to receive all updates and extensions (hardware and software) and include them in the current running version.

Risks and issues: the integration team may not be aware of all extensions and changes going on. In such a case, that is, when changes are implemented without informing the integration team, the system production might stop or undefined system behaviour may be expected.

Mitigation strategy: provide accurate and complete information about the expected timing of updates and extensions to the integration team. It may be advisable to build up a database or intranet reflecting ongoing software updates for communication between the development team and integration team.

Pre-decessing task: ongoing task. Clear cutover dates have to be identified in the release plan of the integration team. These dates have to be consistent with the overall cycle.

Subsequent task: the same for the next cycle.

Success monitoring and quality assurance

Objective: the key is to make quality measurable. This happens at various instances. Initially, performance and service quality targets are defined during the strategy definition. They represent the performance and quality of the whole organisation as they are experienced by the customer. The results should be monitored with an EPM tool based on the balanced scorecard approach. Additionally, during the readiness check, the internal steps necessary to come up with the defined performance are identified. Thus, the readiness check is a built-in quality assurance of the results of the proof of concept phase going on in parallel. Finally, after each deployment, the quality of the release has to be checked for software quality – like the traditional approach with the number of defects and incidents outstanding. The difference, though, is that defects are not checked against a requirement document, but against performance commitments such as service availability, response times and a small number of failed transactions.

Success criteria: at the end of each cycle, an unambiguous statement can be made of how successful it was and to what extent it fulfilled the plans. Quality can be measured, for example, by implementing the balanced scorecard approach.

Responsibilities and dependencies: measuring success should be built into the ongoing design and development tasks. There may be a dedicated unit with a controlling focus keeping track of planned measurements and synchronising them.

Risks and issues: if you do not find the right balance between measuring too little and measuring too much, either you will continue flying blindly through the fog, or you will get a data graveyard.

Mitigation strategy: construct your measurements systematically; use an approach that expresses achievement the same way, no matter which aspect of overall performance and quality is measured (for example, by colour such as red, yellow, green, or by standardised scores such as 1 through 10, or with defined terms such as excellent, mediocre, unacceptable).

Pre-decessing task: first, the targeted measurement dimensions have to be defined — you may use the customer satisfaction areas as outlined in chapter 1 as a guideline. Then, the refinement of those measurements to the actually measurable events has to be driven throughout the cycle.

Subsequent task: the same for the next cycle. In later cycles, the focus will shift from implementing the measurement to fine-tuning the quality by comparing it with industry benchmarks or by reflecting customer comments for improvement.

13.3 Summary

Let me re-emphasise the two key points for implementing the transformation:

❑ you won't get what you don't measure — so express all goals of each cycle in clearly measurable targets, and measure the results;

❑ keep the cycles short, for example, three months.

14

Tools and vendors

@@@ To select the tools, follow the objectives given. @@@ Vendors are listed as examples for your reference. @@@

Using IT architecture as outlined in Section 8.6 (Figure 24), we will take a journey through the various components. Given the different situations of the various enterprises and the wide span of regional support of vendors, I cannot give recommendations for specific products here. What I want to give you instead is a list of criteria to help you evaluate the various available options. When I mention vendors in what follows, these are meant as examples which can clarify my points, or show how they have implemented some leadership concepts.

Before we dig into the details of the various components, let us discuss some general points that will drive the relationship with your vendors, as well as operational dynamics and maintenance. We have already talked about making or buying software and I have expressed my recommendation to buy as much as is reasonable. Additionally, we need to look at tools for design and development processes and at different options for integrating components.

14.1 Tools for design and development

The design and development processes described in the last chapter require the support of good design, development and test tools. In particular joint application design sessions with rapid prototyping activities are much more effective if you have a tool that allows you an immediate adjustment of the layout and contents while the workshop still continues. If your design tool does not support such an immediate adjustment, you need to pull all the team together again and you may lose a few days where the job could have been done right away.

Which rapid prototyping tools exist? There is a wide range: from tools aimed at end users to developer tools. End-user tools (such as NetObjects Fusion, *www.netobjects.com*, or Microsoft FrontPage, *www.microsoft.com*) allow you to manage screen contents easily, but only have a constrained set of navigation options. If you want to have more customised features on your website, you need a developer tool (such as Homesite from Allaire* − *www.allaire.com*) which allows you to write the website code (in HTML) and quickly see the result on a split screen. The major strength of this approach is that it allows easy debugging of the code.

Both types of tools mentioned above assume that the traditional split between marketing on the one hand and developers on the other persists. If you have already successfully transformed your organisation towards holistically approaching website design, and HTML is not enough you are looking for a tool supporting animated graphics with Java or Java 2, then an additional type of tool is recommendable, namely code-generating software. Tools such as Versata − *www.versata.com* − can be learned quickly and allow the web-designer/developer to create contents, design and navigation quickly. With such tools you can create websites with approximately one-third of the effort of the other development approaches. To make this quick website development even slicker, you can include some good graphics, audio recordings and videos provided by a new media and marketing company.

14.2 Close integration versus 'loose coupling'

For the implementation of your system components, you need to decide how neatly to integrate them. For the sake of clarity, we will now discuss the two extreme positions, namely complete integration and loose coupling.

Complete integration means that all the components can be provided from one vendor, ideally even as an off-the-shelf solution. The details of the implementation, such as internal interfaces between the components or data structures, are hidden from the users. The benefit of this approach is the accessibility to the same

---

* Now a subsidiary of Macromedia (*www.macromedia.com*).

information from all components – and that you do not need to deal with many software vendors. Prominent examples for customer care include Siebel (*www.siebel.com*) or Oracle (*www.oracle.com*, with its 11i solution) or ERP tools such as SAP R/3 (*www.sap.com*). The disadvantages are the complexity of the application and the interfaces to other applications. The complexity issue is that the implementation of such tools takes a long time (as does its replacement should you eventually consider that).

Interfacing to other applications is still necessary because no application exists that covers all the needs of a big enterprise. In a particular project, I once assessed some strange architecture at the client site where two-thirds of the data for the CRM tool were redundant, being replicated by data from the operational systems. Can you imagine the necessary synchronisation efforts, and the misunderstandings caused because the data somebody in one department is looking at are different from the data in the leading system? The recommendation in this case was to apply a loose coupling instead.

Loose coupling based on enterprise application integration (EAI) seeks to implement the goal of 'plug and play'. Ideally, any component should be replaceable by another of a similar functionality just by pulling it out and plugging the replacement it. We all like the idea, but we must admit that there is still a long way to go in the IT industry. The big issue is that each component needs to have an adapter or connector to the intermediary architecture. The good news is that many of these adapters or connectors have been produced by the strong players for the various industries. For example, Teknekron (*www.tibco.com*) started off with its bus concept connecting many trading applications of investment banks many years ago, and can still be considered as leading this market. Today, more refined approaches exist such as the message broker concept (like CORBA) that handle which types of messages are to be exchanged between which sources and targets of information. Players in this field are Active Software (*www.activesoftware.com, www.webmethods.com*), or Neon (*www.neonsoft.com)*. The most advanced integration tools add the functionality of representing the integration on a business process level (for example, Crossworlds, *www.crossworlds.com,* or Vitria, *www.vitria.com*). Configuring those tools also means describing your workflows in such a way that they are repeatable and allow measuring of the throughput, that is, the service levels.

This full-scale support of integration of the separate components ought to be the best, in particular because it allows an easy implementation of service level monitoring. In practice, though, you may want to keep an eye on the licensing costs – and you may not like to overchallenge the current capabilities of the organisation for setting the most sophisticated tools up and using them. This question, by the way, that is, if the organisation can adopt the preferred integration tool, should also be considered during the readiness assessment.

Your suspicion is right – there is significant work necessary for this integration. As a rule of thumb, estimate some 10 per cent of the component effort to create the adapter or connector, or even more, if you reflect your overall workflow. Is that not a contradiction of the recommendation to 'buy' rather than to 'make' the software? I still recommend the 'loose coupling' option, because for many of the necessary interfaces, you should be able to find vendors that provide adapters for the key business transactions off the shelf (at least for the strong middleware players such as ActiveSoftware/webMethods or Crossworlds). Moreover, the recommended middleware-based integration approach with loose coupling, combined with using third-party software components, enables you to be more flexible in getting the system support you need for quickly extending your business model.

14.3 Licensed software versus 'open source'

For some system components you have the choice of licensed software versus open source software. Open source, that is software without licence costs, for example, are the Linux (*www.linux.com*) operations system (instead of Unix), or Web server software such Apache (*www.apache.com*) or iPlanet (*www.iplanet.com*) in contrast with licensed application server software such as WebSphere (from IBM; *www.ibm.com*), Netscape's servers, (*www.netscape.com*), or BEA Weblogic (*edocs.bea.com*).

The licensed solutions usually have a wider functionality – one of the leaders is ATG Dynamo (*www.atg.com*), where you have the server integrated with interaction monitoring and personalisation.

The open source advantage is that you have a big community of people and organisations that can make extensions to the tool. Its biggest downside is the lack of reliable planning concerning which features come next. If you select the open source approach, you have to build up a development group who can make all the extensions you need – and who are capable of fixing software errors themselves. For some open source software, companies have now started packaging support services (for example, Redhat for Linux; *www.redhat.com*), so that is the ideal combination for mission-critical applications: free software with services.

14.4 Front-office components

We have already mentioned that you will not have the energy to maintain too many vendor relationships, to have your staff learn how to use too many tools – and to tackle too many integration issues. To minimise the size of these dimensions, I recommend you come up with a matrix as outlined in Table 25. This matrix should reflect all the components you want to have in place for a specific e-cycle. By indicating which components you want to select from which vendor, you can quickly see the breadth of knowledge you need to build up in your organisation.

With such a matrix, you can consecutively build up the IT support for your enterprise – and balance the costs of the IT with the business benefits. The matrix as it stands has more vendors than you should deal with – of course, you need just one supplier for each tool category. I have compiled it as a quick reference summary* reflecting my understanding of the breadth of coverage the various vendors have.

Internet portals

Objective: providing the information for the online customer in a good format.

---

* The focus is on European and North American vendors. Please do not interpret this as a specific recommendation for your business situation – individual requirements are too varied to come up with a generic recommendation. Also, some of the functional coverages are relatively weak, while others are pretty strong, so you need to factor that in when you configure your solution. If a vendor is missing, it does not indicate that I do not like him or her or cannot recommend him or her, he or she may just have missed the deadline to make product information available before the printing of this book. Additional market surveys can be obtained from global Internet and PC publications (for example, *Computer Weekly*, *Internet World*), local publications, my book *Success @ e-business*, or Daniel Amor's software implementation handbook *E-business (R)evolution*.

Table 25 Component coverage by vendors (summary matrix)

Vendor	Portal					Access						Entertainment				Integration		Back office systems			
	Design	Avatar	E-mail	Directory	One-to-one	Search	App server	Security	CRM	DWH/DMS	E-shop	Video	Animation	Content mgmt	Community	DSS/treatmet	EAI/workflow	Billing	ERP/financial rep	EPM/performance	Supply chain mgmt
CommerceOne																					✔
Ariba																					✔
SAP																			✔	✔	✔
SAS																			✔	✔	
PeopleSoft																			✔	✔	
Broadbase																				✔	
XaCCT																		✔			
Portal																		✔			
Kenan/Billing																		✔			
Belle																		✔			
Avolent																		✔			
Adobe																		✔			
Vitria																	✔				
Tibco																	✔				
Neon																	✔				
Crossworlds																	✔				
Sane																✔					
Personify																✔					
NetGenesis																✔					
Epiphany																✔					
AMS/Strata, CACS, Tapestry																✔		✔			✔
WebMethods/Active														✔			✔				✔
Vignette/Storyserver														✔		✔					
Netegrity														✔							
Interworld														✔							
Interwoven														✔							
Infopark														✔							
I:FAO														✔							
Andromedia (Macromedia)													✔	✔							
Paramount												✔									
MGM												✔									
Kirch												✔									
Disney												✔									
Canal +												✔									
BSkyB												✔									
Berlusconi/Mediaset												✔									
AOL/Time Warner												✔									
akami												✔									
wanadoo												✔									
t-online												✔									
BT												✔									
OpenShop											✔										
Open Market											✔		✔								
Intershop											✔										
Sybase										✔						✔	✔				
FileNet										✔							✔				
Vantive									✔												
Siebel									✔												
Oracle (11i)									✔	✔	✔										
Clarify									✔												
Brokat								✔													
IBM/Websphere							✔						✔								
Apache							✔														
PortalOne (Verity)						✔									✔						
Intkomi						✔						✔		✔							
Weblogic (BEA)					✔		✔		✔								✔				
Netscape					✔		✔	✔			✔										
Doubleclick					✔										✔						
Cassiopeia					✔				✔					✔		✔					
Caput					✔									✔		✔					
Broadvision					✔				✔					✔		✔					
Blaze					✔				✔							✔					
ATG/Dynamo					✔		✔		✔							✔					
Planet				✔			✔														
Entrust			✔					✔													
EchoMail		✔																			
Connectify Direct (Kana)		✔																			
Brightware		✔																			
Aptex (Mindwave)		✔																			
Artificial Life		✔										✔									
Versata	✔													✔							
Fusion (NetObjects)	✔													✔							
Frontpage (Microsoft)	✔													✔							
Homesite (Altaire)	✔													✔							

Tool evaluation criteria:

❏ avatars – allow the customers an animated interaction with a customer representative; ideally the customer should have the choice between different genders and styles;

❏ e-mail management – allow automatically personalised responses, monitor the follow-up in customer care and escalate in case of late follow-up; analyse e-mail patterns (for example, complaints, enquiries, time, service levels); support mailing lists;

❏ personalisation – use the profile information per customer segment, track the customer online behaviour (for example, by click stream analysis), apply the treatment strategy to provide customised and personalised Web contents;

❏ directory services – maintain an overview of the subscribers (for example, of overall service, of mailing lists, of communities, of 'buddies online'); support authentication of Web visitor.

Some vendors (examples):

❏ avatars:
   Artificial Life (*www.artificiallife.com*)

❏ e-mail management:
   Aptex (*www.mindwave.com*);
   Brightware (*www.brightware.com*);
   Connectify Direct (*www.connectify.com, www.kana.com*);
   EchoMail (*www.echomail.com*)

❏ directory services:
   Entrust (*www.entrust.com*);
   iPlanet Directory Suite (*www.iplanet.com*)

❏ personalisation:
   ATG Dynamo (*www.atg.com*);
   Blaze (*www.blazesoft.com*);
   Broadvision (*www.broadvision.com*);
   Caput (*www.caput.com*);
   Cassiopeia (*www.cassiopeia.com*);
   Doubleclick (*www.doubleclick.com*);
   Netscape (*www.netscape.com*);
   Weblogic (*edocs.bea.com*)

Internet access

Objective: two types of search engine need to be supported: one is the public search engine leading visitors to your site, the other is the search engine internal to your site helping the visitor navigate within it. For the public search engines, you have to include the metatags in your website that allow the search engines a proper indexing of your site and you should re-register regularly. The internal search engine should allow the visitor navigation which is as easy as possible.

Access management has to allow authorised users access to the Web front-end and to prevent unauthorised users from access.

Security features have to prevent data being intercepted or changed in your or in your customers' systems.

Tool evaluation criteria:

❏ internal search engine – support of single-word searches and phrases, approximate searches and acoustic representation of searches (for example, disregarding spelling mistakes or allowing spelling variations), automatic extension of search index by actual searches, easy administration of search index, multi-language support;

❏ access management – administration of internal users and Web users, access restrictions to be possible for different areas (access to data – read/write/delete, access to transactions – trigger/execute/follow-up/cancel/close, personal areas and public areas);

❏ security – distinction between public website and secure server where personal data are kept, intrusion detection to monitor illegal access, virus check capabilities with frequent updates of virus patterns, secure transfer protocols (for example, HTTPS, SSL, SET), authentication.

Some vendors (examples):

❏ search engine:
  the public search engines are regularly checked and ranked by *www.searchenginewatch.com* and *www.searchenginecolossus.com*. There, you will find which is the best search engine for your targeted customer segments. Many of these providers also offer tools for the search functions necessary for your customers to

navigate within your service. Additional vendors for your internal search engine include:
Intkomi (*www.intkomi.com*)
Lexiquest (*www.lexiquest.com*)
Verity (*www.verity.com*)

❏ access management:
this is usually covered by the application server (see Section 14.3):
Apache (*www.apache.com*)
ATG/Dynamo (*www.atg.com*)
iPlanet (*www.iplanet.com*)
Netscape (*www.netscape.com*)
WebLogic (*e-docs.bea.com*)
WebSphere (from IBM; *www.ibm.com*)

❏ security:
Brokat (*www.brokat.com*)
Entrust (*www.entrust.com*)

Customer relations management (CRM)

Objective: to provide the full information about the customer engagement to the call-centre agent, allow transaction entry by call-centre agents and by the customer, provide help desk facilities.

Tool evaluation criteria:

❏ scalability for wide range of call-centre agents, support of workflow (beginning with an interaction by one agent, followed up by another), conceptually same view on customer in all channels (for call centre, in branch, on the Web), user profiles to control access to information details and to control competencies for triggering transactions;

❏ tracking of customer interactions, for example, last contact (either initiated by the customer or by the provider), pending activities (for example, pending questions from call centre, unresolved complaint);

❏ monitoring of customer online behaviour and click stream analysis (for example, which link from a partner was used, how long a banner was watched, what price information was displayed before the customer decided to purchase).

Some vendors (examples):
  ATG Dynamo (*www.atg.com*)
  Blaze (*www.blazesoft.com*)
  Broadvision (*www.broadvision.com*)
  Caput (*www.caput.com*)
  Cassiopeia (*www.cassiopeia.com*)
  Clarify (*www.clarify.com*)
  Doubleclick (*www.doubleclick.com*)
  Maximize (*www.maximize.com*)
  Oracle 11i (*www.oracle.com*)
  Siebel eSales (*www.siebel.com*)
  Vantive (*www.vantive.com, www.peoplesoft.com*)

Data warehouse and document management

Objective:

❏ data warehouse – storing the data important for an assessment of customer behaviour, customer value contribution and customer risk profile to allow a quick assessment for the call-centre staff and for real-time decision-making on which personalisation and treatment approach to apply;

❏ document management – archiving documents that are relevant for customer relations, for example, contracts, complaints, letters.

Tool evaluation criteria: performance and scalability to very large data volumes, easy access mechanisms for call-centre agents, analysis tools.

Some vendors (examples):

❏ data warehouse:
  IBM (*www.ibm.com*)
  Oracle (*www.oracle.com*)
  Sybase (*www.sybase.com*)

❏ document management:
  Acta (*www.acta.com*)
  BEA weblogic (*e-docs.bea.com, www.bea.com*)
  FileNet (*www.filenet.com*)
  IBM (*www.ibm.com*)

Product catalogue and online shopping

Objective: to provide the information about products that can be purchased online, and to support payment transactions.

Tool evaluation criteria: various presentation types for product or service to be supported (by text, pictures, audio, video); product configurations should be easily maintainable; pricing has to be changeable easily; a broad set of payment options has to be available (direct debit, credit card, customer card, electronic payment) and the payment interfaces have to be supported.

Some vendors (examples):
  InterShop (*www.intershop.com*)
  Netscape ECXpert (*www.netscape.com*)
  OpenMarket (*www.openmarket.com*)
  OpenShop (*www.openshop.com*)
  Oracle 11i (*www.oracle.com*)
  Siebel eSales (*www.siebel.com*)

Entertainment: videos and animation

Objective: in order to keep the customers as much as possible at your website and to keep them interested in your product or service, you should create an entertaining envelope around it. This area is still at an experimental stage (partly due to a lack of 'best practices' and partly due to bandwidth constraints). So you could occupy a unique market position with creative solutions.

Tool and partner evaluation criteria:

❏ for providing video entertainment, you either need to partner with a producer of videos or with a licenser of videos. The contents that can be made available for your customers have to match your target areas.

❏ to make video contents accessible to your customer, an appropriately high bandwidth has to be supported by your telecom partner/Internet service provider (ISP). Consider the maximum number of customers online and simultaneously downloading your video streams. Currently, at small bandwidth Internet lines this is focused on smart technologies to compress video streams and to show the video sequence in a small fraction of the overall screen. With the upcoming broadband services (for example, those based on DSL or UMTS), the ISP has to be capable of pumping high data volumes for your video streams into the network.

❏ animation is necessary to design your website in an attractive way (we have discussed this before, but I want to repeat it to underline the full picture of an entertaining website).

Some vendors or partners (examples):

❏ video tools: Intkomi (*www.intkomi.com*) has acquired the multi media specialist FastForward and offers now (together with Portal, Redhat and Sun), in addition to search functions, audio and video management as well as broadcasting features. Another vendor of video streaming equipment is Akamai (*www.akamai.com*). Top ambitions can be supported with specifically produced videos. If you plan to have large numbers of customers watching your video contents, you should partner with an ISP who specialises in streaming huge video streams; this is well supported in most countries by the incumbent telecom provider (for example, British Telecom, *www.bt.co.uk*; Wanadoo, *www.wanadoo.fr*; t-online, *www.t-online.de*).

❏ video contents: entertainment producers and licensers have started to complement their entertainment broadcasting proposition with online sales activities (starting with video on demand and merchandising goods); check with:
AOL/Warner (*www.aol.com, www.warner.com*) – global
Berlusconi/Mediaset (*www.mediaset.it*) – Italy
BskyB (*www.sky.com*) – UK
Canal Plus (*www.mon.cplus.fr*) – France
Disney (*www.disney.com*) – global
Kirch/PremiereWorld (*www.premiereworld.de, www.kirchnewmedia.de*) – Germany
MGM (*www.mgm.com*) – global
Paramount (*www.paramount.com*) – global
An overview of the players in this market is maintained by *www.screendigest.com*

❏ animation: basic animation, such as changing banners, rotating symbols or waving flags, can be implemented with Java and with the Java generating tools. The next level of animation is the integration of avatars (see 'Internet portals' on page 231), as well as some basic audio files, images and brief audio or video streams (those, for example, supported by *www.shockwave.com, www. macromedia.com, www.realplayer.com*).

Content management and communities

Objectives:

❑ allow a broad set of content publishers (for example, corporate marketing, a Web agency, external news providers, community members) to contribute contents to your website while maintaining navigation and structural integrity;

❑ communities should be created in a way which leads to a positive circle of growth – community members have to attract others and they should organise the contents of the community by themselves;

Tool evaluation criteria:

❑ support of expert users (for example, Web agency) and inexperienced users (for example, customers), definition of Web layout for all types of contents, rules for quality checks, thesaurus with words and phrases indicating preferred contents to be highlighted on the website and prohibited words (for example, politically incorrect terms), maintenance of discussion forum;

❑ personalisation of community pages (individual layout, preferences, and bringing the appropriate community members together).

Some vendors (examples):

❑ content management systems:
Andromedia (*www.macromedia.com*)
i:FAO (*www.ifao.net*)
Infopark (*www.infopark.com*)
Interworld (*www.interworld.com*)
Interwoven (*www.interwoven.com*)
Netegrity (*www.netegrity.com*)
Vignette Story Server (*www.vignette.com*)

❑ community support: same vendors as personalisation (see 'Internet portals' on page 231).

Treatment strategy and personalisation (DSS)

Objective:

❏ to understand customer behaviour (for example, usage of
Internet, buying behaviour), assess the value contribution of
various customer profiles, and assign appropriate treatment and
personalised web contents.

Tool evaluation criteria:

❏ analysis tools − analyse website traffic (hit counts, click stream
analysis from/to website and within website), usage patterns;

❏ customer value management − provide models describing value
contribution, risk profiles, buying propensity, assign specific
profile to each individual customer, high performance for real-
time evaluation (for example, credit worthiness check, loan
approval, collections profiles);

❏ assigning treatment and personalisation − select the message to be
displayed automatically (for example, the banner advertisement, a
special offer, the price plan); allow the customer to configure his
or her preferences ('mysite', favourites)

Some vendors (examples):

❏ analysis tools:
   Acta Analytical eCaches (*www.acta.com*)
   Andromedia Aria (*www.macromedia.com*)
   ATG Dynamo (*www.atg.com*)
   Doubleclick (*www.doubleclick.com*)
   NetGenesis / CartSmarts (*www.netgenesis.com*)
   Sane: NetTracker (*www.sane.com*)

❏ for customer value management:
   AMS Strata and CACS (*www.ams.com*)
   Experian (*www.experian.com*)
   FairIsaac (*www.fairisaac.com*)
   Personify Essentials (*www.personify.com*)

❏ for personalised treatment, most of the vendors as for personalised
front-ends (see 'Internet portals' on page 231) plus
   E.piphany (*www.epiphany.com*)
   Vignette StoryServer (*www.vignette.com*)

Performance management (EPM)

Objective: in addition to the planning and controlling of financial figures, service levels, client satisfaction and the readiness to innovate have to be monitored. Please refer to Section 5.6 for a description of the balanced scorecard approach.

Tool evaluation criteria: the tool has to reflect all geographic and organisational entities. It has to support data aggregation and in-depth analysis by offering integrated and flexible views of individual customers and customer segments, individual products and product segments, business process service levels, treatment strategy performance, and staff development.

Some vendors (examples): generic tools include SAS (*www.sas.com*) which allow you to develop your own reporting based on some basic data models. There are also tools geared at the optimisation of customer touch points such as online interactions, call-centre treatment and marketing campaigns, offered for example by Broadbase (*www.broadbase.com*). Extensions to ERP systems can be configured, for example, for SAP (*www.sap.com*). The best solution, though, is an integrated tool that ties back into the various business units' planning and monitoring activities and that can roll up the figures (or take an in-depth look at the results) according to your organisational structure, for example, PeoleSoft 8, a solution suite of fifty-nine collaborative applications (*www.peoplesoft.com*).

Back-office integration and payment

Objective: to integrate Web front-end components with back-office processing.

Tool evaluation criteria:

❏ adaptability to your needs, flexibility for future requirements, scalability to additional processing power, integration with your existing systems and robust operations are the key criteria for the various tools.

❏ in the billing and payment area, you can process in-house or outsource to a service provider such as a credit card acquirer, a bill consolidator, or a collections or factoring company. The vendors indicated below reflect an in-house solution, because the bill consolidation and payment collection is heterogeneous in the various countries.

Some vendors (examples):

❏ EAI:
Active Software/webmethods (*www.webmethods.com*)
CrossWorlds (*www.crossworlds.com*)
Neon (*www.neon.com*)
Tibco (*www.tibco.com*)
Vitria (*www.vitria.com*)

❏ billing and payment:
Adobe (payment built into documents, music or video: *www.adobe.com*)
AMS/Tapestry (billing of any events, for example, for telecom calls or bill consolidator payments: *www.ams.com*)
Avolent (online bill presentment: *www.avolent.com*)
Belle (*www.bellesystems.com*)
Kenan/Arbor (telecom billing: *www.kenan.com, www.lucent.com*)
Portal (Internet billing: *www.portal.com*)
XaCCT (Internet billing: *www.xacct.com*)

Glossary

ATM	In banking – automatic teller machine: where you get cash; often also used as self-service terminal, for example, for account statements.

In telecoms – asynchronous transfer mode: data transmission which can happen either in one direction, or in the other direction or in both directions at the same time. |
Avatar	Representation of a human being in a virtual reality environment. Can serve as a guide in a shopping mall. Example: see Einstein alive, from *www.artificiallife.com*
Backbone	Network connection for high speed exchange of Internet services, in particular between ISPs.
Bandwidth	The throughput capability of data connections; measured, for example, in megabit per second. ISDN connections, for example, have 64 kBit/second. DSL (fixed-wire) or UMTS (mobile) will have 2 megabit/second or more.
Banner	Advertising block from third parties inserted on a website. The viewer can get to the website of the advertiser by clicking on the banner. The display of banners can be suppressed by special software.
Bookmark	The preferred websites of a user can be defined in some browsers. So the user can simply select the bookmark without needing to type the whole URL. Also called favourites.
Browser	Shows the information stored on the Internet (which is expressed in HTML or Java) on the screen of the user and allows print-out. Two primary products exist currently for PCs: Netscape Navigator and Microsoft Internet Explorer.

For mobile phones, the manufacturers still have their proprietary browsers. For PDAs Microsoft is developing software to allow a similar user interface as for PCs. |

| Certification | For online payment transactions, trust centres issue electronic certifications to consumers. With the certification, consumers can obtain e-cash from their bank. The trust centre together with the bank guarantee to exchange digital cash against real money. This digital cash can be transferred electronically, for example, to a service provider to pay for his services. The service provider then can cash it in. |

| Chat | A real-time conversation between two or more visitors of a website using a chat room. The text typed by any of the visitors shows up on the screen of all participants in the chat. The conversation is usually deleted when the conversation is finished. Often, access to the chat room is restricted to the members of a community. |

| Community | A group of individuals sharing particular interests, for example, the customers or partners of a company. Usually, the community members have to identify themselves, for example, by a user-ID and password. In business communities, the authenticity of a user needs to be checked, in private communities the members can use nicknames.

The members of the community communicate with each other, for example, via chat and on the forum. For business communities, it may be advisable to trigger discussions on certain topics, for example, to obtain feedback of the market perception of the products and services offered.

Communities on private topics (for example, flirting and dating) are run by telecom operators to create additional Web traffic, or by marketing and advertising companies to generate banner placement revenues. |

| Cookies | Files downloaded from the Web to the PC of a user. The cookies can contain the name of the user, profile information, for example, buying preferences, and can be read back by the information provider. Well-designed websites should inform the users about the fact that a cookie is to be placed on his or her PC and what the content is. Cookies should not contain |

sensitive data, for example, credit card numbers, as they could be read by a hacker who could intercept the Internet session.

CSR	Customer service representative (also: customer care representative, call-centre agent).
Cybercash, cybercoin	Trademark of Cybercash; see e-cash.
Dial-up connection	Communication between computers (for example, your PC and the servers of your Web host) is built up on each occasion when you need to transmit data. See also: leased line connection.

The telephone costs will usually be charged by unit (for example, by second or minute) according to the tariff for such connections, for example, local tariff, long-distance tariff.

This approach is advisable if you have only occasional data transmissions, for example, to check a little incoming mail or to update your website contents infrequently.

Digital cash	See certification and e-cash.
Domain	The Internet domain is a semantic label for the URL of a website, for example, mcgraw-hill.co.uk. The domain name contains the top-level domain (for example, .com for North American companies or .de for German providers). The domain names are assigned by specific institutions in each country.
Download	To get files from the Internet and load them on to your own computer. Such files can contain text, pictures, audio, video, software or business data. These data do not need to be encoded in HTML, but can use the format of any application.
DSL	Digital subscriber lines: in contrast with ISDN, no dial-up is necessary, because with DSL a permanent connection is switched to the operator.
Dual band	Mobile phones that can be used in two different GSM environments.
Dual mode	Mobile phones that can also be used as cordless phones using the fixed-wire connection in the house.

e-business	Overall business approach exploiting electronic interaction in all areas. Types of services and products reflect the opportunities provided by interactive marketing and selling, interactive production and supply-chain management, inter-active ('just in time') delivery and integration with suppliers and partners.
e-cash	Electronic cash. The customer loads electronic cash from his bank on to his computer. E-cash is certified by a trust centre and is only valid if it is presented together with the certificate. At each transmission of electronic cash, validity needs to be verified by the trust centre. The owner of the electronic cash can obtain real money in exchange for digital cash (provided it is properly validated). See also certification.
ECML	Electronic commerce modelling language: format standardising the primary features necessary for electronic commerce, for example, order, payment. Developed jointly by AOL, American Express, Cybercash, IBM, Mastercard, Microsoft, Setco, Sun, Transactor Networks, Trintech, Visa.
e-commerce	The use of Internet transactions on a particular channel for exchanging data without changing the overall business approach, for example, for allowing customers the Web entry of orders.
EDI	Electronic data interchange: standards agreed before Internet activities were established in a business context. EDI is performed via the normal telephone network or packet-switched data transmission, respectively. Electronic procurement approaches were implemented via EDI in the 1970s (for example, in the automotive industry). Now, some EDI standards have been upgraded for use on the Internet.
e-mail	Electronic mail: messages exchanged between the mail partners. Most of the ISPs also allow the attachment of data files. The strengths of e-mail are that delivery is much quicker than traditional mail, there are virtually no costs for exchanging information, and there are mailing lists that allow

a distribution of messages and data to a large group of addressees.

Encryption

In order to protect transmitted data against interception and illegal copying, the data are encrypted. The recipient needs to decrypt the data with the same key in order to make them readable again.

Encryption algorithms are the more secure the longer the encryption key is. Currently 64-bit keys are the minimum, and good encryption should use 128-bit keys or more.

Extranet

Making an intranet accessible for selected external partners, for example, suppliers or customers, for exchanging data and applications. The users of an extranet are a well-defined group and access is protected by identification routines (for example, user-id and password).

Favourites

On PC-based Internet: see bookmark.

For mobile Internet: customers can select their preferred websites which are then placed for quick access at the top of their personalised mobile phone screen. Within each of the websites, they may also have favourites, for example, the stocks they are most interested in.

Firewall

A security device put between an in-house IT environment and the Internet. Usually runs on a specific server in order to encrypt confidential data which are transmitted via the Internet and to prevent unauthorised access from outsiders to the in-house IT environment.

Forum

A discussion between various visitors of a website. The contribution of each visitor is stored in a database and can be retrieved and presented to subsequent visitors. Often, the access to a forum is restricted to the members of a community.

Frame

Method developed by Netscape to split the window visible by a browser into multiple separate areas.

FTP

File transfer protocol: set of rules on how data files can be transmitted between two or more computers. Needed for uploading your website definition to your host, for transmitting data, for example, from a dynamic catalogue, order entry and similar databases.

GSM
Groupe spécial mobile/global system for mobile communication:

The standard for communication for mobile telephony and data transmission. GSM 900 is implemented in approximately 100 countries, GSM 1800 in twenty countries, GSM 1900 in particular in the US.

GUI
Graphical user interface: displayed on the screen of a computer using colour icons, radio buttons, pull-down menus (to name some key elements) and allowing multimedia features. Initially developed by Xerox and later used by Apple for the Macintosh computers, now widely used. In contrast to this, the earlier 3270-screens were only able to display 24 lines of 80 characters each in black and green (or white).

Home page
The cover page of a website. This is the entry to your whole Internet presentation of a provider. Home pages often contain the sitemap, that is, a table of contents, and search functions to directly access the desired information. Usually all underlying pages should refer back to the home page.

HTML
Hypertext mark-up language: description syntax for Web pages; most of the text-rich websites are stored in HTML format. Non-graphical HTML documents can be created by text-editors (for example, Microsoft Word); graphical HTML documents require a more sophisticated editor. The display functions are included in the browser software for end users.

HTTP
Hypertext transfer protocol: document trans-mission rules between computers. Each system linked to the Internet must be able to handle HTTP; for end-user devices this is included in the browser software.

Hypertext
An overlay structure to traditional text documents. In hypertext documents, references

('hyperlinks') are included to specific parts of the text itself or to external items. Within hypertext documents, you can use the hyperlinks to jump directly to the location of the referenced text.

Identrus	International banking consortium dealing with security approaches.
Interconnect	Agreement between fixed-wire telco providers to mutually use their lines and to reimburse each other appropriately.
Intermediary	Agent in touch with buyers and with sellers who matches demands and supplies. Traditional examples include real-estate brokers, investment brokers or travel agencies. Internet examples include online auctioneers. In a broader sense: everybody in the supply chain.
Internet	Network of millions of servers around the globe who are connected by using the same standards for data interchange. Can be accessed by the general public via PC (connected to a telephone wire), mobile phones, and soon also by TV (connected via TV cable or satellite). Internet servers are run by private persons, companies, public services and ISPs.
Intranet	Network of servers within one enterprise, where only the staff has access to provided data and information. The same standards for data interchange are used as in the Internet. Intranets are shielded against outside intruders by firewalls and additional password protection.
IP-number	Unique physical address of each computer connected to the Web (e.g. 162.70.95.131).
ISDN	Integrated services digital network: allowing telephony using digital transmission of the signal (instead of analogue transmission). ISDN offers better transmission quality than analogue lines. The standard bandwidth is 64 kBit/sec, but higher bandwidth is possible depending on local implementations.
ISP	Internet service provider; tier 1 = large organisations organising global data interchange,

	Tier 2 (and below) = providing access to the retail market. The ISPs can also host the websites of the content providers, in particular private persons and small businesses that cannot afford their own server for the website.
Java	Programming language for applications on the Web developed by Sun to reflect the latest research in software engineering such as object orientation. Java allows the building of websites with more user-friendly navigation and complex animations not supported by HTML. Additionally, Java is used to build small applications ('applets'), which can be run on the consumer's PC, for example, to calculate a repayment schedule for a loan.
Leased line connection	The communication between computers (for example, your in-house Web server and your Internet provider), kept up permanently. See also: dial-up connection.
	Telephone costs are charged on a 'rental' basis, for example, monthly, depending on the bandwidth you have subscribed to. This approach is advisable if you have frequent data transmissions, in particular, if you run your own Web server.
Link	Connection between two websites. One presentation can refer to another presentation to allow the user quick jumps between the websites just by a mouse click.
Mall	Website combining several online shops and added services in a user-friendly GUI.
Micro-payments	See: e-cash.
MIME	Multipurpose Internet mail extensions; standard for formatting e-mail messages and attachments.
Mobile services	Mobile services use the fact that the location of the mobile phone or PDA can be identified. Services include travel-related recommendations (hotels, restaurant) as well as navigation support (for example, around traffic jams), or special shopping offers in the environment.

Modem	Modulator/DEModulator: used to translate digital signals for data transmission (for example, Internet) to analogue signals used in traditional voice telephone connections.
MOLAP	Multidimensional OLAP: prepares internal data for often-used enquiries in such a way as to allow very efficient responses to complex analytical analysis.
Name server	The server that translates the URL (for example, *http://www.success-at-e-business.com*) into the physical location of the website. This translation can be handled by global name servers (for example, with the company where the site is registered), by national name servers, or by a server in your own company.
OLAP	Online analytical processing: tool to define *ad hoc* queries in large databases. Often used to identify customer segments and profiles, for example, for customer relations management.
PDA	Personal digital assistant: a very small laptop. Usually has a colour display, a numeric and character keyboard, electronic storage of handwriting and functions necessary for people on the road such as an electronic calendar, electronic business card archive, e-mail. Often combined with mobile communication feature. With UMTS, PDAs will allow Internet surfing with a quality similar to today's PCs.
Plug-in	Software which can be downloaded from the Internet on an as-needed basis. It is configured to be immediately executable on the user's PC without additional set-up.
PoP	Point of presence: physical locations where the services of an ISP can be accessed. Ideally, the nearest PoP should allow you to dial in with a local call.
Portal	In the portal, the provider has packaged all his or her services and those of his or her partners. The benefit for the visitor is 'one stop shopping'. The benefit for the portal provider is to increase traffic by channelling many value-added services and to

generate additional revenues such as sponsoring or advertising fees for customer-specific links and banners.

POS

Point of sales.

Roaming

Agreement between mobile telco providers to mutually use their infrastructure and to reimburse each other appropriately. International roaming is common, because so far nobody has built up truly cross-border mobile infrastructures. National roaming is only applicable in countries with little mobile infrastructure.

Router

Tool to select the best physical connection to the server where the website is located. Frequently used websites can be stored redundantly on routers in order to minimise the cost of data transmissions between the router and the physical website location.

Server

The hardware where websites are stored. These servers can be accessed from remote places via routers in order to view the contents of the website. Also, the maintenance of the website can be done remotely. The software for the administration of the websites is also part of the server.

SET

Secure electronic transaction.

Set-top box

Device to connect a standard household TV with the Internet by using the fixed-wire telephone lines or cable TV wires.

Site

See website.

SLA

Service level agreement: measurable commitment for certain service qualities, for example, waiting time in a call centre, time needed to fix a complaint.

Smart phone

Mobile phones combining telephone capabilities with palmtop computer functions.

SME

Small and medium enterprise.

SMS

Short message service: brief text provided on the display of the mobile handset.

SOHO	Single office/home office.
SSL	Secure socket layer: approach for data encryption using a private key and a public key for secure HTTP data transmissions. It is supported by all Web browsers and the industry standard for data encryption.
Surfing	Viewing the Internet contents via a browser by moving from website to website in order to get entertaining or research information.
TCP/IP	Transmission control protocol/Internet protocol: standard for data transmission used between all Internet routers and servers.
TriBand	Mobile phones that can be used in three different GSM environments.
UMTS	Universal mobile telecommunication system: new global standard for mobile telephones (used from 2002). With UMTS, data transmission up to 2 megabit/sec will be possible. With mobile UMTS devices, for example, PDAs, the Internet use will have a similar quality as today's PCs.
Unified messaging	Approach to make messages accessible via different devices (for example, e-mail, SMS, voice mail), no matter how the message was originally sent. This means that the provider needs to perform conversions, for example, from text to speech, or from PC-text to WAP-text.
Upload	Copying data files from the user's PC to the Internet. Opposite of download.
URL	Unified resource locator: globally unique address within the Internet of a website.
Virtual reality	Representation of reality on computer. Covering at least visual aspects (usually three-dimensional) and acoustic aspects. For video games and robot applications, sensor gloves can be used to simplify the steering of a device (for example, a camera), which was previously done by commands, function buttons, cursor steering or joy sticks.
WAP	Wireless access protocol: allows the transmission of website contents to mobile phones.

Website	Totality of the presentation of a company, private person or public service. The website is usually accessed through the home page. Specific subdivisions of the website can be accessed, if the internal structure of the website is known, or if a link from another website refers to specific subdivision.
WWW	World Wide Web: was developed by the European CERN in order to allow easy access to a user-friendly display of information stored in distributed locations. Uses HTML to define presentation. This presentation can include multi-media components, that is, text, images, audio and video.
XML	Extended mark-up language: allows adding more 'tags' describing the contents of the document. With XML, Internet documents can be formatted as a data entry form for the customer in such a way that the data can be directly further processed by the content provider's software. Also, searches for specific contents can be simplified for the customer provided that XML tags have been set accordingly as an additional index.

Further reading

Douglas F. Aldrich, *Mastering The Digital Market Place*, John Wiley and Sons, 1999

Daniel Amor, *The E-business (R)evolution*, Prentice Hall, 1999

AMS, *Uncovering e-business performance. A study of e-business project performance within 131 European companies.* American Management Systems, 51-55 Gresham Street, London EC2 7JH, 2000

AMS, *Catalyst, Premiere Edition*, Winter 2000: American Management Systems, 4050 Legato Road, Fairfax, Virginia 22033.

Daryl R. Conner, *Managing at the Speed of Change*, Villard Books, New York, 1992

Tom DeMarco, *The Deadline. A Novel about Project Management*, Dorset House Publishing Co Inc., New York, 1997

Larry Downes, Chunka Mui and Nicholas Negroponte, *Unleashing the Killer App. Digital Strategies for Market Dominance*, Harvard Business School Press, 1998

Allan Drexler, David Sibbet and Russell Forrester, *Team Building: Blueprints for Productivity and Satisfaction*, Drexler & Associates, Route 1, Box 131-A, Rockbridge Baths, VA, 24473 USA

Euromoney, European Electronic Banking, Review 2000/2001, edited by Virginie Stephens, *gina@euromoney-yearbooks.co.uk*

Jerrold M. Grochow, *Information Overload! Creating Value With New Information Systems Technology*, Yourdon Press, Upper Saddle River, NJ, 1997 *www.prenhall.com*

Gary Hamel, *Leading the Revolution*, Harvard Business School Press, 2000

Harvard Business School, Banc One – 'This Company Knows How to Motivate People to Act as if They were Entrepreneurs', Case Study 9-394-043, 21.6.1994

Harvard Business School, 'A Measure of Delight: The Pursuit of Quality at AT&T Universal Card Services'. Case Study 9-694-047, 19.5.1994

William H. Inmon, *Building the Data Warehouse*, John Wiley & Sons, 1996

Bruce Judson, *Hyperw@rs: 11 Strategies for Survival and Profit in the Era of Online Business*, Scribner, New York, 1999

Dr Ravi Kalakota, *e-Business: Roadmap for Success*, Addison-Wesley, Reading, MA, 1999

Otto Kalthoff, Ikujiro Nonaka and Pedro Nueno, *The Light and the Shadow − How Breakthrough Innovation is Shaping European Business*, Capstone, Oxford (UK), 1997 *www.bookshop.co.uk/capstone*

Robert Kaplan and David Norton, *Balanced Scorecard. Translating Strategy into Action*, Harvard Business School Press, 1996

Robert S. Kaplan and Robin Cooper, *Cost & Effect*, Harvard Business School Press, 1997

W. Chan Kim and Renee Mauborgne, 'Creating New Market Space', *Harvard Business Review*, reprint 99105

W. Chan Kim and Renee Mauborgne, 'Knowing a Winning Business Idea When You See One', *Harvard Business Review*, reprint 00510

Wolfgang Koenig, Norbert Hoppen, Rudolf Beck and Thomas Weitzel, *Simulation of Network Effects*, J. W. Goethe University, Frankfurt, 2000, *Koenig@wiwi.uni-frankfurt.de*

Jordan D. Lewis, *Trusted Partners: How Companies Build Mutual Trust and Win Together*, The Free Press, May 2000.

Meridien Research, *Corporate Financial Services on the Internet*, 1998

Meridien Research, *Electronic Channels vs. The Branch: The 30 Years' War*, 1998

Meridien Research, *Extranets and Intranets in Corporate Financial Services*, 1998

Meridien Research, *Internet Banking for Small Business*, 1999

Meridien Research, *One-to-One Marketing and CRM*, 1999

Meridien Research, *Retaining and Expanding Customer Relationships with Call Centres*, 1998

Meridien Research, *Videotex – The World's Largest Channel for Home Banking*, 1998

Peter Morath, *Success @ e-business, Profitable Internet Business & Commerce*, McGraw-Hill, London, 2000

Frederick Newell, *Loyalty.com*, McGraw-Hill, New York, 2000

Ikujiro Nonaka and Hirotaka Takeuchi, *The Knowledge-Creating Company: How Japanese Companies Create the Dynamics of Innovation*, Oxford University Press, 1995

PeopleSoft, *Think Value – Improving Shareholder Value in the eWorld*, Essentials document, 2000

PeopleSoft, *Think Change – Managing Change in the eWorld*, Essentials document, 2000

PeopleSoft, *Think Customer – CRM as Strategy*, Essentials document, 2000

PeopleSoft, *Workforce Analytics – Aligning the Workforce with the Organisation's Strategic Objectives*, White Paper, July 2000

PeopleSoft, *PeopleSoft's Enterprise Warehouse 8.0/Deploying Enterprise Performance Management*, White Paper, 2000

Michael E. Porter, 'On Competition', *Harvard Business Review*, 1997 – 1998

David S. Pottruck, Terry Pearce, *Clicks and Mortar, Passon Driven Growth in an Internet Driven World*, Jossey-Basse, San Francisco, 2000

Jonas Ridderstrale, Kjell Nordstrom, *Funky Business*, BookHouse Publishing AB, Sweden, 2000

John Schmidt, 'Enabling Next Generation Enterprises', *eAI Journal*, July/August 2000, *John_Schmidt@ams.com*

Index

D

Y